Hárcek

elena Gomm & Jon Hird

Inside Out

Teacher's
Book

Intermediate

£ 23.70

Macmillan Education
Between Towns Road, Oxford OX4 3PP, UK
A division of Macmillan Publishers Limited
Companies and representatives throughout the world

ISBN 0 333 75758 0 (International Edition)
ISBN 0 333 96758 5 (Level III)
ISBN 0 333 96761 5 (Level III pack)

Designed by Jackie Hill at 320 Design
Illustrated by Andrew Peters p 8. Cartoon on p 8 reproduced by
kind permission of Harry Venning.
Cover design by Andrew Oliver

Printed and bound in Spain by Edelvives SA

2004 2003
10 9 8 7 6

Introduction

At the heart of 'Inside Out' is the belief that the most effective conditions for language learning come about when students engage in activities on a personal level rather than 'going through the motions'. Engagement can be triggered by anything from understanding and smiling at a cartoon to talking at length to a partner about what life was like when you were eight years old.

Intermediate students can more or less 'get by' in many situations. Very often they're eager to speak and use the English they know. But, as a rule, they still aren't fluent communicators.

- Although they've covered most of the basic grammar, they still make elementary mistakes. Virtually all intermediate students know this, and most are inhibited by it, some more than others. But the truth is that they're going to carry on making these mistakes for some time to come. It takes a lot longer to learn the present perfect than it does to teach it.

- They typically have an active lexicon of somewhere between 1,000 and 2,000 words and can recognise many more. But while they probably know 'now' and 'again', they may not know 'now and again'. They may say goodbye to you with a rather poetic 'until tomorrow' instead of the boring but more appropriate 'see you tomorrow'. Most intermediate students don't know enough about using the words they know – how they collocate, when they are appropriate.

- Speaking usually implies listening. When you give a lecture or listen to the radio you relinquish one of these roles, but in most situations you move back and forth fairly freely between them. People interrupt each other, or even talk at the same time. Words blur together. Some people have novel accents. As a result, students still find much of what happens in a natural conversation difficult to deal with. It's hard to participate enthusiastically in anything if you aren't sure what's going on.

Because they can get by in simpler situations, and because these problems are so frustrating, there is a great danger that at this level students will allow their language to 'fossilise': ie that their language deficiencies will become permanent features of their competence.

The challenge this poses to the teacher is to create a situation in the classroom where students consolidate what they know, become more fluent in how they use it and improve their comprehension skills. And at the same time, students need to continue to develop their writing skills and move on to learn more new language. *Inside Out* aims to help you do this as easily and efficiently as possible.

Teaching strategies

All the strategies employed in *Inside Out* aim to promote learning by focusing on personal engagement, both intellectual and emotional.

Accessible topics and texts

Each unit is built around a set of two or three related topics. These have been selected to be meaningful to virtually all students: they are subjects about which most people have something to say.

Grammar awareness/grammar practice

The course covers the main grammar areas you would expect in an intermediate course book, but in a way appropriate to the needs of intermediate students.

At intermediate level, there is little point in teaching the present perfect in the same way as at lower levels, ie as if the students had never seen it before. Intermediate students already know a lot about the present perfect – and this applies to most of the structures that are generally taught at this level. But students still want, expect and need grammar to fill gaps in their knowledge and deepen their understanding.

To provide appropriate grammar study, *Inside Out* includes 'Close up' sections. These follow a three stage approach: language analysis; practice; personalisation.

1 The language analysis stage promotes 'noticing' of language features and usage. Working with example sentences and text from the book, students articulate and organise what they know, and incorporate new information.

   This stage will work both as individual study or as pair/groupwork. In general, we recommend pair/groupwork as this provides a forum for students to exchange and test out ideas before presenting them in the more intimidating arena of the whole class.

   Unlike other books which use the 'guided discovery' approach to grammar, we have avoided gap fills and multiple choice questions. Research showed us that most students are unenthusiastic about using these techniques to study grammar. This may be because they associate them with practice and testing rather than learning. Instead, we provide questions and discussion points.

2 In the practice activities students manipulate or select structures, testing their theories. As they do this, they also become more comfortable with the grammar point.

   The sentences in this section are designed to be realistic rather than relying on invented scenarios about imaginary people. Many can be applied to the students' own lives, and this facilitates the next stage.

3 The personalisation stage is not a conventional free practice, where students, for example, take part in a role play which 'requires' the target structure. As Michael Lewis has pointed out, very few situations in real life actually require a particular structure. Furthermore, when they are faced with a challenging situation without time to prepare, many students will, naturally, rely on what they know, rather than what they studied half an hour ago.

For these reasons, personalisation is based on actual examples of the target structure. Students apply these examples to their own lives, opinions and feelings. Sentences from the practice stage are often recycled for the personalisation. For example:

- Are the sentences true for you?
- Do you think these sentences are true for your partner? Rewrite them changing the adverbs if necessary.
- Use the same structures to give your own opinions about different sports.

All the Close up sections are followed by Language reference boxes, which give accurate, clear explanations backed up with examples. These appear in the unit, right where they're needed, rather than being tucked away at the back of the book.

Personalised speaking tasks

Inside Out is filled with speaking tasks. Their main purpose is to develop fluency. While they are not intended principally as grammar practice, they are linked to the topics, lexis and grammar in the unit so as to include opportunities for students to turn input into output.

The tasks do not require complicated classroom configurations. They are easy to set up and enjoyable to use. Most of them encourage students to talk about things that matter to them, rather than playing roles or exchanging invented information.

Personalised, authentic tasks challenge and engage students, and this encourages linguistic 'risk taking': Can I use this word here? Is this how this structure works? Research into second language acquisition suggests that when students take risks they are experimenting, testing theories about how the language works. This is an essential part of language learning.

Anecdotes

There are also extended speaking tasks, where students tackle a longer piece of discourse. We've called these 'anecdotes'. They are based on personal issues, for instance, memories, stories, people you know. When you learn a musical instrument, you can't spend all your time playing scales and exercises: you also need to learn whole pieces in order to see how music is organised. Anecdotes give students a chance to get to grips with how discourse is organised.

The anecdotes are set up through evocative questions. Students read or listen to a planned series of questions and choose what specifically they will talk about; shyer students can avoid matters they feel are too personal. As they prepare for the anecdote, students also think about the language they will need. This student preparation is a key stage. Research, by Peter Skehan among others, has shown that learners who plan for tasks attempt more ambitious language, hesitate less and make fewer basic errors.

The simplest way to prepare students for an anecdote is to ask them to read the list of questions in the book and decide which they want to talk about. The questions have check boxes so that students can tick the ones they are interested in. Ask them to think about the language they will need. Encourage them to use dictionaries and make notes but not to write out what they will actually say. Finally, put them into pairs to exchange anecdotes.

A variation is to ask students to read the questions in the book

while listening to you read them aloud. Then ask them to prepare in detail for the task, as above.

Alternatively, ask students to close their books – and then to close their eyes. Ask them to listen to the questions as you read them aloud and think about what they evoke. Some classes will find this a more involving process. It also allows you to adapt the questions to your class: adding new ones or missing out ones you think inappropriate. After the reading, give them a couple of minutes to finalise their preparation before starting the speaking task.

In some cases, there is a recording of native speakers performing the same, or similar, tasks for students to listen to before they begin their preparation.

Repeating anecdotes

Consider going back to anecdotes and repeating them in later classes. Let students know that you are going to do this. This will reassure them that you are doing it on purpose, but more importantly, it will mean that they can dedicate some time and thought to preparation. When you repeat the task, mix the class so that each student works with a new partner, ie one who has not previously heard the anecdote.

Repeating complex tasks reflects real interactions. We all have our set pieces: jokes, stories. And we tend to refine and improve them as we retell them. Many students will appreciate the opportunity to do the same thing in their second language, and research has shown that given this opportunity they become more adventurous and more precise in the language they use.

You can also repeat the anecdotes as a speaking component to accompany the tests in the Teacher's Book.

Realistic reading

In theory, no matter how difficult a text may be, the task that accompanies it can be designed to be within the competence of the student, ie 'grade the task not the text'. But conversations with students and teachers have convinced us that this is an insight of only limited value. However easy the task, students are quickly disillusioned by an incomprehensible text.

At the other extreme, many of the texts that have appeared in ELT coursebooks in the past have obviously been written merely in order to include examples of a given grammatical structure. Texts like this are often boring to read and unconvincing as discourse.

The solution adopted in *Inside Out* has been to base all reading texts on authentic modern sources, including magazines, novels, newspapers, etc. Where necessary, the source texts have been edited and graded so as to make them challenging without being impossible. The texts have been selected not only for their language content but also for their interest and their appropriacy to the students who will use this course.

Varied listening work

The listenings include texts specially written for language learning, improvisations in the studio and authentic recordings. There are dialogues, conversations, monologues and real pop songs by the original artists. There is a variety of English accents – British, American, Irish, Australian, etc – and some examples of non-native speakers. The tasks are designed to develop real life listening skills.

Contemporary lexis in context

Selecting vocabulary to teach becomes more difficult at higher levels. It's relatively easy to predict the needs of beginners: 'hello', 'please', 'thank you'. As learners progress to higher levels, their vocabulary needs come to depend more and more on their individual situations: jobs, exams, personal interests, etc.

In *Inside Out*, vocabulary is selected to be generally useful and appropriate to the typical student, who is likely to be 17–35 years old and relatively well educated. It is always presented in context and is related to the themes and topics in the unit.

Lexis is first of all highlighted in exercises which draw attention to it, then recycled in back up exercises. The Workbook provides further recycling, as do the photocopiable tests in the Teacher's Book. The exercises encourage students to deal with lexis as part of a system, rather than as a list of discrete words, through tasks focusing on collocation, connotation and social register.

Motivating writing practice

The Student's Book contains ten structured writing tasks which offer students opportunities to get to grips with a variety of formats: e-mails, postcards, reports, formal and informal letters.

This is backed up by a self-contained writing course which runs through the Workbook.

Components

Each level of *Inside Out* includes a Student's Book, a Teacher's Book, a Workbook, Class Cassettes, a Workbook Cassette and a photocopiable Resource Pack.

Student's Book

The Student's Book covers about 90 hours of classroom teaching. It is made up of 14 main units (1–7 and 9–15) and two review units (8 and 16). The units do not follow a rigid template: the flow of each one comes from the texts, tasks and language points in it.

The book includes all the tapescripts, plus a glossary of grammatical terminology, a list of irregular verbs, a guide to the phonemic alphabet and verb tables for the structures covered in the book.

Class Cassettes (2)

These have all the listening materials from the Student's Book.

Workbook

The Workbook provides revision of all the main points in the Student's Book, plus extra listening practice, pronunciation work and a complete self-contained writing course.

Workbook Cassette

This contains listening practice and pronunciation work, plus recordings of many of the reading texts.

Teacher's Book

In this book you'll find step-by-step notes and answers for every exercise. These include closed-book activities to warm the class before beginning a new set of work. The tapescripts are included in the body of the notes for easy reference.

For every one of the main units there is a one-page photocopiable test, for use as soon as you finish the unit or a couple of weeks later. There are longer mid course and end of course tests which go with the two review units (8 and 16).

At the beginning of the book there is a zero unit. This consists of two parts.

The first part is a quiz about the Student's Book to help familiarise students with it: how language is described, the kinds of activities they will do, how the list of contents works, what they can find at the back of the book.

The second part is a Student profile. It aims to discover something about each student's language learning history and reasons for studying English, for example: for an exam, for work reasons, out of personal interest, etc. Students can fill the form out individually or by interviewing each other in pairs. The Student profile is similar to needs analysis, which has been used in business English for many years. But it is not only business students who have reasons for learning. General English students also have needs and wants. Knowing about them will help you to plan lessons, to use the Student's Book more appropriately and to get to know your students better.

Resource Pack

The Resource Pack contains forty photocopiable worksheets designed to supplement or extend the Student's Book. The worksheets are based on the themes and grammar points in the book and are linked to the book unit by unit. They were written for this project by eleven different ELT teachers. They are very varied, but one thing they have in common is that they provide practical, useful classroom practice. There are full teaching notes for every worksheet.

Over to you

If you have any comments about *Inside Out* – suggestions, criticisms or even praise – you can send an e-mail direct to the editorial team at: inside.out@mhelt.com

Or check out our website at: insideout.net, where you can register to receive extra teaching materials free every week by email and contact other teachers who are using *Inside Out*.

Your opinions will help to shape our future publishing.

Zero Unit answers:

(Page numbers refer to the Student's Book)

1 a) 16 (p 2/3)   b) They are review units. (p 2/3)

2 a) write (p 147);   b) pen (p 146);   c) We (p 153)

3 a) Style (unit 14)(p 3);   b) Party (unit 7)(p 2);
c) Friends (unit 1)(p 2);   d) Basics (unit 12)(p 3)

4 Passive (p 54)

5 Question forms; subject questions; prepositions; using questions (p 8)

6 a) Friends (unit 1, p 10);   b) Kids (unit 5, p 46);
c) Age (unit 15, p 128)

7 1,000 (p 14)   **8** Nine (p 29)   **9** 1966 (p 41)

10 Alex Garland (p 92)

0 *Zero unit*

Book quiz

Look through your book and find the answers to these questions:

1 a) How many units are there in the book?

_____

b) Why are units 8 and 16 different?

_____

2 a) What is the last verb in the table of irregular verbs?

_____

b) Which word illustrates the sound /p/ in the table of phonetic symbols?

_____

c) What is the first word of tapescript 32?

_____

3 Look at the list of contents. In which units can you:

a) listen to a song called *Ugly*?

_____

b) read about a festival in Spain?

_____

c) write an e-mail?

_____

d) study food vocabulary?

_____

4 What grammar structure is dealt with in the Language reference section in News?

_____

5 What can you study in the Close up section in Friends?

_____

6 Look at the list of contents. Decide which units you think these pictures are in and then check in the unit.

a) _____   b) _____

c) _____

7 How many words are there in *The Little Book of Calm*?

_____

8 How many personality numbers are there in *Ki Astrology*?

_____

9 When did Ike and Tina Turner record *River Deep, Mountain High*?

_____

10 Who wrote *The Beach*?

_____

Student profile

- **Name**

_____

- **Have you studied English in the past?**

No ☐   Yes ☐ → When and where? _____

- **Have you got any English language qualifications?**

No ☐   Yes ☐ → What are they and when did you take them? _____

_____

- **Do you use English outside the class?**

No ☐   Yes ☐ → When do you use English and where? _____

_____

- **Are you studying English, or in English, outside this class?**

No ☐   Yes ☐ → Please give details _____

_____

- **Do you speak any other languages?**

No ☐   Yes ☐ → Which ones? _____

_____

- **Why are you studying English?**

I need it for work.

No ☐   Yes ☐ → What do you do? _____

_____

I need it to study.

No ☐   Yes ☐ → What are you studying? _____

_____

Where? _____

I'm going to take an examination.

No ☐   Yes ☐ → What examination are you going to take? _____

_____

When? _____

For personal interest.

No ☐   Yes ☐ → What do you like doing in your free time? _____

_____

1 *Friends* Overview

The topics in this unit are people and relationships. The main grammatical focus is on question forms and using auxiliary verbs.

The speaking activities give students the opportunity to practise asking and answering different types of questions and to talk about close friends. They read about how a friendship develops and is maintained over several years, listen to the song *You've got a friend* and practise writing e-mails.

Section	Aims	What the students are doing
Introduction page 4	*Conversation skills*: fluency work	Talking about friends, relatives and famous people.
Fame pages 4–5	*Conversation skills*: fluency work	Talking about famous people. Talking about family resemblances by matching photos of famous people to their relations.
Test your questions page 5	*Grammar*: testing students' knowledge of questions	Writing interview questions for one of the people in the photos and comparing the questions with a recording.
	Pronunciation: sentence stress	Practising stress in questions.
Close up pages 6–7	*Grammar*: question forms; subject questions; prepositions	Studying question forms: subject questions; questions ending with prepositions. Practising using questions.
Noughts & Crosses page 7	*Grammar*: questions	Playing a game, *Noughts & Crosses*, based on a general knowledge quiz.
Friends for life pages 9–10	*Reading skills*: predicting; for gist	Making predictions about a text.
	Lexis: friendship expressions	Finding expressions from the text about friendship.
	summarising	Summarising the text.
	Listening skills: listening for detail	Listening to a conversation about a close friend.
	Conversation skills: fluency work	Anecdote: talking about a close friend.
You've got a friend pages 11–12	*Pronunciation*: vowel sounds	Distinguishing between long and short vowel sounds.
	Listening skills: predicting; listening for detail	Making predictions about a song, *You've got a friend*. Checking comprehension by matching the lines of the lyrics.
	Lexis: slang	Analysing slang vocabulary used in songs.
You've got mail page 13	*Writing skills*: giving personal information;	Reading and writing e-mails introducing yourself.
	editing a text	Correcting mistakes in an informal letter.

1 *Friends* Teacher's notes

Closed books. Whole class. Before students open their books, ask them what qualities a good friend has. List their suggestions on the board.

Write 'God gives you your family. Fortunately you can choose your own friends.' on the board. Students talk about whether they agree with the message of the sentence – that families are an obligation and friends a pleasure.

Write on the board the names of three people who are important to you: a friend, a relative and somebody famous, as in the Student's Book. Students ask you questions about the three people: *Who's Greg? How did you meet him? When did you meet him? How long have you known him?*, etc. Answer their questions and correct obvious or important errors.

Open books. Students write the names of their three people. Then, if the classroom layout permits, students mill about and ask each other about their lists. Otherwise, they work in pairs or small groups.

Fame (p 4)

1 Groupwork. Students discuss the three questions.

Whole class. Groups report back to the class who they think are the most famous men/women in the world. List on the board all the people mentioned by at least two groups. Then hold a class vote to decide the most famous person in the world from amongst the candidates on the board.

Note: in monolingual classes, you may prefer to hold a vote for the most famous person in their country.

2 Pairwork. Students identify the six people in the photographs and say what they know about them.

> 1 Mick Jagger (British rock singer, lead singer of the Rolling Stones)
> 2 Claudia Schiffer (German supermodel)
> 3 Yoko Ono (Japanese performance artist and musician, widow of John Lennon)
> 4 Arantxa Sánchez Vicario (Spanish tennis player)
> 5 Bob Marley (influential Jamaican reggae musician who died of cancer)
> 6 Ronaldo (Brazilian soccer player)

3 Pairwork. Students match the famous people and their relatives.

> a) Arantxa Sánchez Vicario's father
> b) Ronaldo's brother

> c) Yoko Ono's son (Sean Lennon)
> d) Claudia Schiffer's mother
> e) Bob Marley's son (Ziggy)
> f) Mick Jagger's daughter (Jade)

Test your questions (p 5) (Workbook p 4)

1 Whole class. Do the first question as an example.

Pairwork. Students write the questions for the answers. Allow plenty of time for this activity – but don't worry if slower students do not finish all of it.

Whole class. Go through the exercise, accepting any correct answer – even if it is not the same as the recording.

2 ▭ 01 SB p 148

Play the recording. Students compare their questions to the ones on the recording.

> ▭ 01
>
> Interview with a celebrity
> (I = Interviewer; C = Celebrity)
> I: *Could you tell us a little bit about yourself?*
> C: *Sure.*
> I: *First of all, where were you born?*
> C: *I was born in London, but I've got dual nationality because my mother's from Nicaragua.*
> I: *Do you still live in London?*
> C: *No, I'm living in Ibiza now.*
> I: *Oh, really? How long have you been there?*
> C: *Not long. I moved from London with my two daughters, Assisi and Amba, about six months ago.*
> I: *Are you happy there?*
> C: *Yeah, very happy. We love the outdoor life. Also, my mother's a Spanish speaker and I feel more comfortable in a Latin country.*
> I: *Have you made any new friends?*
> C: *Yeah, I've made lots of new friends here. A few English, but my two best friends are Argentinian and Spanish.*
> I: *What do you do for a living?*
> C: *I'm a painter, but I've recently started a jewellery business with a friend, and that takes up most of my time. I also do some modelling when I need the cash!*

I: And what do you do in your free time?

C: Well, with a business and two young children I don't have much free time, but I love reading and listening to music.

I: What sort of music do you like?

C: All sorts: pop music and classical.

I: Do you ever listen to the Rolling Stones?

C: No, never, but don't tell my father.

I: How often do you see your parents?

C: Not very often. My mother's in New York and my father's often on tour. But we all love big family get-togethers.

I: You've obviously travelled a lot. What's your favourite place in the world?

C: That's a difficult question because I've been to so many amazing places, but I think Brazil is my favourite. The children love it there too.

I: Finally, can I ask one last question – who chose your name?

C: I think my father chose it. My mother wanted me to have a Spanish name.

Pronunciation (p 5) (Workbook p 6)

Closed books. Whole class. Ask one student *Where were you born?* Make the primary stress on 'born' very clear. Show some interest in the answer, then get the student to ask the person next to them: *Ask Maria the same question.* Students practise the question. Try snapping your fingers to show the rhythm:

•   •   •   ●

Where were you born?

Get them to mill around for a minute or so asking each other:
Student A: Where were you born?
Student B: Rome. What about you?

1 📼 **02 SB p 148**

Open books. Students look at tapescript 02 on page 148 and underline the word they think will be the primary (strongest) stress in each question. If they are having difficulties, explain that the primary stress comes on the word most important to the meaning of the sentence.

Notes: (1) Primary stress depends on meaning and context, but the examples in the book are clear. (2) In longer sentences, each clause will have a primary stress. All the questions here have only one clause.

📼 **02**

a) Where were you born?

b) Do you still live in London?

c) How long have you been there?

d) Are you happy there?

e) Have you made any new friends?

f) What do you do for a living?

g) What do you do in your free time?

h) What sort of music do you like?

i) Do you ever listen to the Rolling Stones?

j) How often do you see your parents?

k) What's your favourite place in the world?

l) Who chose your name?

Students listen and check. Do not correct the answers yet.

Pairwork. Students compare answers. Play the recording again if necessary.

Whole class. Go through the answers. Break up the pace and provide extra practice by drilling some of the sentences with the whole class.

a) born   b) London   c) long   d) happy
e) friends   f) living   g) time   h) music
i) Stones   j) parents   k) favourite   l) name) who??

Pairwork. Students practise saying the questions from the interview.

2 Pairwork. If your students are already friends, encourage them to ask more questions in order to find out details that they didn't already know.

Close up (p 6) (Workbook p 4, p 5, p 6)

Before the class. Get a sheet of paper for each student – half a sheet of A4 should be big enough. At the top of each sheet, write a question. For example:

What do you do? Are you free on Saturday? What did you think of the movie? Where did you get that tie? How's the new job going? What have you done to your hair? Is that your Porsche? Where are you going for your holidays? Who was that boy I saw you with last night?

If you know the class well, adapt the questions to suit them.

Closed books. Whole class. Give each student one sheet. Tell them they have the first line of a conversation, and they have 30 seconds to write the next one. After 30 seconds, call 'time'. Students pass the paper to the right. Repeat until every student has written one line in every conversation. As the conversations get longer you will have to allow slightly more time – but keep the pace up. At the end, choose pairs to read out conversations to the rest of the class. Ask the class to correct any important grammar errors – and help them if they can't. If the class is bigger than about twelve students, you may want to divide them into groups of six or so to do this activity.

A more challenging version for more able classes is to insist that each line must finish in a question:
Where did you get that tie?
In the market. Do you like it?
Yes, I do. Was it expensive?

Question forms (p 6)

Open books. Pairwork. Students go through the grammar awareness questions. They check their answers in the Language reference section.

> a) Subjects: she; you; John; you. Auxiliaries: has; did; is; do. Main verbs: been; have; staying; do.
>
> b) After.
>
> c) 1 present perfect simple 2 past simple 3 present continuous 4 present simple
>
> d) continuous – am perfect – have simple – do
>
> e) will, shall, should, may, might and must
>
> f) why, what, who, whose and where. There is also whom, but it is less used.
>
> g) At the beginning.

Subject questions (p 6)

Closed books. Write the sentence from 1 on the board: *Mark Chapman shot John Lennon in December 1980*. Students think about which person is the subject and which is the object – but ask them not to answer yet.

1 Open books. Pairwork. Students read the question and exchange answers.

> The subject is the person who did the shooting: Mark Chapman. The object is the person who was shot: John Lennon.

If necessary, give them some more sentences to work on: *Pete Sampras plays tennis; Picasso painted Guernica ...*

2 Pairwork. Students discuss the questions.

> 1   John Lennon
>
> 2   Mark Chapman (did)
>
> a) In the first question *who* is the object; in the second it is the subject.
>
> b) The first question uses an auxiliary: did.

3 Students put the words in the correct order and add the auxiliary *did* when necessary. Then they match the questions and answers.

> a) Who trains Arantxa Sánchez? Her father.
>
> b) Which band did Bob Marley play with? The Wailers.
>
> c) Who writes songs with Mick Jagger? Keith Richards.
>
> d) Who did Yoko Ono marry? John Lennon.
>
> e) Who paid Claudia Schiffer $1 million to appear in a car advert? Citroën.
>
> f) Who did Ronaldo play for in the 1998 World Cup? Brazil.

4 Students make five true sentences with one item from each box.

> a) Elton John performed *Candle in the Wind* at Princess Diana's funeral.
>
> b) Madonna played Evita in the film of the same name.
>
> c) Edith Piaf sang *Je Ne Regrette Rien*.
>
> d) Frank Sinatra died in 1998.
>
> e) Verdi wrote *La Traviata* in 1853.

5 Students write two questions for each answer.

> b) Who played Evita in the film of the same name? Which part did Madonna play in the film *Evita*?
>
> c) Who sang *Je Ne Regrette Rien*? Which famous song did Edith Piaf sing?
>
> d) When did Frank Sinatra die? Which American singer died in 1998?
>
> e) When did Verdi write *La Traviata*? Who wrote *La Traviata*?

Prepositions (p 7)

Closed books. Write *Where do you come _____ ?* on the board. Ask students to supply the missing word (*from*). They will almost certainly know the sentence from earlier classes. Point out that the question finishes with a preposition. This is normal in English – but not in many other languages.

1 Open books. Students add the missing prepositions.

> a) with   b) for   c) on   d) of   e) about   f) to

As you check the answers, drill the questions, getting the whole class to repeat. Get them to say them as quickly and rhythmically as they can: WHO-do-you-usually-have-lunch-WITH?

2 Pairwork. Students ask and answer the questions. Alternatively, get them to stand up and mill around and ask several people.

Using questions (p 7)

1 This exercise can come at any time during this grammar section as a break from concentrating on structure.

> a) Have you got any children? Yes, three.
>
> b) Have you got a pen? Yes, here you are.
>
> c) Have you got a moment? Sure. What do you want?
>
> d) Have you got enough potatoes? Yes, plenty, thank you.

a) Is that your father? Yes. That's the day he joined the army.

b) Is that my pen? Yes, it is. I'm sorry, it looks just like mine.

c) Is that your dog? Yes, I'm sorry. Is he bothering you?

d) Is that the time? We'd better get a taxi.

a) Would you like to go out for a coffee? Good idea. Where shall we go?

b) Would you like to call me tomorrow? OK. What time would be good for you?

c) Would you like to live in the country? It's always been my dream to do that.

d) Would you like to wait here for a moment? Certainly. Is it OK if I smoke?

2 Whole class. Discuss the questions in turn. There is room for interpretation in this exercise. Some questions could be exponents of more than one function. All of them are asking for information – but they are primarily about something else. Feel free to expand on the possibilities below, or to let your students do so.

Have you got ...?

a) In an official context, this might just be asking for information. More frequently, the person who says it is likely to be socialising: making polite, friendly conversation.

b) making a request

c) making a request

d) making an offer

Is that ...?

a) socialising

b) pointing out a mistake

c) making a complaint

d) taking leave

Would you like to ...?

a) making a suggestion

b) making an arrangement

c) socialising

d) making a request

Noughts & crosses (p 7)

Students work in teams to prepare questions for a quiz. With large classes, you may find it easier to divide the class into four teams: two As and two Bs.

Go through the rules of the game with the whole class. Draw a grid on the board and demonstrate the way to play noughts and crosses if necessary. Direct them to the Language toolbox for useful expressions.

Alternatively you can run the quiz as a simple competition between the two teams, keeping the score on the board.

Optional activities

Twenty questions. One person thinks of a thing and tells the class whether it is animal, mineral, vegetable, abstract or a combination of these. The rest of the class can ask twenty yes/no questions to find out what it is, for example: *Have you got one? Is there one in this room? Is it bigger than a house? Can you eat it?*, etc.

The yes/no game. One person stands at the front of the class. The others ask questions in an attempt to get that person to say either yes or no. The object of the game is to answer as many questions as possible without saying yes or no. Keep the score on the board as students take turns at answering the questions. If necessary, go through some ways of answering questions without saying yes or no with the class beforehand. For example: *I do, I have, I don't think so*, etc.

Friends for life (p 9) (Workbook p 8)

Closed books. Ask a few students how long they have known their oldest friends. Ask if anyone had a close friend at school that they no longer see. Ask them why some friendships last your whole life, while others die. Allow a couple of minutes for discussion.

1 Open books. Go through the preamble and the prediction questions.

Pairwork. Students look at the title of the article and the photographs and predict the answers to the questions.

2 Students read the text and check their predictions.

Note: this text is not designed to work as a jigsaw reading.

Lexis (p 10)

1 Students complete as much of the exercise as they can without rereading. They can compare their answers with a partner before going back to the text to check.

a) We clicked straightaway; We hit it off straightaway.

b) We had a lot in common.

c) We got on very well together.

d) We became close friends.

e) We fell out.

f) We went our separate ways; We drifted apart.

g) She'll always be there for me.

2 Pairwork. Students work together to put the summary in the correct order. They should try to do this first without looking back at the article.

(1) Tina and Will hit it (2) off immediately when they first (3) met. They became close (4) friends and got on (5) well together. They had a lot (6) in common. Now they have gone their (7) separate ways and they've drifted (8) apart. They haven't fallen (9) out and they say that they are still (10) there for one another.

Anecdote (p 10)

1 🔲 **03 SB p 148**

See Introduction, page 4, for more ideas on how to set up, monitor and repeat 'anecdotes'.

As this is the first 'anecdote' type activity in the book, make sure that students understand what they have to do. Go though the questions with students. Play the recording once, then ask them to compare their answers in pairs.

🔲 **03**

(B = Balvir; T = Tim)

B: … No, I went out with my friend last night. Well, actually, she's my best friend. Have you ever met her?

T: Er, I don't know.

B: Lisa?

T: You told me about her.

B: I did. She's the Greek girl.

T: Er, yeah.

B: Really pretty … and she's got long, dark hair and she's um, she's very petite. Um, yeah, we had a great time. We met … gosh … we've known each other now … about 15 years. Can you believe that?

T: Oh, wow.

B: Yeah, we met … I was working for her dad. He had a casino. Oh, I tell you, those were wild days but, er, we met working there together and um, she's a sister, a younger sister, and she doesn't get along with her very well, so I always like to say that I'm like her sister. I'm like the sister she never had.

T: Hah, hah, hah …

B: We don't have a lot in common, but, er … cause she doesn't work, she's a full-time mum. She's got a little boy.

T: Oh, yeah.

B: He's about … he's about 11 now … difficult age. Hum. Uhm, um, but we still get together about once or twice a month, and it's always good to see her.

T: Nice.

B: Yeah.

---

2 Play the recording again. Pause, if necessary, to allow time for note-taking.

3 Allow time for students to go through the questions again and decide what they want to talk about. One way is for students to close their eyes as you read out each question in turn, with a short pause between each question for students to have time to think about how they will answer it. This gives them time to relive the experience. They should not attempt to talk about all the topics, and no one is required to talk about anything they feel uncomfortable about or to give away any information which they feel is private.

Pairwork. Students tell their partner about their close friend. The listening partner can make comments and ask questions.

You've got a friend (p 11) (Workbook p 6, p 7)

Vowel sounds

Closed books. Write *feel* and *fill* on the board. Check the meaning – by translation if necessary. Say the words and ask students which word sounds longer. If they have difficulty in hearing the difference, repeat the words, moving your hands – or thumb and forefinger – apart as you say them. Encourage students to make the gestures themselves as you say the words.

1 Open books. Pairwork. Students decide which words go in which group.

Note: this activity introduces all the pure vowel sounds. Be prepared for lots of problems with individual sounds – especially in multilingual classes – and do not try to rush things along.

Long vowels:	call, darkest, hurt, need, soon
Short vowels:	come, friend, good, got, winter, thank, think

2 🔲 **04 SB p 148**

Before the class. You should have dictionaries available for this activity. Most good monolingual and bilingual dictionaries now use the IPA or a variation on it.

Focus attention on the phonetic symbols. Ask if anyone can tell you what they mean (they are symbols representing the seven short vowel sounds in English) and why they are used (the International Phonetic Alphabet enables a word in any language to be written in symbols showing exactly how it is pronounced).

Go through the phonetic symbols with the whole class, making sure they know what sound each one represents.

Pairwork. Students listen to the recording and match the words to the phonetic symbols.

Note: students should see that most phonetic symbols are easy to identify. Different nationalities may react differently, partly depending on if and how the International Phonetic Alphabet (IPA) has been used in their school system.

Long vowels: / ɔː / call, / ɑː / darkest, / ɜː / hurt,
/ iː / need, / uː / soon

Short vowels: /ʌ/ come, /e/ friend, /ʊ/ good,
/ɒ/ got, /e/ let, /ɪ/ spring, /æ/ thank,
/ɪ/ think

04

a) *call* b) *come* c) *darkest* d) *friend*

e) *good* f) *got* g) *hurt* h) *need* i) *soon*

j) *winter* k) *thank* l) *think*

3 Students think of other words they know for each sound. Go round the class, helping where necessary.

4 **05 SB p 148**

Pairwork. Students read the instructions and suggest how the words could be used in the song. Some, such as *get* are too general to predict accurately. Ones which are more limited in meaning – like *darkest* – are more obvious.

Play the song.

05

You've Got a Friend by the Brand New Heavies

When you're down and troubled
And you need some loving care
And nothing, no, is going right
Close your eyes and think of me
Oh, and soon I will be there
To brighten up even your darkest night

You just call out my name
And you know wherever I am
I'll come running, yeah, to see you again
Don't you know that winter, spring, summer or fall
All you've got to do is call
And I'll be there, yes I will
You've got a friend
(You've got a friend in me)

Ain't it good to know that you've got a friend
People can be so cold
They'll hurt you and desert you
Take your very soul if you let them
So don't let them

You just call out my name ...

The word that isn't in the song is 'thank'.

5 Pairwork. Make sure students understand how the exercise works. The lines are jumbled within each verse and the chorus, not across the whole song. Students try to match up the lines before listening for a second time. Once most pairs have finished, play the song again while they listen and check.

Verse 1
1   When you're down and troubled
2   And you need some loving care
3   And nothing, no, is going right
4   Close your eyes and think of me
5   Oh, and soon I will be there
6   To brighten up even your darkest night

Chorus
1   You just call out my name
2   And you know wherever I am
3   I'll come running, yeah, to see you again
4   Don't you know that winter, spring,
      summer or fall
5   All you've got to do is call
6   And I'll be there, yes I will
7   You've got a friend

Verse 2
1   Ain't it good to know that you've got a friend
2   People can be so cold
3   They'll hurt you and desert you
4   Take your very soul if you let them
5   So don't let them

Lexis (p 12)

1 Ask students what *ain't* means.

Ain't is a slang form of *isn't*. It is often heard in American English, particularly in songs. It is also used in some variations of British English – for example, cockney. It can also substitute for *am not*, *aren't*, *haven't* and *hasn't*.

2 Students write the 'correct' forms of the underlined words.

a) want to b) going to c) isn't d) yes, doesn't
e) any f) have got to

3 Pairwork. Students match the lines with the singers or bands. They can check their answers on page 141.

a) the Beatles
b) Lighthouse Family
c) Bob Dylan
d) All Saints
e) the Rolling Stones
f) Oasis

You've got mail (p 13) (Workbook p 9)

Closed books. Ask who has e-mail, how often they use it and what for. Ask if any have or have had penfriends.

1 Groupwork. Students discuss which e-mails they think are most interesting and which they would most like to answer and why.

2 Students write short e-mails introducing themselves. Try setting a word limit – for example, 30 words. Circulate and monitor.

As an alternative, tell students not to sign their e-mails. Collect the finished e-mails and put them up on the walls of the classroom. Students go round the room and try to guess who wrote each one.

3 Students read the letter and decide which of the people from the e-mails in 1 wrote it.

> Francine

4 Students go through the letter looking for spelling mistakes and miscapitalisations.

> paragraph 1: address; writing; boring; Thank; Olivier; Sonia
>
> paragraph 2: especially; Saturday; I'm; English; Spanish
>
> paragraph 3: travelling; useful; studied; English; Chicago; Spain
>
> paragraph 4: too; married
>
> paragraph 6: apologies

You might point out that *traveling* in paragraph 3 is not a mistake in American English.

5 Students write a letter introducing themselves to a penpal. They can write in reply to one of the e-mails if they wish.

Test

At the end of each unit there is a photocopiable test. Use it at the end of the unit, or a couple of lessons later. Allow about 30 minutes for it. It scores 40 points: to get a percentage, multiply the student's score by 2.5. You may not wish to use a grading system, but if you do this is a possibility.

35–40 = A (excellent);   25–34 = B (good);   20–24 = C (pass)

To make the test more complete, add an oral and/or a written component. For example, ask the students to talk in pairs about their best friends and/or write an e-mail introducing themselves to a new penfriend.

> Scoring: one point per correct answer unless otherwise indicated.
>
> **1** 1 have; 2 did; 3 does; 4 Are; 5 Am
>
> **2** 1 Who wrote *The Moonlight Sonata* in 1853? (Beethoven)
>
>   2 Which instrument did Miles Davis play? (the trumpet)
>
>   3 Which group had five records in the American top ten at the same time in 1965? (The Beatles)
>
>   4 What song do you sing in Britain on New Year's Eve? (*Auld Lang Syne*)
>
>   5 Which pianist and singer changed his name from Reginald Dwight? (Elton John)
>
>   6 Which note comes after 'fa'? (soh)
>
> **3** 1 on; 2 for; 3 about; 4 with
>
> **4** 1 met; 2 off; 3 friends; 4 on; 5 common; 6 apart; 7 out; 8 ways; 9 there
>
> **5** 1 Would you like to
>   2 Can you
>   Would you like to
>   3 Is that
>   4 Is that
>   5 Can you
>
> **6** (½ point each)
>   1 again S; 2 darkest L; 3 Fall L; 4 good S; 5 got S; 6 hand S; 7 hurt L; 8 let S; 9 need L; 10 soon L; 11 Summer S; 12 Winter S
>
> **7** 1 What do you <u>do</u>?
>   2 Can I <u>help</u> you?
>   3 Would you like a <u>drink</u>?
>   4 What <u>time</u> is it?
>   5 Whose <u>turn</u> is it?

1 *Friends* Test

Name: **Total:** ____ /40

---

1 Auxiliaries in questions *5 points*

Add appropriate forms of *be*, *do* or *have*.

1 How long _____ you known your best friend?

2 How _____ you meet him?

3 Where _____ he live?

4 _____ you seeing him this weekend?

5 _____ I asking too many questions?

2 Subject and object questions *6 points*

The sentences below are incorrect. Correct them.

1 Who did *The Moonlight Sonata* write in 1853?

_____

2 Which instrument played Miles Davis?

_____

3 Which group did five records have in the American top ten at the same time in 1965?

_____

4 What song sings you in Britain on New Year's Eve?

_____

5 Which pianist and singer did his name change from Reginald Dwight?

_____

6 Which does note come after 'fa?'

_____

3 Questions with prepositions *4 points*

Add appropriate prepositions.

1 I gave you £100 only last week – what did you spend it _____ ?

2 You idiot! What did you do that _____ ?

3 You don't know? What are you talking _____ ?

4 Who was that girl I saw you _____ ?

4 Vocabulary – friendship *9 points*

Complete the text.

I first (1) _____ Jerry at university. We hit it

(2) _____ immediately and became close (3) _____ .

I suppose we got (4) _____ well together because we

had a lot in (5) _____ : we both played football, we liked the same music. Since we left university we've drifted (6) _____ . These days we almost never see each other. We've never actually fallen (7) _____ or anything; we've just gone our separate (8) _____ , I suppose. Still, I'd like to think that in a crisis we'd still be (9) _____ for one another.'

5 Using questions *5 points*

Use *Is that*, *Would you like to* and *Can you* to complete this conversation.

A: Take a seat. (1) _____ begin straight away or shall we have a coffee?

B: Oh, coffee, please.

A: Sarah, (2) _____ bring us a coffee?

B: (3) _____ your son?

A: Yes. He's just started university.

B: He looks very like his father.

A: Yes, everybody says that. (4) _____ your bag?

B: Oh, sorry. Let me move it out of your way.

A: OK, let's get started. (5) _____ finish the job by Friday or do you need help?

6 Vowel sounds *6 points*

Are the underlined vowels in the words below long or short? Mark them L or S.

1	ag<u>ai</u>n	_____	7	h<u>ur</u>t	_____
2	d<u>ar</u>kest	_____	8	l<u>e</u>t	_____
3	F<u>a</u>ll	_____	9	n<u>ee</u>d	_____
4	g<u>oo</u>d	_____	10	s<u>oo</u>n	_____
5	g<u>o</u>t	_____	11	S<u>u</u>mmer	_____
6	h<u>a</u>nd	_____	12	W<u>i</u>nter	_____

7 Sentence stress *5 points*

Underline the strongest stress in each question.

1 What do you do?   4 What time is it?

2 Can I help you?   5 Whose turn is it?

3 Would you like a drink?

2 Relax *Overview*

The topic in this unit is relaxation and what people do to relax and to enjoy their leisure time. The main grammatical focus is the present tense: simple, continuous and perfect, and adverbs of frequency.

Students listen to four people discussing *The Little Book of Calm*, a book which recommends certain daily activities to deal with stress. Students discuss how they deal with stress. They then read an article in which a busy working mother gives her opinion on *The Little Book of Calm*.

Students listen to people talking about books they have read or films they have seen, and then discuss their feelings about books, films and music. The unit finishes with students reading film reviews from the Internet and they write their own film review.

Section	Aims	What the students are doing
Introduction page 14	*Conversation skills:* fluency work	Students talk about what they did yesterday and how much time they spent working, studying and relaxing.
The Little Book of Calm pages 14–15	*Listening skills:* predicting; listening for detail	Making predictions from photos about four people's reaction to *The Little Book of Calm*.
	Speaking skills: summarising	Summarising the four people's views on the book.
Close up pages 15–16	*Grammar:* adverbs of frequency	Identifying adverbs of frequency in a listening text.
		Analysing the positions of adverbs of frequency in a sentence.
		Practising adverbs of frequency by talking about habits and routines.
Sally sees herself as she really is pages 17–18	*Reading skills:* skimming; scanning	Skimming a text for gist and scanning for specific information.
	Lexis: collocations	Learning expressions about stress, mannerisms and self-control.
Close up pages 18–19	*Grammar:* present tenses: the present simple; the present continuous; the present perfect	Identifying different uses of present tense structures.
		Practising using present tense structures.
Books, films & music page 20	*Listening skills:* listening for gist to expand vocabulary; to generate interest	Listening to dialogues about either a book, a film or a piece of music, to identify the topic.
		Reviewing and learning vocabulary to do with books, films and music.
		Listening to extracts from film soundtracks to generate interest in the topic.
A good read page 20	*Lexis:* adjectives with *-ed* & *-ing*	Choosing correct adjective endings of words in a reading text.
How are you feeling page 21	*Conversation skills:* fluency work	Talking about feelings.
		Giving opinions on various topics.
		Anecdote: talking about a film you have seen or a book you have read recently.
Net reviews page 22	*Reading skills:* scanning; for detail	Scanning a web-page for specific information.
		Checking comprehension by using the information in film reviews in order to give a rating score.
A film review page 23	*Writing skills:* giving detailed information; expressing opinions	Writing a film review.

Closed books. Whole class. Ask students what is the best way to relax. List their suggestions in a column on the board. Then ask what things in life cause the most stress. List their ideas in a second column.

Pairwork. Students discuss and number the ways of relaxing in order, with 1 being the most relaxing. Then they do the same with the causes of stress.

Open books. Students list things they did yesterday under the three headings.

Pairwork. Students compare their lists and find out how much time they each spent working/studying and relaxing. They decide if yesterday was typical.

Ask several students to read their lists and the rest of the class to raise their hands if they also did the activities mentioned. Find out who spent the most time working/studying and who spent the most time relaxing.

The Little Book of Calm (p 14)

(Workbook p 10)

1 Whole class. Students look at the main photograph and describe what they see. If necessary, prompt them with questions like *What is the woman reading? Does she look relaxed? What do you think are the causes of stress in her life?*

Ask if anyone has read or seen *The Little Book of Calm*. Establish that it contains short pieces of advice for stressed people.

Optional activity

Pairwork. Once you have established what *The Little Book of Calm* is, students work in pairs and imagine that they have been asked to contribute a new piece of advice to the book. They should write their advice out neatly on pieces of paper which can be displayed on the classroom wall for everyone to read and enjoy.

2 Whole class. Students look at the photographs and say whether they think the people look stressed or relaxed.

Pairwork. Students read through the activities in the list and check vocabulary. They guess which of the people in the photographs do which activities. You could draw a chart on the board and get students to vote on whether or not each person does a particular activity. Leave the chart on the board for students to compare with their answers after they have done the listening activity.

Students look at the photos and try to guess the people's reactions to the book.

3 📼 **06 SB p 148**

Students listen to the recording and check their predictions. Elicit what activities in 2 the speakers mentioned.

> a) Peter   b) no one   c) Robert   d) Barbara,
> Robert, Peter, Sally   e) Peter   f) Peter   g) Peter
> h) no one   i) Peter   j) Barbara   k) Sally
> l) Peter   m) no one

📼 **06**

Barbara
(I = Interviewer; B = Barbara)

I: *Do you think you're a relaxed person?*

B: *Yes, I think so.*

I: *What do you think of 'The Little Book of Calm'?*

B: *Well, I think it's interesting, but I work from eight thirty in the morning until about seven in the evening, so I don't have much time to relax. I never have time for a nap during the day. I have a massage from time to time, but I hardly ever have a leisurely bath.*

I: *Do you ever do any physical exercise?*

B: *Yes, I go to the gym two or three times a week and I sometimes walk to work.*

I: *And how do you relax in the evenings?*

B: *I have a glass of wine and watch television.*

Robert
(I = Interviewer; R = Robert)

I: *Do you think you're a relaxed person?*

R: *I don't know – I thought I was until I read 'The Little Book of Calm'.*

I: *What do think of it?*

R   *Hah ... I think it's rubbish. I mean, I like warm water, but only if it's got tea or coffee in it. And I've never had a massage or a nap during the day, but I don't get stressed out very often.*

I: *How do you relax when you're not working?*

R: *Well, I go for a walk in the park now and again. I often read in the evening. I like reading, but I'm so tired after work that I frequently fall asleep with a book in my hands and the light on.*

Peter

(I = Interviewer; P = Peter)

I: *Do you think you're a relaxed person?*

P: *Oh yes, definitely.*

I: *What do you think of 'The Little Book of Calm'?*

P: *I think it's brilliant. It's changed my life.*

I: *Really? Which advice do you follow?*

P: *I never drink tea or coffee. I drink two glasses of milk every morning and a cup of hot water in the evening. Um, I go running every morning before work and I spend at least 10 minutes alone in a quiet room when I get home in the evening. Then I float in the bath for about 20 minutes.*

I: *What does your wife think about that?*

P: *She thinks I'm mad.*

Sally

(I = Interviewer; S = Sally)

I: *Do you think you're a relaxed person?*

S: *Not really.*

I: *Why not?*

S: *I don't think I'm very good at relaxing. I don't like sitting around doing nothing.*

I: *So what do you do in your free time?*

S: *Well, I've got three children so I don't have much free time. But once a month, I get a babysitter and go dancing with my friends. We laugh a lot, and that's what I find relaxing.*

I: *What do you think of 'The Little Book of Calm'?*

S: *I don't think it was written for people with three children.*

Close up (p 15) (Workbook p 10)

Adverbs of frequency

1   🔲   **06 SB p 148**

Whole class. Students turn to the tapescript on page 148, listen to the recording again and underline all the time expressions they hear which tell them how often someone does something.

Barbara:	never; from time to time; hardly ever; two or three times a week; sometimes
Robert:	never; (not) very often; now and again; often; frequently
Peter:	never; every morning; every morning
Sally:	once a month

2   Pairwork. Students match the time expressions they underlined with the words and expressions in the box.

often:	two or three times a week; often; frequently; every morning
regularly:	once a month
sometimes:	from time to time; sometimes
not very often:	hardly ever; not very often; now and again
don't ever:	never

3   Pairwork. Students ask and answer questions. If students did it, encourage them also to ask about the activities they thought of in the optional activity where they put their advice on the walls. Encourage them to make a note of the answers they get so they can report back to the class at the end.

Whole class. Pairs report back to the group. Find out which are the most popular and which the least popular of the activities. You could also find out who did the most activities most frequently and ask them if they think they are very relaxed.

Pairwork. Students continue asking and answering questions, this time to find out how similar or different they are from each other. They can use the topics in the book to form their questions, but encourage them to think of some topics of their own. Again, they should make notes of their partner's replies so that they can report back to the class.

4   Whole class. Discuss the sentence, eliciting that *often* goes before the main verb (*Bob often walks to work*) and *every morning* at the end of a clause (*Bob walks to work every morning*), though it can also go at the beginning (*Every morning, Bob walks to work*).

5   Pairwork. Students decide whether the adverbs go in position (a) or position (b). They can check their answers in the Language reference section on page 16 before you go through the answers with the whole class. This will get them used to referring to the Language reference section and encourage them to try to find out information for themselves first before coming to you.

Position a: frequently, always, hardly ever, never, occasionally, usually, rarely, sometimes, normally

Position b: from time to time, now and again, occasionally, once a month, once in a blue moon, sometimes, twice a year, once every two weeks

Note: *sometimes* and *occasionally* are included in both lists as they can also go at the beginning or end of a clause.

6 Students do this individually then compare answers with a partner.

> a) I eat out in restaurants once in a blue moon.
> b) I go to the hairdresser's once every six weeks.
> c) I hardly ever argue with my brothers and sisters.
> d) I check my e-mails every day.
> e) I listen to classical music now and again.
> f) I sometimes forget where I've put my keys.
> g) I'm often late for appointments.
> h) I go for a run once or twice a week.

7 Pairwork. Students decide if the sentences are true for a partner and change the adverbs to make them true. They then check with their partners, asking questions to find out if they were right.

8 Pairwork. Students ask and answer questions to find out how similar or different they are.

Sally sees herself as she really is (p 17)

1 Whole class. Students look at the photo and describe what they see. Tell them that this is a photo of Sally, the woman they heard in the listening exercise and that the photo was taken at her sister's wedding.

Read the questions and ask students to look quickly at the article and find out the answers. The two questions are designed to encourage students to scan the text for the answers rather than read it in detail. To encourage them to do this, you could set this activity up as a race with the first student or pair of students to find the answers raising their hands.

> a) Sally thought she was a relaxed person, but changed her mind when she saw her sister's wedding video. The video showed that she had several habits which we associate with people who are not relaxed.
> b) She doesn't think much of *The Little Book of Calm* because she doesn't think it is relevant to someone with her busy lifestyle.

2 Students read the text again more carefully and decide if the sentences are true or false. Check answers with the whole class.

> a) true   b) false   c) true   d) false   e) false

Ask one or two students to explain why sentences b), d) and e) are false.

3 Whole class. If you have a story to tell about seeing yourself on video, it would be a good way to start the students off and encourage them to speak.

Pairwork. Students discuss the questions. Go around and make a note of any interesting stories you hear.

Lexis (p 18)

1 Whole class. Encourage students to try to do this from memory first, before they look back at the text about Sally. Check answers. Ask students if any of them have these habits.

> a) always fidgeting
> b) non-stop
> c) fiddle with
> d) make an appointment ... to deal with
> e) at the crack of dawn
> f) have a lie-in
> g) take a break

2 Whole class. Ask several students to suggest endings for each one.

> *Possible answers*
> a) Nobody can ever get a word in because you talk non-stop.
> b) Don't phone me before eleven tomorrow. I want to have a lie-in.
> c) Did you remember to ring the dentist and make an appointment?
> d) You look tired. Why don't you take a break?
> e) Sit still! Stop fidgeting!
> f) Carla, you'll break that if you keep on fiddling with it.
> g) In this job you'll have a lot of new problems to deal with.
> h) Our flight leaves at 8.05 so we need to get up at the crack of dawn.

3 Pairwork. Students choose A) and B) according to which they think is true of their partner. They should not ask their partner at this stage. They should also decide which is true for themselves. When they have finished, students ask their partners which sentences are true for them and find out how accurately they guessed.

4 Whole class. Make sure students understand that sentence B) in each case describes a relaxed person, so the more B) answers are true of them, the more relaxed they are. Find out who is the most relaxed person in the class, and who is the least relaxed.

Close up (p 18) (Workbook p 10, p 11)

Present tenses

1 Whole class. Students read each sentence and decide which tenses are used.

a)	present simple
b)	present perfect
c)	present continuous
d)	present perfect
e)	present simple
f)	present perfect
g)	present continuous
h)	present continuous
i)	present simple

2 Pairwork. Students look at the sentences in 1 and match them to the uses.

a)	true all the time
b)	something which started or happened in the past is important now
c)	in progress and temporary
d)	something which started or happened in the past is important now
e)	true all the time
f)	something which started or happened in the past is important now
g)	in progress and temporary
h)	in progress and temporary
i)	true all the time

3 Students put the verbs into the correct tenses. When they have finished, elicit what each paragraph is about.

A	(1) wake up; (2) have given up; (3) haven't gone; (4) don't want; (5) hurry – (a man with a new baby)
B	(1) sleep; (2) go out; (3) visit; (4) walk; (5) hears; (6) wash; (7) eat; (8) have used up – (a cat)
C	(1) have finished; (2) don't know; (3) want; (4) am working; (5) wear; (6) serve; (7) smell; (8) have worked – (someone working in a fish and chip shop or a fast food restaurant)
D	(1) am getting; (2) make; (3) invest; (4) have travelled; (5) have worked; (6) eat; (7) drink; (8) have been – (a model)

4 Whole class. Students write three true sentences about themselves on a piece of paper or each sentence on a different piece of paper. Collect the papers and shuffle them. Each student takes a piece of paper and guesses who wrote the sentences.

Books, films & music (p 20)

(Workbook p 12, p 13, p 14)

Optional activity

Closed books. Divide the class into three groups, or multiples of three. Give each group one of the topics (books, films or music) and get each to brainstorm as many words as possible connected with their topic for a few minutes. Students should write these down on a piece of paper. After a few minutes, pass the papers to another group and get them to add more words. Repeat this so that each group has had the opportunity to write words about each topic. As a whole class, ask students to read out the words and check understanding.

1 In smaller classes, get students individually to mingle around the class, asking and answering the questions and producing a survey. In a large class, divide students into groups to discuss the points. Or you could simply ask for a show of hands for each point and put the results of the survey on the board.

2 🔲 07 SB p 149

Students write the numbers 1 to 7 on a piece of paper. As they listen to the recording, they note down their answers next to the numbers. Students compare their answers with a partner and then listen again. Check answers with the class.

1 music	2 film	3 book	4 film	5 book
6 film	7 music			

🔲 07

1
A: *Which is your favourite track on the album?*
B: *The last one – it's amazing. I can't wait to see them live.*

2
C: *What did you think of it?*
D: *I thought the acting was brilliant and the photography's superb. Apart from that, it was dead boring.*

3
E: *Have you finished it yet?*
F: *Nearly.*
E: *What's it like?*
F: *Really good. I reckon it's going to be a best-seller.*

4
G: *I enjoyed that. What did you think of it?*
H: *I thought it was rubbish – a sentimental tearjerker – and the ending was so predictable.*
G: *Well, it made you cry anyway.*
H: *No, it didn't – I've got a cold.*

5

I: *Are you enjoying it?*

J: *Yeah, I found it a bit difficult to get into, but now that I'm past the first few chapters, I can't put it down.*

6

K: *What did you think of the special effects?*

L: *What special effects?*

K: *It was all done with computers.*

L: *Oh no ... I thought it was real. You've spoilt it now.*

7

M: *Did you have a good time?*

N: *Not really ... I can't stand all that techno stuff. I like it when you can actually hear the lyrics.*

M: *Old hippy.*

N: *What did you say?*

M: *Nothing.*

3 Tell students that you are going to play the recording again and that they should note down the words and expressions that helped them find the answers to 2 on a piece of paper. Pause after each extract if necessary to give them time to write.

When they have finished, ask them to transfer their notes into the table, putting the words and expressions in the correct columns. As you check answers, elicit or explain the meaning of some of the more idiomatic expressions, for example:

difficult to get into: used of books which are initially hard to read, perhaps because the story isn't immediately understandable or interesting, but which often turn out to be very good if you don't give up.

tearjerker: used of a film which makes you cry because it deals with a tragic or sentimental story. To jerk is to pull something sharply.

can't put it down: used of books which are so good that you don't want to stop reading them in order to do something else.

Books	Films	Music
bestseller	acting	track
difficult to get into	photography	album
chapters	tearjerker	performing live
can't put it down	special effects	techno
	computers	lyrics

4 Pairwork. Students find the words and put them in correct columns of the table. You could do this as a race with the first pair to finish raising their hands. You might want to warn students that several of the words can go in more than one column.

Check answers with the class and make sure that everyone understands the meaning of the words. Encourage them to ask a partner to explain any that they don't know before they ask you or look them up in the dictionary.

Books	Films	Music
storyline	premiere	reggae
paperback	plot	hit
novel	musical	hiphop
short story	science fiction	blues
plot	horror	opera
science fiction	subtitles	dance
horror	soundtrack	musical
	director	classical
		stereo system
		band
		orchestra
		soundtrack

Get students, individually or in pairs, to add some more words to the lists, maybe the more useful/interesting ones from the brainstorm session if they did it.

5 08

Before you play the recording, go through the list of film types with the class and make sure that everyone understands them.

A romantic comedy: an amusing film about love
A gangster film: a film about violent gangs/groups of criminals
An action film: a film containing a lot of exciting events, often violent
A thriller: a film that tells an exciting story about murder or crime
A western: a film about life in the 19th century in the west of the USA

Ask students to write numbers 1 to 6 on a piece of paper and to jot down the film types next to the numbers as they listen.

Play the recording. Students discuss and compare their answers in pairs before checking with the whole class.

Possible answers.
a) western b) horror c) love story d) comedy
e) action f) thriller

6 You could make this a race with the different groups competing to be first to find, say, two films for each type. As soon as they have finished, they should raise their hands. The winners are the first team to produce a correct list.

A good read (p 20) (Workbook p 13)

Adjectives with -ed & -ing

Closed books. Whole class. Ask several students what books they are reading at the moment and what books they have just read. Make sure they use the present continuous and present perfect tenses correctly in their replies. If any student shows enthusiasm for a particular book, ask them to talk about it to the class and give reasons why they would recommend reading it. If there are several students who are reading a book at the moment, divide the class into groups and get students to tell their group about the book(s). If the class need encouragement to talk, start by telling them something about a book you are reading at the moment. Encourage them to ask you questions about the book – what it is about, who wrote it, why you like it, etc.

1 Open books. Whole class. Students look at the magazine article. Point out that there are alternatives for some of the words. Get students to read through individually and decide which is the correct alternative. Once this is done, ask an individual (confident) student to read out the comments that the people made and to try to choose the correct word in each case. Ask the rest of the class whether they think the student made the right choice. Don't confirm answers at this stage.

Elicit the difference between *interesting* and *interested*. If students have difficulty, write the following sentences on the board and see if they can explain the difference:

I am interested in books.

The book was very interesting.

> 1 interesting, disappointed
> 2 interesting
> 3 excited, disappointed
> 4 boring
> 5 fascinated, inspiring
> 6 interesting

2 Establish that we use adjectives ending in *-ed* to describe how people feel and adjectives ending in *-ing* to describe the person or the thing that causes that feeling.

Go back over the text and check answers with the whole class.

3 Pairwork. Students say if they agree with any of the comments in the text and discuss how they choose a book.

How are you feeling? (p 21)

1 Pairwork. Establish that all the adjectives in the box can be used to describe the way someone feels. Students tell each other how they are feeling today. They can use some of the adjectives from the list or any others that they know. Encourage them to give reasons for their feelings.

2 Whole class. Demonstrate the activity with a confident student. Ask them to choose another adjective from the list (or another feeling adjective that they know) and tell the class what makes them feel like this. With weaker students, you might prefer to give them a few examples about yourself, for example: *I feel pleased when all my students pass their tests, I feel tired when I have had five classes in one day, I feel embarrassed when I can't remember somebody's name*, etc.

Pairwork. Students choose three more adjectives and tell their partner what makes them feel like this. Go round helping and encouraging and note any interesting answers you hear. Alternatively, get students to choose three adjectives for their partner to talk about.

3 Groupwork. Read the topics with the class and check vocabulary.

Students are describing things as well as their feelings about them so they can use *-ing* adjectives as well as *-ed*. You could demonstrate the activity with one of the topics, encouraging them to use an example of both types of adjective. For example, say *I think motor-racing is really exciting. I feel really excited when I hear the engines revving up.*

Give students time to choose their topics and prepare what they want to say about them, then put them in groups of three or four to discuss the topics and exchange opinions.

Anecdote (p 21)

See Introduction, page 4, for more ideas on how to set up, monitor and repeat 'anecdotes'.

4 Pairwork. Students choose items from one of the lists and decide what they want to talk about.

5 Pairwork. Students tell their partner about the film or book they have chosen. The listening partner can make comments and ask questions.

Net reviews (p 22)

Closed books. Ask students if they use the Internet, how often and what for. If any students are unfamiliar with the Internet, encourage those who use it to explain what it is, how they use it and how it works.

1 Open books. Whole class. Ask if anyone can explain why we use the words *web* and *net* in connection with the Internet (because the interconnecting nature of the system is likened to a spider's web or a net).

Ask if anyone has ever looked for information about a film on the Internet. What film did they look for? Did they get the information they wanted? What other information did they find there?

2 Closed books. Whole class. Find out if anyone has seen the film *The Horse Whisperer*. (Maybe it has a translated or different title in their country.) If so, ask them to tell the class what it is about and who is in it.

Pairwork. If no one has seen the film, elicit or explain the meaning of *whisperer* and then ask students to write or discuss a short summary in pairs of what they think the film might be about. Emphasise that you are not expecting them to know the answer and that they should use their imaginations to write an account of what a film with this title could be about.

Pairs read/tell their summaries to the class. Find out which they like best.

Open books. Students look at the headings and the review of *The Horse Whisperer* on the Internet page. They match the headings to the sections of the review. Give them a few minutes to do this. Compare answers in pairs before checking with the class.

> a) 3 b) 6 c) 7 d) 5 e) 8 f) 2 g) 4 h) 1

Ask students what they think of the film review and whether it would encourage them to see the film or discourage them from seeing it. If any of them have seen the film, ask them to say whether they agree or disagree with the reviewer.

3 Pairwork. Students read the comments and give ratings out of ten.

Check answers with the class.

> Jim, New York: 7/10
>
> Anna, Geneva: 9/10
>
> Ángel, Salamanca: 3/10
>
> Agnes, France: 7/10
>
> D.J. Mico, Sweden: 2/10

A film review (p 23)

Writing

Refer students back to the Internet review of *The Horse Whisperer*. Tell them that they are going to write a review for the Internet of a film they have seen and that they can use this as a model. Go through the list of points which they should include with the class and refer them to the useful expressions in the Language toolbox.

You may want to set the writing task for homework, but it is useful to do some preparation for it in class as this allows students to raise any questions or problems they have and will often generate enthusiasm for the task. You could allow students to work in pairs and to discuss the films they are going to write about and prepare notes for each of the points in the list.

Encourage students to present their work clearly and attractively, perhaps including illustrations they have drawn themselves or pictures cut out of newspapers or magazines. You might want to check and correct students' work before they do the final presentation.

Display the completed film reviews in the classroom and allow some class time for students to read each other's reviews. If having students moving around the classroom is a problem, you might like to mount the reviews in a book which you can circulate round the class.

Test

> Scoring: one point per correct answer unless otherwise indicated.
>
> **1** 1 We hardly ever see …
> 2 They never did their …
> 3 He is often late …
> 4 I usually walk …
> 5 We phone each other from time to time.
> 6 has always lived there.
> 7/8 I generally go to the cinema once or twice a month.
>
> **2** 1 interested
> 2 boring
> 3 relaxing
> 4 excited
>
> **3** 1 work, am working (2 points)
> 2 has worked
> 3 is playing
> 4 have finished
> 5 am starting
> 6 go
> 7 comes
> 8 love
> 9 is staying
> 10 think, have lost (2 points)
> 11 am, am doing (2 points)
> 12 have you lived
> 13 visit
> 14 have been
> 15 am listening
>
> **4** 1 crack of dawn
> 2 lunatic
> 3 sit back
> 4 lost my temper
> 5 edge of my seat
> 6 fiddling
> 7 fidget
> 8 bite my nails
> 9 switch off
> 10 lie-in

2

Relax Test

Name: **Total:** _____ /40

---

1 Adverbs of frequency *8 points*

Put the adverbs into an appropriate place in the sentence.

1   We see them these days. (hardly ever)

2   They did their homework on time. (never)

3   He is late for school. (often)

4   I walk to work. (usually)

5   We phone each other. (from time to time)

6   She has lived there. (always)

7/8 I go to the cinema. (generally/once or twice a month)

2 Adjectives ending in *-ing* or *-ed* *4 points*

Add the correct ending to the adjectives.

1   I've been interest__ in it for years.

2   That was the most bor__ film I've ever seen!

3   You need a nice relax__ bath.

4   He's really excit__ about going on holiday.

3 Present tenses *18 points*

Choose the correct tense.

1   Usually I **work/am working** in Bilbao, but at the moment I **work/am working** in Madrid for a couple of months.

2   She **works/has worked** for the BBC for over ten years now.

3   He isn't here at the moment. He **is playing/plays** golf with Juan.

4   At last – we **finish/have finished**!

5   I **start/am starting** to feel much better thanks.

6   We **are going/go** to a restaurant every week.

7   This is my friend Luis – he **is coming/comes** from Mexico.

Put the verbs into an appropriate present tense.

8   Thanks – I _____ (love) chocolate.

9   He _____ (stay) in the Star Hotel at the moment.

10 Oh no! I _____ (think) I _____ (lose) my keys.

11 I _____ (be) a bit busy at the moment – I _____ (do) my homework.

12 How long _____ you _____ (live) in Prague?

13 We _____ (visit) our grandparents every weekend.

14 They _____ (be) here for over twenty minutes so far.

15 Sssssh! I _____ (listen) to the radio.

4 Vocabulary – stress and relaxation *10 points*

Complete the text by rearranging the mixed-up words.

Am I a relaxed person? Well, yes and no I suppose. During the week, I get up at the (1) rckac of nwda, rush around like a (2) ultcani and then sit in traffic for anything up to an hour. I always try to (3) tsi cbka and relax, but it never works and I've generally (4) sotl my eptmer at least once before I even get to work. On top of that, things can get a bit stressful from time to time in my job and you'll very often find me sitting on the (5) deeg of my aset, deep in thought and (6) glidfndi non-stop with my hair. I also (7) ditegf a lot – the people in the office are always shouting at me to sit still! Another bad habit I've got is that I (8) tbie my slina. You can tell what kind of week I'm having by looking at my hands!

However, I am lucky that I find it easy to (9) chistw fof from work when I'm not there. I always begin the weekend by having a long, long (10) ile-ni followed by breakfast in bed and the newspaper – heaven! But before I know it, it's Monday morning again and I'm sitting in that damn traffic …

1 _____   6 _____

2 _____   7 _____

3 _____   8 _____

4 _____   9 _____

5 _____   10 _____

Photocopiable

3 *Dating Overview*

The topic in this unit is dating and how people meet their life partners. The main grammatical focus is the past simple and present perfect.

Students do a jigsaw reading and listening activity in which they discover two modern ways of starting a relationship and explore vocabulary related to the unit theme. They then read about the different ways in which four women met their life partners. They are encouraged to discuss the texts and talk about their own experiences or people they know.

Students are given further opportunities to discuss the theme of the unit by reading about the nine personality types in Chinese astrology, and an article about a boyfriend's worst nightmare, describing his fear when his girlfriend's penfriend comes to stay.

Section	Aims	What the students are doing
Introduction page 24	*Conversation skills:* fluency work	Students talk about various first experiences and what they remember about them.
Twenty-first century dating page 24–25	*Reading skills:* jigsaw reading; exchanging information;	Comparing information from two extracts in a magazine article, *Twenty-first century dating*, on how two couples started their relationships.
	summarising	Summarising the two extracts.
	Lexis: collocations	Focusing on collocations about love and relationships used in the article: *Twenty-first century dating*.
	Listening skills: listening for gist	Finding out if the relationships from the article survived one year later and checking comprehension.
Close up pages 25–26	*Grammar:* past simple & present perfect	Identifying the difference between past simple for finished time and present perfect for time-up-to-now.
	since & *for*	Reviewing the difference between *since* and *for*.
How we met page 27	*Reading skills:* scanning;	Scanning for information about how a relationship began.
	for detail	Completing three more texts on the same topic with appropriate time expressions and verbs.
Dream date pages 28–29	*Pronunciation:* sounds	Listening to and practising schwa sounds.
	Lexis: adjectives	Reviewing and practising simple and compound adjectives describing personality.
	Reading skills: skimming	Skimming an article on Chinese astrology and following instructions to calculate *Ki* astrology signs.
	Lexis: criticisms & generalisations	Finding expressions to do with criticisms and generalisations within the text.
I don't fancy yours much page 30	*Listening skills:* listening for gist; for detail	Listening to a conversation about a new boyfriend first for gist, and then for detail, by comparing the listening to the printed conversation.
A boyfriend's worst nightmare page 31	*Reading skills:* predicting; for gist	Making predictions about an article: *A boyfriend's worst nightmare*.
	Writing skills: writing a final paragraph	Writing a final paragraph to predict how the story ends and comparing it with the final paragraph in the article.
	Lexis: get	Forming expressions with *get* with the meaning 'become'.

3 *Dating* Teacher's notes

Note: if dating is too sensitive a theme in your students' culture to allow them to discuss it comfortably, most of the exercises can be changed to talk about how to meet and make friends rather than life partners.

Closed books. Ask students what they think the best way is to meet your life partner. (Or the best way to meet a friend, if preferred.) List their ideas on the board and perhaps have a class vote on which is the best way.

Open books. Pairwork. If possible, students sit face to face. They choose at least three topics from the list which they feel comfortable about discussing. They then take turns to tell their partner what they remember about these topics. The listening partner should listen carefully and ask follow-up questions to find out further details.

Twenty-first century dating (p 24)

(Workbook p 15)

Groupwork. Students look at the photograph and discuss what they can see. Ask them to decide who the people are and what is the relationship between them.

1 Pairwork. Read the introduction with the class. Then students decide in pairs what they think happened before the two couples first met or spoke to each other. Several pairs report what they think happened. Don't confirm or deny any suggestions at this stage.

2 Pairwork. One student reads about couple 1 on page 139 and the other couple 2 on page 140. This jigsaw reading activity creates a communication gap – each student in a pair reads different information. They then have a good reason for communication when they tell each other what they have read.

Give students at least five minutes to read their texts, then tell them to close their books and tell each other about the two dates.

Ask individual students to tell the class about the date their partner told them about. Other students can supply any information that is omitted.

Ask students what they think of these two ways of meeting a partner. Which one would they prefer? Would they agree to marry someone they 'won' in a radio competition?

Couple 1

The couple met on the Internet. They e-mailed each other for two months before their first 'date' and exchanged pictures by e-mail.

Couple 2

The couple agreed to marry each other as part of a radio competition. Joel was chosen by the station as the 'most eligible bachelor' and Lisa was one of 300 single women who called the station offering to marry him.

Lexis (p 25)

1 Most of the answers can be found by looking back at the couple 1 and couple 2 texts, but encourage students to try the exercise first without looking at the texts. Allow them to work in pairs if they prefer.

Check answers with the class to make sure that everyone has filled in the statements in the same way before you do 2.

Possible answers

a) I don't believe in love at first sight.

b) Somewhere in the world there's a Mr or Miss Right for everybody.

c) People don't usually marry the man or woman of their dreams.

d) Most women enjoy their independence whereas many men tend to be keen to get married.

e) A man should propose to a woman. It isn't natural for a woman to ask a man to marry her.

f) A marriage is more likely to succeed if both partners have had a relationship/other relationships before getting married.

g) If the bride and groom are in love then it doesn't really matter what the parents think.

h) It's better to save the money than spend it on an expensive honeymoon/wedding in some exotic location.

---

2 Pairwork. More than one answer may be possible for some of the statements in 1, so decide as a class on one version of each statement for discussion.

Students discuss the statements. Go around giving help where needed and encouraging students to give reasons for their opinions.

When several pairs have reported what they decided, encourage further discussion.

Listening (p 25) (Workbook p 18)

1 ▭▭ **09 SB p 149**

Whole class. Tell students that one of the relationships they read about has survived and one has not. They are going to hear an interview with the two couples. Before you play the recording, ask for a show of hands on which relationship they think has survived. Encourage students who voted differently to give their reasons. Elicit also what problems they think each couple might have had. Students listen to the recording to check their predictions and note down the couples' problems.

> Lisa and Joel (the couple who met through a radio competition) are still together one year later.
>
> Problems:
>
> Kathy and Tom lived a long way away from each other, so Kathy had to fly to America to meet Tom.
>
> Kathy and Tom's relationship ended the moment they met face to face. Kathy was put off Tom as soon as they met because she hated his shoes.
>
> Joel and Lisa have a problem with Joel's mother, who is still opposed to the marriage and won't talk to them.
>
> Joel and Lisa had to move away from their home town because of all the publicity. Strangers kept asking them personal questions.

▭▭ **09**

Tom and Kathy

(J = Journalist; K = Kathy)

J: *Kathy, we last heard from you when you were about to meet Tom for the first time.*

K: *That's right. It was easier for me to take time off work, so I booked a flight to Denver.*

J: *Wow! That's a long way to go for a date! And rather expensive too.*

K: *Oh, we shared the cost of the flight. Tom's a very generous man. Anyway, he arranged to meet me at the airport.*

J: *And when was that?*

K: *It was almost a year ago. I felt really nervous, but I couldn't wait to meet Tom.*

J: *And was he there?*

K: *Oh, yes. I spotted him immediately. He looked just like his photograph.*

J: *Hah. Was it love at first sight?*

K: *I'm afraid not. I couldn't have predicted what happened but something put me off him straightaway. I didn't even leave the airport. I just turned round and came straight back to Ireland. We haven't been in touch since that day.*

J: *Wow, what was it that put you off?*

K: *Well, it's going to sound really stupid, but I hated his shoes.*

Lisa and Joel

J: *Lisa and Joel, are you still married?*

L: *Oh, yes, very much so. We've been married for a year now. In fact we've just celebrated our first wedding anniversary.*

J: *Oh, congratulations! How have your lives changed since your unusual marriage?*

Jo: *Well, my mother hasn't spoken to me since the day we got married! Hah. That's the good news.*

J: *Hah, hah, hah.*

Jo: *But, no, I'm joking. We're really upset about it. But we've moved away from our home town.*

J: *Really? Why did you decide to do that?*

Jo: *Well, everybody knew about the competition and the wedding and we turned into tourist attractions. We couldn't walk down the street without strangers coming up to us and asking us all these personal questions.*

J: *So, where do you live now?*

Jo: *In Adelaide. Er, we've been there for about six months now, and we love it.*

2 Whole class. Read the sentences. If students are unclear about the meaning of any of them, encourage other students to explain them. Then read each statement in turn and ask students to say whose story it belongs to. Play the recording and check answers or refer students to the tapescript.

a)	Tom and Kathy
b)	Tom and Kathy
c)	Lisa and Joel
d)	Tom and Kathy
e)	Lisa and Joel
f)	Tom and Kathy
g)	Lisa and Joel
h)	Lisa and Joel
i)	Tom and Kathy
j)	Lisa and Joel

Elicit students' reactions to the two stories. Do they think Lisa and Joel will still be together five years from now? What do they think about the reactions of Joel's mother and the people in their home town? Do they think hating someone's shoes is a good enough reason for not having a relationship with them? Have they ever decided against a potential partner for a seemingly trivial reason? Conversely, have they ever been attracted to someone because of something trivial?

Close up (p 25) (Workbook p 15, p 16, p 17)

Present perfect & past simple

1 Whole class. Students look at the two sentences and the questions underneath. Elicit answers and make sure everyone is quite clear about the difference between the past simple and the present perfect.

> a) No, they don't.
>
> b) Yes, they are.
>
> c) The past simple is used to describe something that happened in the past but is no longer happening. Kathy and Tom had an e-mail relationship in the past, but they don't have this relationship now.
>
> The present perfect is used to describe something that started in the past and is still happening now. Joel and Lisa started living together a year ago and they are still living together now.

2 Whole class. Students read the sentences and decide which situations are still going on now. Do the first one as an example. Ask if Kathy is still single and elicit that she is and that the use of the present perfect means that this is a situation which is still going on now.

Allow students to compare their answers with a partner before you check them with the class.

> Situations a), c), d), e), f) and g) are still going on now.

since & for (p 26)

1 Whole class. Students look at the sentences in the previous exercise and underline the words *since* and *for*. Elicit from students when we use *since* and when we use *for*. Get students to write down in two columns words/expressions we use with *since* and words we use with *for*. Get them to compare with a partner before an open-class check. Explain that we use *since* when we are talking about a point in time (for example: *since 1997, since June 10th, since I was a child*) and *for* when we are talking about a period of time for example: *for ten years, for six hours, for a long time*.

Do the first two as examples to make sure they understand that to complete the 'for' column they need to calculate the time that has passed since the point of time given in the 'since' column, and that to complete the 'since' column, they need to calculate the point in time which the length of time given in the 'for' column refers to.

Pairwork. Students complete the table. Check answers with the class.

Answers here are personal, depending on the time and date of the class and the age of the students. The following is a guide.

since	for
1995	[the number of years between 1995 and the present year]
[the time five minutes ago]	five minutes
my last birthday	[the number of days or months since the birthday]
[the date 10 years ago]	10 years
I was born	[the age of the student]
[the date two weeks ago]	two weeks
Christmas	[the number of days or months since last Christmas]
[the time an hour ago]	an hour

Optional activity

You could play a game here. Tell students that when they hear an expression that is used with *since*, they stand up and when they hear one that is used with *for* they sit down. If, for example, they are already standing and they hear an expression that is used with *since*, they do not move and remain standing. Say an expression that is used with either *since* or *for*, for example 'ten minutes' and the students respond appropriately. The last student to respond or a student who responds inappropriately, is 'out' and no longer takes part. This continues until one student, the winner, is left.

2 Closed books. As an introduction to and model for the next activity, write five sentences that include the target language on the board, one of which is false. Students guess which is the false sentence. You could get a show of hands before you reveal the false sentence.

Open books. Students work individually to write their five sentences. Make sure they understand that four should be true and one false and that they should be based on the time expressions in the table or similar ones. Ensure that they hide the false sentence amongst the true ones and don't necessarily make it the fifth sentence. Go round to give help where necessary and discourage them from discussing their sentences with other students.

Pairwork. If possible, students work with partners they do not know well and with students who are not sitting next to them. They take turns to read their sentences and guess which sentence is false.

Direct students to the Language reference section for more information on the present perfect and past simple.

How we met (p 27)

1 Tell students that they are going to read some more accounts of how two people met, beginning with Karen and David. Go through the questions with them and explain or elicit the meaning of *fate*.

Pairwork. Students read the text and answer the questions.

Check answers with the whole class.

> a) last summer
> b) a few months ago
> c) at a party
> d) three months, two weeks and three days

2 Students read Emma's account of how she met Paul. Make sure they understand that the gaps represent missing time expressions. Students work individually to fill in the missing time expressions. Make sure they understand that there is no one correct answer to this and a variety of expressions are possible as long as a logical sequence of events is maintained.

Allow students to compare their completed texts with a partner before checking with the class. Make a list of the various time expressions students suggest on the board. See how many they can add to the list and encourage them to keep a written list in their notebooks which they can add to from time to time.

> *Possible answers*
>
> 1 Last year   2   A week later   3   for six months
>
> *Other time expressions students might have used include:*
>
> 1   When I was (18), One day last (summer), Some (years) ago
>
> 2   Later that week, After a few (days), A (month) ago
>
> 3   A time expression using *for* fits most easily here, but it must follow logically from the ones chosen in the first two gaps.

3 Students read another gapped text and this time they put the verbs in the correct form. Make sure they are clear about the difference between the present perfect and the past simple. Do the first gap with the class, eliciting that the time expression *when I was sixteen* refers to something that happened at a finished time in the past and that, therefore, the past simple form of *see* should be used. Students fill in the gaps individually or in pairs. Check answers with the whole class.

> 1 saw   2 liked   3 went   4 got   5 have been
> 6 haven't had

4 In this third gapped text, students complete the account with appropriate verbs in the correct form. Encourage them to read the whole text through, ignoring the gaps, before they start so that they have a clear idea of what happened. This will help them to choose the correct tenses. Do the first one with the class as an example.

Students compare their answers in pairs before checking with the whole class. Elicit or explain the meaning of the expression *I haven't looked at another man* = I haven't been interested in another man.

> *Possible answers*
> 1   met
> 2   was
> 3   went
> 4   wanted
> 5   stopped
> 6   didn't hear
> 7   sent/wrote
> 8   had
> 9   didn't want
> 10 began/started
> 11 wrote
> 12 received/got
> 13 proposed
> 14 got
> 15 have been
> 16 haven't looked

Elicit some suggestions as to what happened to Basil's letters.

> *Possible answer*
> Elena's mother destroyed the letters because she wanted her daughter's relationship with Basil to end.

5 Allow students time to read the four stories again and to decide which is the most romantic. You could have a class vote on this. Encourage students to give their reasons.

6 Pairwork. Students discuss couples they know and how they met.

Dream date (p 28) (Workbook p 17)

The schwa

Whole class. Read the introduction and the example words. Students practise saying them.

Closed books. To help students say and appreciate the sound, ask them to totally relax every muscle in their body, drop their shoulders and, with an absolute minimum of effort and no movement of the mouth, make a sound. Something approximating to schwa will probably be uttered! Provide a model if necessary.

1 ☐ **10 SB p 149**

Pairwork. Students listen to the recording.

> ☐ **10**
>
> a) *What's a nice girl like you doing in a place like this?*
>
> b) *You know, I'm not just an interesting person, I have a body too.*
>
> c) *I'm in advertising. Would you like to be in our next photo shoot?*
>
> d) *Do you believe in love at first sight or do I have to walk past you again?*
>
> e) *A: Do you have a boyfriend?*
> *B: Yes.*
> *A: Want another one?*
>
> f) *Your father must be a thief, because he's stolen the stars from the sky and put them in your eyes.*
>
> g) *I've just moved next door and I was wondering if you could recommend a good restaurant nearby. Would you like to join me?*

2 Pairwork. Students discuss the sentences. They decide which ones they like best and least. Then they choose four and practise saying them to each other.

3 Whole class. Elicit some chat-up lines and translate them into English. If your students are from different countries, ask other students if these chat-up lines would work in their countries.

Lexis (p 28) (Workbook p 19)

Closed books. Elicit a few, say six or eight, character adjectives and write them on the board in two columns: positive and negative. Get students, in pairs, to brainstorm a few more to add to each column. In open class, ask students for some of the adjectives they have come up with. Check understanding. Depending on the array of adjectives elicited, you could play a game. You say one of the adjectives and the first student to say the opposite, or something approximating to it, gets a point and so on. The student, or team if you wish, with the most points after, say, ten adjectives is the winner.

1 Pairwork. Students look at the list of qualities and choose the six most important for an ideal partner (or friend).

2 Students make compound adjectives and match them to the descriptions.

> a) self-centred
> b) big-headed
> c) narrow-minded
> d) old-fashioned
> e) two-faced
> f) absent-minded
> g) over-sensitive

3 Note: if astrology is a taboo subject in your students' culture, you could omit this section or avoid spending too much time on it, leaving out the calculation of students' own signs and moving straight from a quick reading of the text to the 'Criticisms and generalisations' section.

Closed books. Ask students if they know what astrology is and what their own astrological star signs are. Find out how many people read their horoscopes in the newspaper or in magazines, how often they read them and whether they believe in them. Elicit that astrologers claim to be able to predict the future and to classify people's characters according to the configuration of the stars and planets at the time they were born. Astrologers also suggest that the stars affect our relationships and people of certain star signs are most suited to form relationships with those of certain other star signs.

Ask students what other ways they know of predicting the future, for example, palm reading, reading tea leaves, tarot cards, etc.

Open books. Whole class. Students have to decide which description fits them best. Give them plenty of time to read the text and make their choices. Ensure that they make a note of the numbers they choose.

Start a discussion by saying which number you would choose. Go over any difficult points of the text with them and explain any difficult vocabulary. Students turn to page 141 and calculate their *Ki* Astrology signs. If you are happy for your students to know your age, you could calculate your own *Ki* Astrology sign on the board as an example. Otherwise use the one in the book. Give students two to three minutes to calculate their signs.

Go through the list of compatible signs with them and make sure students understand that these are the signs of people who would make good partners for them. Ask whether the numbers the students have calculated match the numbers they chose.

Criticisms & generalisations (p 29)
(Workbook p 17)

1 You could do this as a race with students in teams. Ensure they cover the list of sentences and only look at the text on *Ki* Astrology. Read out each sentence in turn, giving the number so that students know where to look. As soon as a team finds the expression in the text they raise their hands. Award a point for each correct answer.

> a) Your cool manner is attractive, but it can frighten people off.
>
> b) ... you tend to choose partners who will take advantage of your generous nature.
>
> c) ... you're easily bored and tend to flit from one thing to the next.
>
> d) ... you can be stubborn ...
>
> e) ... because you like to experiment you can be unfaithful.

f) ... you like to be the boss. You tend to be attracted to softer partners.

g) ... you tend to get bored quickly and your relationships do not always last very long.

h) You tend to be very private and difficult to get close to.

i) You appear strong and in control, but underneath you're easily hurt. You can be over-sensitive at times.

2 Make sure students understand that *tend(s) to be* and *can be* are often used to make criticism softer. Read the five statements with the class and ask them to make the first one softer using *tend(s) to (be)* or *can be* as an example. Give students five minutes to rewrite the sentences. Allow them to compare their answers with a partner before checking with the whole class.

Possible answers

a) Women tend to be/can be more sensitive than men. Men tend not to be as sensitive as women. Men can be less sensitive than women.

b) People of the older generation tend to be/can be narrow-minded.

c) Very good-looking people can be/tend to be big-headed.

d) Women tend to be more faithful in relationships than men. Men tend not to be as faithful in relationships as women. Men tend to be less faithful in relationships than women.

e) People from hot countries tend to be/can be more outgoing than people from cooler climates. People from cooler climates tend not to be as outgoing as people from hot countries. People from cooler climates tend to be/can be less outgoing than people from hot countries.

Ask students if they agree with the statements. Encourage them to give reasons for agreeing or disagreeing. Direct their attention to the Language reference section on page 30 where they will find more information about tactful criticism.

I don't fancy yours much (p 30)

Closed books. Elicit how students express in their language the idea that someone is interested in someone of the opposite sex. If your students are from different countries, invite them to put the various expressions on the board. Explain that in English we use the verb *fancy*. We can say *I fancy him, He fancies her*, etc. Note that the verb is also used for things that you would like to do, for example, *I fancy going to the cinema tonight*. Elicit other verbs to do with liking someone or something, for example, *like, love, be attracted to, adore*, etc.

1 🔲 **11 SB p 149**

Open books. Whole class. Focus attention on the title *I don't fancy yours much*. Ask students to say what they think this means (*yours* here refers to a girlfriend or boyfriend and this expression is often used by one person teasing another about their choice of partner, particularly if the partner is unattractive in some way).

Go through the instructions with the class, making sure they are clear who Meg, Rose and Jake are. Students listen to the dialogue and find out what Meg thinks of Rose's new boyfriend. Although they will see that the script of the dialogue is printed in the next exercise, discourage students from reading it as they listen. There are differences between the recording and the script and this may distract them from the main purpose of the first listening. If necessary, have students close their books while they listen for the first time.

She doesn't like him.

🔲 **11** ▸

(R = Rose; M = Meg)

R: *What do you think of Jake?*

M: *He's all right.*

R: *You don't like him, do you?*

M: *Well, he wasn't exactly friendly.*

R: *Oh, he's just a bit shy, that's all.*

M: *Shy? You must be joking. Five minutes after meeting me he asked me to buy him a drink! That's not what I call shy!*

R: *OK, that was a bit cheeky, but he's broke.*

M: *Huh. I'm not particularly well-off myself and I'm trying to save up for my holiday.*

R: *All right, all right, I'll pay you back. He's not bad-looking, though, is he?*

M: *No, I suppose not – but he knows it. I think he's really big-headed.*

R: *You're just jealous.*

M: *No, I'm not. I don't want him. He's mean, big-headed and stupid.*

R: *What do you mean stupid? You're not exactly Miss Einstein yourself.*

M: *Shut up!*

R: *No, you shut up!*

M: *Mum!*

2 🔲 **11 SB p 149**

Get two students to read the tapescript aloud and ask the rest if they can spot any differences between the script and what they have just heard on the recording. Do not confirm or deny any answers at this stage.

Students listen to the dialogue again and underline anything in the tapescript which is different. Students compare answers with a partner before checking with the whole class. Play the recording again, if necessary.

> The students should have underlined the following (the recorded version is given in brackets):
>
> he was unfriendly (he wasn't exactly friendly)
>
> He's just shy (He's just a bit shy)
>
> that was rude (that was a bit cheeky)
>
> I'm poor myself (I'm not particularly well-off myself)
>
> He's good-looking, though, isn't he? (He's not bad-looking, though, is he?)
>
> Yes, I suppose so (No, I suppose not)
>
> You're stupid too (You're not exactly Miss Einstein yourself)

3 Students look at the tapescript on page 149 and compare what was said on the recording with the expressions they have underlined. Ask them which expressions the sisters use to avoid saying things directly.

> All the expressions in brackets in the answer key for 2 are used to avoid saying things directly.

4 Whole class. Direct students' attention to the Language reference section on this page for more about tactful criticism. Go through the information with them, focusing particularly on the last part.

Read the critical comments with the class and invite them to suggest several other ways in which the first example could be made less direct and more tactful. (*He's a bit short-tempered, He's a little short-tempered, He's not particularly patient.*)

Students rewrite the other comments. Check answers with the class.

> *Possible answers*
> a) She's not exactly/particularly sensitive. She's a bit insensitive.
> b) He's not exactly/particularly modest. He's a bit big-headed.
> c) They're not exactly/particularly clever/intelligent. They're a bit stupid.
> d) She's not particularly hard-working. She's a little lazy.
> e) She's not exactly generous. She's a bit mean.
> f) They're not particularly broad-minded. They're a bit narrow-minded.

Optional activity

Divide the class into two teams. Give them a few minutes to make a list of critical statements, one for each member of the team. Discourage them from making personal criticisms of anyone in the class. Go round and monitor, offering help where necessary.

Give each member of the team a number. The first member of Team A reads out a critical statement and the first member of Team B has twenty seconds to reply with a less direct and more tactful way of giving the same criticism. A point is awarded for each correct tactful criticism. Adjust the length of time given to reply to suit the ability of your students. Team members take turns to give the criticism and to soften it.

A boyfriend's worst nightmare (p 31)

(Workbook p 20)

1 Closed books. Groupwork. Tell students that they are going to read a magazine article called *A boyfriend's worst nightmare*. Ask them to make a list of ideas about what a boyfriend's worst nightmare could be. Alternatively, you could ask them to discuss this in pairs or small groups. You could also ask them to think about and discuss what a girlfriend's worst nightmare could be. Perhaps some groups could discuss the former and some the latter. Assigning the discussions to single-sex groups and comparing ideas could lead to interesting discussion.

2 Open books. Students read the text and find out if anyone suggested the same 'boyfriend's worst nightmare' as is described.

Closed books. Whole class. Ask a student to start telling the story. Invite additions and corrections from the class, and change the student who is telling the story a few times.

Groupwork. Students discuss and decide what happens at the end of the story. They should agree on an ending and work together to write two or three short paragraphs to finish the story. One member of each group reads out the ending of the story.

3 Students turn to page 143 and read the end of the story.

4 Groupwork. In the same groups, students compare the ending of the story in the book with their version. Direct students' attention to the expression *an enormous weight was lifted from my mind*. Elicit that we use this expression when we are really worried or depressed about something and then hear some good news that tells us our worries are unnecessary. Ask students to suggest some circumstances in which this expression could be used.

Pairwork. Students discuss the last time they had a weight lifted from their mind. Encourage them to report to the class any interesting or amusing stories they heard in their pairs.

Lexis (p 31)

1 Students look back at the text and find the answers to the two questions. Check answers with the class.

> a) He got involved in the excitement of university life and lost touch with them.
>
> b) He got more and more jealous.

2 Focus attention on the use of *got* in the answers to 1. Ask students if they know of any other expressions using *got*. Make a list of any suggestions on the board. Encourage students to group words together when they record them in their notebooks. They can start a page of expressions which use *got* and add to the list as they come across more of them. Go through the five *got* expressions with the class and make sure that they understand them. Invite suggestions for other ways of finishing the example. Students complete the other sentences on their own.

Allow students to compare their sentences with a partner before you check answers with the whole class. Write any particularly interesting sentences on the board. Elicit from students that in these expressions *get* approximates to *become*. Brainstorm/Elicit other expressions using *get* and check meaning.

3 Groupwork. Students read the ends of their sentences to other students. The others try to guess which sentences they belong to.

Test

Scoring: one point per correct answer unless otherwise indicated.

1 1 self-centred
2 old-fashioned
3 easy-going
4 hard-working
5 over-sensitive
6 big-headed
7 absent-minded
8 good-looking

2
A: Where <u>are</u> <u>you</u> going? /ə/ /ə/ (2 points)

B: T<u>o</u> the cin<u>e</u>ma t<u>o</u> see *Star Wars*. /ə/ /ə/ /ə/ /ə/ /ə/ (5 points)

A: Who <u>are</u> <u>you</u> going with? /ə/ /ə/ (2 points)

B: Paul <u>a</u>nd Jane. /ə/ (1 point)

3 (½ point each)
1 for ages
2 for five weeks
3 since last Friday
4 since 15th May
5 since 1999
6 since five minutes ago
7 for five minutes
8 since I came here

4 1 met   2 got married   3 have known
4 were   5 lost   6 hasn't played   7 shared
8 haven't seen   9 lived   10 went   11 saw
12 didn't go   13 has been   14 ran off
15 have you worked   16 was   17 did you work
18 left

7 — actively fuested

3 *Dating* Test

Name: _____   **Total:** _____ **/40**

---

1   Vocabulary – qualities and character *8 points*

Complete the eight compound adjectives using the words in the box. Use each word only once.

> sensitive   centred   going   working   minded
> fashioned   looking   headed

1 self- _____

2 old- _____

3 easy- _____

4 hard- _____

5 over- _____

6 big- _____

7 absent-_____

8 good- _____

2   Pronunciation – /ə/ *10 points*

The following dialogue contains ten /ə/s. Mark them on the dialogue.

1   A: Where are you going?
2   B: To the cinema to see *Star Wars*.
3   A: Who are you going with?
4   B: Paul and Jane.

3   *since* and *for* *4 points*

Which of the following are used with *since* and which are used with *for*?

1 _____ ages

2 _____ five weeks

3 _____ last Friday

4 _____ 15th May

5 _____ 1999

6 _____ five minutes ago

7 _____ five minutes

8 _____ I came here

4   Past simple and present perfect *18 points*

Put the verbs into the present perfect or the past simple.

We (1) _____ (meet) in Tokyo in 1998.

They (2) _____ (get married) in Barcelona.

I (3) _____ (know) her since we (4) _____ (be) at school together.

He (5) _____ (lose) his passport when he was on holiday.

She (6) _____ (not/play) tennis since last year.

We (7) _____ (shared) a flat for two years, but I (8) _____ (not/see) him for over five years.

He (9) _____ (live) in São Paulo until he (10) _____ (go) to university in Rio.

I (11) _____ (see) her yesterday.

We (12) _____ (not/go) on holiday last year.

He (13) _____ (be) single since his girlfriend (14) _____ (run off) with a Spanish plastic surgeon two years ago.

A: How long (15) _____ you _____ (work) for CNN?

B: Since last January. I (16) _____ (be) at CBS before that.

A: How long (17) _____ you _____ (work) for CBS?

B: For seven years. Ever since I (18) _____ (leave) school.

4 *Adrenalin* Overview

The topic in this unit is excitement, particularly in relation to sport. The grammar focus of the unit is past experiences using the present perfect, past simple and past continuous. There is also work on absolute and gradable adjectives and intonation in expressive sentences.

Students talk about feelings they experience in certain situations or when they do certain activities. They go on to read a webpage about a man who continues to take part in a dangerous sport even after a near-fatal accident. They are then given the opportunity to tell a story about a time when they felt a rush of adrenalin.

The listening activities include an interview with Jane Couch, a female boxer, and the Ike and Tina Turner song *River Deep, Mountain High*.

The Adrenalin Game provides students with an opportunity to talk about past events and experiences.

Section	Aims	What the students are doing
Introduction page 32	*Conversation skills*: fluency work	Talking about frightening or exciting experiences.
My name is Mike & I'm a skydiver pages 32–34	*Reading skills*: scanning;	Generating interest in a text, *My name is Mike & I'm a skydiver*, by talking about parachute jumping. Scanning text for specific information.
	for detail	Correcting a summary of the text.
	Lexis: collocations;	Reviewing collocations about risk and excitement in the text.
	grading adjectives	Making synonyms from adjectives, and then grading them.
	Pronunciation: intonation	Practising stress to express strong feelings.
A sporting life page 35	*Lexis*: sports	Reviewing and categorising vocabulary to do with sport.
	Listening skills: note-taking	Listening to an interview with a female boxer and taking notes.
Close up pages 36–38	*Grammar*: past experience: past simple; past continuous & past perfect	Finding the correct endings of grammatically correct sentences that make no sense so that they make sense.

Listening to five people talking about past experiences and identifying the differences between past tenses used to describe past experience. |
	Conversation skills: fluency	Anecdote: talking about a past experience that produced an adrenalin rush.
The Adrenalin Game: truth or dare? page 39	*Grammar*: past simple; past continuous & past perfect	Playing a game, *The Adrenalin Game*, to practise talking about past events and experiences.
Close up page 40	*Lexis*: sports	Reviewing vocabulary to do with sports.
	Grammar: comparisons	Reviewing comparative and superlative structures and modifiers in the context of sports.
River deep mountain high page 41	*Listening skills*: predicting;	Making predictions about a song, *River Deep, Mountain High*, by completing a love letter.
	listening for detail	Listening to the song and comparing it with the completed love letter.

4 *Adrenalin* Teacher's notes

Closed book. Pairwork. Elicit or explain the meaning of the word adrenalin. Students make a list of the subjects/activities they think might be included in a unit entitled Adrenalin. Get feedback from the whole class and write any interesting ideas on the board. You could get students to rank the activities in terms of how adrenalin-inducing they are.

Open books. Whole class. Students look at the definition of adrenalin in the margin. Elicit some situations in which they have been aware of a rush of adrenalin. Brainstorm some words for how they felt, other reactions in the body (for example, increased heart rate), etc.

Whole class. Students look at the photograph and identify the sport (skydiving or parachute jumping). Find out if any of them have ever done it or know of anyone who has. Encourage them to tell their stories to the rest of the class. Elicit some reactions to the picture, for example, how many of them would like to or would be willing to skydive; how they would feel before, during and after jumping from a plane.

1   Whole class. Go through the lists of emotions and situations to make sure everyone understands them.

Pairwork. Students discuss how they would feel in each situation. Give them two to three minutes for this. Pairs report back to the class. Perhaps have a show of hands for each situation and emotion to see how much agreement there is across the class.

2   Pairwork. Students compare their experiences and discuss which gave them the biggest adrenalin rush, that is which caused the strongest emotion. Again, you could have a show of hands to find out who has been in each of the situations and then ask them to tell the class how they actually felt.

My name is Mike & I'm a skydiver (p 32)

Note: the text is about someone who says he is 'addicted' to skydiving. The title of the text is a play on the formula used by societies which help people to overcome alcohol addiction. New members are encouraged to face up to their addiction by introducing themselves to the group with the words *My name is ... and I am an alcoholic.*

1   If you discussed these questions fully when looking at the photograph in the last section, move on quickly to 2. If not, have a show of hands to find out how many people would agree with each statement.

2   Whole class. Go through the three questions with the class and then get them to scan the text quickly to find the answers. As a way of encouraging students to scan read for the necessary information only and not to spend time on every word, you could do this as a race with the first student to find the answers putting up their hand.

> *Possible answers*
> a)   He was bored with the routine of his life and looking for more excitement and he saw an ad for skydiving on the television.
> b)   He had a rush of adrenalin; it was amazing.
> c)   Another skydiver crashed into his parachute and he fell 80 feet to the ground. He has continued because he is addicted to skydiving: it is his life.

Whole class. Students read the text again more carefully and underline any words they don't know. Go through the underlined words, encouraging students who do know the meanings to explain them to the rest. Make sure they understand *voluntarily, took my breath away, free-falling, cord, hooked, addicted* and *collided*. Elicit what kind of person might say *There must be more to life than this* (someone who is bored with the dull routine of their life, someone who has no excitement in their life).

Ask students what they think of the text. Could they imagine getting hooked on skydiving or any other sport? Do they think Mike is mad or brave to continue skydiving after his accident?

3   Pairwork. Go through the sentences with the class. Students then discuss and correct the details that are wrong. Check answers with the class.

> a)   Mike was watching television when he saw the ad.
> b)   He phoned the skydiving centre the next day and booked a jump.
> c)   After a day's training, he wondered if he was completely mad.
> d)   It was a beautiful evening. At first he felt nervous, then he began to feel more relaxed.
> e)   After a 20-minute flight, he jumped out of the aeroplane, and after free-falling to 5,500 feet, he opened his parachute.
> f)   After his first jump, he knew he would do it again.
> g)   During his free time, he skydived. He thought about skydiving a lot when he was working.
> h)   The accident happened when another skydiver collided with his parachute.
> i)   Correct
> j)   Correct

Lexis (p 34)

1 Pairwork. Students complete the questions. Encourage them do this without looking at the text first.

2 Students then look at the text, check their answers and discuss/in pairs ask and answer the questions. Check answers with the whole class and get feedback from the discussions.

> a) live
>
> b) take part
>
> c) put; risk
>
> d) took; breath away?
>
> e) addicted

Grading adjectives (p 34)

1 Students look at the adjectives in the box and match pairs with similar meanings.

2 Whole class. Students look at the example. Elicit that *furious* is a stronger version of *angry*. We call *furious* an 'absolute' adjective and *angry* a 'gradable' adjective.

Go through a few of the adjectives in the list with the class and elicit whether they are gradable or absolute. Give students a few minutes to classify the rest and check the answers with the class.

Get students to go back over the text about Mike the skydiver and to circle any absolute adjectives they find. They may circle the following: *(completely) mad, (absolutely) incredible, (most) amazing*. Elicit that absolute adjectives are qualified by strong adverbs (for example, *completely, absolutely*) and it would not be possible to say 'very mad' or 'fairly incredible'. Students can look at the Language reference section on this page for more information about gradable and absolute adjectives.

Gradable	Absolute
angry	furious
tired	exhausted
strange	incredible
bad	awful
funny	hilarious
good	brilliant
excited	thrilled

You could elicit/brainstorm a few more and add them to the lists.

Optional activity

To consolidate the language, a quick game or two is a good idea. (1) You or a student calls out a gradable adjective and students respond with its absolute equivalent. (2) Bingo – students write down any four absolute adjectives on a strip of paper and pass it to another student. Call out a succession of gradable adjectives and students cross off the absolute equivalents on their papers. The first to cross off all four shouts 'Bingo!' and is the winner.

Intonation (p 34)

1 🔲 **12 SB p 149**

Pairwork. Encourage students to go through the dialogues in pairs before they listen to the recording and to predict which words go in the gaps. They could write their guesses in pencil beside the dialogues. Students listen to the recording and complete the dialogues. They then compare their answers with a partner. Check answers with the class.

> 🔲 **12**
>
> **A**
>
> A: Have you ever been skydiving?
>
> B: Yes, I have.
>
> A: Was it **good**?
>
> B: **Good**? It was absolutely **incredible**!
>
> **B**
>
> C: Have you ever been surfing?
>
> D: Yes, I have.
>
> C: Were you **scared**?
>
> D: **Scared**? I was absolutely **terrified**.

2 🔲 **12 SB p 149**

Students listen to the recording again and note the pronunciation of the words in bold type. These are heavily emphasised by the speakers to enhance their meaning and make their utterances more exciting.

Try reading the dialogues to the class without emphasising these words and allow them to see how flat and boring it sounds.

3 Pairwork. Students practise the dialogues. Go round and encourage them to exaggerate the intonation for effect. Then get some pairs to perform their dialogues for the class, making them as interesting as possible by exaggerating the intonation. Make sure they understand that exaggerated stress is not appropriate for gradable adjectives.

4 Pairwork. Students make up similar dialogues using gradable and absolute adjectives. As they practise them, go round the class listening to their dialogues and pick out any really good ones to be performed for the class. If students are slow to produce ideas of their own, start them off by telling them about a dangerous sport or some activity you have participated in (you can make this up if you wish); get them to ask you if you were scared, if it was good, etc. and then use an absolute adjective in your reply. Encourage students to use a range of adjectives, for example, *tired/exhausted, bad/terrible*, etc., and not just the ones in the examples. It is probably a good idea to model and encourage students to make up an array of shorter dialogues, for example, *Was she angry? Angry? She was furious!* as the *Have you ever ... ?* model is quite limiting and does not facilitate too many absolute adjectives.

A Sporting Life (p 35)

Lexis

1 Make sure that students know all the names of the sports. Explain any that they do not know. In small groups, students think of categories for each of the sports. Then they group them into each category.

> *Possible answers*
>
> Swimming, surfing, sailing and scuba diving are all water sports.
> Aerobatics, bungee jumping and skydiving are all sports you do in the air.
> Ice hockey, skating and snowboarding are all sports you do on ice or snow.
> Baseball, basketball, football, rugby, table-tennis, tennis and volleyball are all sports you play with a ball.
> Athletics, cycling, horse riding, basketball, judo, karate and weightlifting are all Olympic sports.
> Climbing, horse riding, bungee jumping and skydiving are all dangerous sports.

2 Students decide which verb, *go, play* or *do*, is used with each sport.

> *go*: bungee jumping, climbing, cycling, horse riding, sailing, scuba diving, skating, skydiving, snowboarding, surfing, swimming, weightlifting, windsurfing
>
> *play*: badminton, baseball, basketball, football, ice hockey, rugby, table-tennis, tennis, volleyball
>
> *do*: aerobatics, athletics, judo, karate

3 Pairwork. Students see if they can add to the lists in 2.

4 Groupwork. Students discuss the three questions.

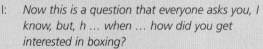 **13 SB p 149**

5 Open books. Students look at the photograph and read the introduction. Elicit their reactions. Find out if anyone has heard of Jane Couch and if women's boxing takes place in their countries.

Whole class. Read the interview questions.
Groupwork. Students predict some possible answers to questions 2, 3, 4, 5, 6 and 7. Get some groups to report their answers to the whole class.

Students listen to the interview and make notes about Jane's answers to the questions. When they have finished, they can compare notes with a partner.

Play the recording again to allow students to get any information they missed the first time round. Let them compare in pairs again before checking answers with the whole class.

Questions asked with answers

Q: How did you get interested in boxing?
A: Saw a documentary on TV.

Q: Were you interested in sport at school?
A: No.

Q: How long did it take you to get fit?
A: About 2 years.

Q: Do you know how many professional female boxers there are?
A: Three hundred women boxing as amateurs and eight women boxing professionally in the UK. Thirty thousand women boxing throughout the world.

Q: What do your critics say?
A: Women shouldn't box.

Q: What do you think are the prime skills to have as a boxer?
A: You've got to have a good brain, know your skills and be fit.

Q: How do you relax?
A: She doesn't relax.

Q: How do you prepare for a match?
A: At a training camp near Bristol for eight weeks.

Q: Have you ever been seriously hurt in a match?
A: No.

Q: Do you think you've changed since your success?
A: Lifestyle has changed, but not as a person.

Q: When's your next big fight?
A: At the end of February / the beginning of March.

Q: Where will it be?
A: In London.

13

Interview with Jane Couch
(I = Interviewer; JC = Jane Couch)

I: *Now this is a question that everyone asks you, I know, but, h ... when ... how did you get interested in boxing?*

JC: *I saw a documentary about women boxing in America about six years ago, it was there, just a li ... a little television programme, it was about an hour long, and I ... I watched the programme and it just changed my life, I was just fascinated from there on in, from like a half an hour programme, I just went ... 'I'm going to do that'.*

I: *And were you interested in sport at school?*

JC: *No, nothing. I wasn't even fit or anything. I used to smoke. I used to drink. Um, just didn't look after meself at all. Didn't eat very well, and this just changed my life. Hah ...*

I: *How long did it take you to get fit?*

JC: It took me, I'd say, to get to the level that I'm at, it took me ... about two years to reach ... to reach the level I needed to be at.

I: And do you know how many female boxers there are in ... the ... in Britain?

JC: In the UK, um, there's ... there's about three hundred women boxing as amateurs, and there's about eight women boxing professionally in the UK at the moment, but throughout the world there's about thirty thousand women, throughout the world.

I: And what do your critics say?

JC: Um, at ... at the ... at the outset it was difficult. It was, like, women shouldn't box, you know, ... they shouldn't be doing this, and they shouldn't be doing that, and should be at home looking after the kids, and everything. But, um ... and she's never be as good as a man, but my last three fights have been live on TV. I've just signed a five fo ... fight deal with Bravo Television.

I: What do you think are the prime, um, skills to have as a boxer?

JC: Um, believe it or not, you've got to be ... you've got to have a pretty good brain to be a good boxer. Anyone can fight, but to make it to the top you've to know your skills, and you've to have a pretty cute brain, and ... and the fitness ... the fitness side of it is very, very important.

I: And how do you relax?

JC: I don't. I never do ... I ... I nev ... I don't sleep much. I just ... and when I do, I dream about boxing, and when I'm trying to get to sleep it's about my fights. I'm just, I can't ... I work really hard. I'm just constantly working, working ...

I: How do you prepare for a match?

JC: Um, for a ... for a ten-round, um, world title fight, obviously I go to training camp just outside Bristol, for eight weeks before each fight, and, um, once I go to training camp that's it. I don't do anything. I've got a ... a very good trainer, I've got a very good team round me, so ...

I: Have you ever been seriously hurt in a match?

JC: Er, not really seriously. Not lasting damage. Things that take a couple of weeks to mend, like broken cheek bone, broken nose, lost a few teeth, but just, er ...

I: Your teeth look great to me from where I'm sitting, I can tell you ...

JC: Hah ... no, I only lost the back ones. Hah, hah ...

I: Now, just finally, do you think you've changed since your success?

JC: Um, changed as a person? I ... I ... I think ... I think I've changed as in ... in the lifestyle that I live now, is um, it's just constantly I'm travelling. I live out of a suitcase. But I think, um, as a person, definitely not, no, I've j ... my feet are just so firmly on the ground, you wouldn't believe it. Um, ...

I: I would believe it, having met you. I can assure you.

JC: Hah.

I: And, just lastly, when's your next big fight?

JC: Er, the next one's going to be the end of February, beginning of March. I'm going to be defending my world ... my three world titles.

I: And where will it be?

JC: In London! Hah, hah.

I: Well, that's great. Thank you very, very much.

Close up (p 36) (Workbook p 21, p 22, p 23, p 24)

Closed books. Ask a few students *Have you ever ... ?* questions to establish the idea, check understanding of the concept and check pronunciation. Make it clear that *ever* means *in your whole life*.

Past experience

1 Pairwork. Students sort out the mixed up sentences. Check answers with the class.

a) Have you ever ridden a horse on the beach?

b) Have you ever been asked to make a speech?

c) Have you ever met a famous person?

d) Have you ever driven a Ferrari?

e) Have you ever been to the top of a mountain?

f) Have you ever crossed a desert?

g) Have you ever appeared on a television programme?

h) Have you ever caught a snake?

2 Students work individually to decide how their partner (the same partner they had in 1) would answer the questions. Go through the possible answers with the class first. They should make a note of the answer next to each question, but should not consult their partner at all.

Pairwork. Students compare their answers and confirm or deny the answers guessed by their partners.

3 In the same pairs, students discuss their answers and practise asking more *Have you ever ... ?* questions. You could start them off by allowing them to ask you some questions about your experiences. You could write a few key words on the board to give students some ideas, for example, *eat/meet/see*.

4 [cassette] 14 SB p 150

Go through the table with students and explain that each speaker on the recording is going to be asked one of the

Have you ever ... ? questions. They must make brief notes for each person as they listen. Emphasise that these are notes and they do not have to write full sentences.

Students listen to the recording and make notes. Play the recording again for them to find any missing information.

a)	Y	playing rugby, jumping up to catch the ball	knocked off balance, fell on left leg, twisted ankle, couldn't play for more than 3 months
b)	Y	walking across field with sister and dog	chased by mad horse, ran away
c)	Y	playing football, playing tennis	broke nose twice: once hit in face by other football player, once missed tennis ball and got hit on nose
d)	Y	driving in Spain	car drove up fast, pulled in front of her and stopped
e)	Y	playing in sea	pulled away from beach by sea, panicked and swallowed water; almost drowned, rescued by someone

🔲 **14**

a
(I = Interviewer; B = Ben)

I: *Have you ever had a sports injury?*

B: *Yes, I have. I was playing rugby for the local team and it was just after kick-off. I was jumping up to catch the ball when a player from the other team knocked me over and I fell heavily on my left leg.*

I: *Oh, dear. Were you badly hurt?*

B: *Ah, yes, I twisted my ankle and couldn't play rugby for more than three months.*

b
(I = Interviewer; D = Dina)

I: *Have you ever been in a dangerous situation?*

D: *Yes, I ... I have. I was walking my dog one day with my sister and we were crossing this field. There was a horse in it and it suddenly started running towards us, looking really mad.*

I: *What did you do?*

D: *Well, I know you're not supposed to run away from animals because they can sense your fear. But we ran away as fast as we could.*

c
(I = Interviewer; F = Frank)

I: *Have you ever broken a bone?*

F: *Yes, I've broken my nose twice. The first time I was playing football and one of the other players hit me in the face. The second time, I was playing tennis. I missed the ball and it hit me right on my nose.*

d
(I = Interviewer; P = Paula)

I: *Have you ever been really frightened?*

P: *Yes, I have. Last summer I was driving on the motorway in Spain and we were getting close to Barcelona. So I got into the right-hand lane ready to turn off the motorway when this car screeched up next to me, pulled in front of me and slammed on his brakes. I don't know how I managed to slow down fast enough to avoid him. I've never been so frightened in my life.*

e
(I = Interviewer; G = Glen)

I: *Have you ever thought you were going to die?*

G: *Yeah. It was when I was eight or nine and I was at the beach with my parents. I was playing in the sea, but on the edge because I couldn't swim. Suddenly, I realised that I couldn't feel the bottom and the sea was pulling me further away from the beach. For a few seconds, I panicked and I started swallowing a lot of water. Then I felt really calm, as if I was floating away. I was drowning. Fortunately, someone saw me and pulled me out in time.*

5 Pairwork. Students compare their answers and then ask each other questions from the table. Give them plenty of time to do this and encourage the questioner to add follow-up questions to find out as much information as possible. Encourage students to report back to the class any interesting facts or stories they heard from their partners.

6 Students look at the three headings in the table (*Have you ever ... ? What were you doing? What happened?*). Elicit that the tenses are the present perfect, past continuous and past simple.

7 Pairwork. Students look at the tapescript and find further examples of each of the tenses. They then discuss the questions. Encourage students to check their answers in the Language reference section on page 38 before you check answers with the class.

a)	present perfect
b)	past simple
c)	Both beginnings are grammatically correct, but 1 is more interesting because the use of the past continuous suggests that this is background information and something is about to happen. In 2 the past simple tells us what happened but gives no suggestion that there is more to tell.

8 Pairwork. Students look at the timelines and decide which timeline goes with which tense. Refer them to the Language reference section if they have difficulty with this. Check answers with the class.

> 1 past simple
> 2 past continuous
> 3 present perfect

9 Pairwork. Students read the conversations and complete the gaps with the correct forms. Check answers with the class.

> **A** (1) Have you read; (2) I read;
> (3) I was travelling; (4) did you think;
> (5) I loved
>
> **B** (1) you have lost; (2) I left; (3) Did you ring
>
> **C** (1) We bought; (2) was it; (3) we haven't paid
>
> **D** (1) were you doing; (2) I was watching;
> (3) did you watch; (4) Have you ever been;
> (5) That was; (6) I have changed

10 Students work individually to write their six sentences on a sheet of paper or, to encourage more interaction and make it more challenging, students could write on six different strips of paper. Emphasise that they mustn't show their sentences to anyone.

11 Collect the papers and shuffle them. Give out the papers to the class. Each student must guess who wrote the sentences they have received. When they have decided who it is, they put up their hands. Invite them to read out the sentences and say who they think wrote them. The 'accused' person confirms or denies it.

Optional activities

When you have collected the papers and shuffled them, read out one set of sentences and elicit guesses from the class as to who wrote them. Each student could write five true sentences and one false one. A partner or the rest of the class have to decide which sentence is false.

Anecdote (p 38) (Workbook p 25)

See Introduction, page 4 for more ideas on how to set up, monitor and repeat 'anecdotes'.

1 Whole class. Remind students of the expression *a rush of adrenalin*. Previously they have discussed this in terms of sports. Now the discussion is broadened to include other experiences. Tell students that they are going to prepare and tell a story to a partner about a moment when they felt a rush of adrenalin.

Students look at the Language toolbox which gives a framework for storytelling. Get them to identify the different tenses used here. Elicit that a good structure makes a story easier to follow and more interesting.

Go through the list of questions with the class and explain that these are here to help them structure their stories successfully. Give students ten to fifteen minutes to work on their stories individually. Go round and give help with vocabulary and structure as needed. Encourage them to write notes which will help them tell the story in the right order, rather than writing the story down to be read out.

2 Pairwork. Students take turns telling their stories. Encourage the listeners to listen carefully and attentively and to save any questions until the story is finished. Go round listening and noting any interesting stories you hear.

Ask if any students particularly enjoyed the stories they heard. If so, get the relevant student to recount the story again for the rest of the class. If no one volunteers, ask to hear any of the stories that seemed particularly good as you were going around.

The Adrenalin Game: truth or dare? (p 39)

This board game should provide a welcome change of pace, while providing further opportunities for students to practise talking about events and experiences in the past. You will need dice and counters for each team.

Establish the meaning of *dare* (an invitation to someone to do something difficult or dangerous to show how brave they are).

Go through the rules of the game with the whole class, then divide them into teams to prepare their 'truth' questions and their 'dares'. Monitor their lists discreetly and discourage them from asking any questions that are too personal and from suggesting dares that are too embarrassing or which involve actual physical danger.

Play the game as outlined in the Student's Book. Team members should take turns to be the person who answers the question or performs the dare.

Close up (p 40) (Workbook p 23)

Comparisons

1 Whole class. Students find the names of twelve sports. Find out how many people have done each one.

> baseball boxing bungee jumping cricket
> football formula one skydiving rugby running
> scuba diving skiing snowboarding

2 ▭ 15 SB p 150

Pairwork. Students listen to the recording and identify the four sports. They note down the key words that helped them.

> 1 snowboarding (similar to skiing, a board, bindings to attach your feet to the board)
> 2 scuba diving (sea, lake, equipment, wetsuit, dive)

3 football (Notts Forest, Man U, team, match, sent off, first half, referee)

4 bungee jumping (elastic, jump, free fall, bounce up and down)

📼 15

George

(I = Interviewer; G = George)

I: George, is this similar to skiing?

G: Actually, it's slightly easier and I think it's a lot more exhilarating.

I: Is it cheaper?

G: No, not really. The equipment is just as expensive.

I: What do you need?

G: A board, of course, and that can cost about £400. Then you have to have bindings to attach your feet to the board, and you also need special clothes and boots which are quite expensive.

I: Is it as popular as skiing?

G: With young people, yes.

Katrina

(I = Interviewer; K = Katrina)

I: Katrina, where did you learn?

K: I did my preliminary certificate in Malta when I was on holiday.

I: I suppose you have to learn in the sea, don't you? I mean, you don't live near the sea, do you?

K: Er, no, but I could have had lessons at home in a lake, although it's much more pleasant to learn in the Mediterranean because it's nice and warm.

I: Did you have to buy all the equipment?

K: No, you can hire it but it's far better to have your own wetsuit because it's important for it to be exactly the right size.

I: Are lessons very expensive?

K: Quite expensive, but it's worth having lessons with professionals because it's much safer.

I: Were you nervous on your first dive?

K: Yes, but it was one of the most amazing experiences I've ever had.

Paul

(I = Interviewer; P = Paul)

I: Paul, who do you support?

P: I used to support Notts Forest, but then I changed to Man U.

I: Why?

P: Because they're by far the most exciting team in England.

I: Did you watch their last match?

P: Yes. They didn't play as well as usual and one of their best players was sent off in the first half.

I: Why?

P: Er, the referee said that he kicked a player from the other team.

I: So, did they lose?

P: No, it was a draw.

Eva

(I = Interviewer; E = Eva)

I: Eva, was it your first time?

E: Yes, and it was amazing.

I: What did you have to do?

E: Well, the first time you do it they attach the elastic around your waist and you just jump. At first, you free fall, and then the elastic pulls you back and you bounce up and down a few times.

I: How did it feel?

E: Incredible ... I can't explain the feeling ... it's ... it's much better than anything else I have ever done. It's exciting, but it isn't nearly as frightening as you imagine.

I: What made you do it?

E: It was a birthday present and it's definitely the best birthday present I've ever had.

3 Students listen again and fill in the gaps in the sentences. Allow them to compare answers in pairs. Check answers with the class.

Possible answers

a) Snowboarding is slightly easier than skiing.

b) Snowboarding is just as popular as skiing.

c) Scuba diving was one of the most amazing experiences I've ever had.

d) Man U are by far the most exciting team in England.

e) Bungee jumping is much better than anything else I've ever done.

f) Bungee jumping isn't nearly as frightening as you imagine.

4 Groupwork. Students discuss their own opinions about sports, using the structures in 3.

5 Pairwork. Students discuss the rules for comparative and superlative adjectives. You might want to get them to discuss the rules with their books closed to see how much they remember before they look at the Language reference section at the bottom of the page which outlines the rules.

River Deep Mountain High (SB p 41)

1 Students make a list of three or four things for each adjective. Encourage them to be as imaginative as possible.

2 Pairwork. Students work together to compare their lists and see if there are any common items. Get one or two students to read out the things they have chosen in each category.

3 Go through the letter with the students and get them to suggest words which might fit into each gap. Students then work individually to complete the letter.

4 🔊 16 SB p 151

Play the recording while the students compare their list of images with the ones in the song. Ask students if any of the images are the same. Play it again and ask students to list the images in the song.

> 🔊 **16**
>
> *River Deep Mountain High* by Ike and Tina Turner
>
> *When I was a little girl*
> *I had a rag doll*
> *Only doll I've ever owned*
> *Now I love you just the way I loved that rag doll*
> *But only now my love has grown*
> *And it gets stronger, in every way*
> *And it gets deeper, let me say*
> *And it gets higher, day by day*
> *And do I love you my oh my*
> *Yeah, river deep mountain high*
> *Yeah, yeah, yeah*
> *If I lost you would I cry*
> *Oh how I love you baby, baby, baby, baby*
>
> *When you were a young boy*
> *Did you have a puppy*
> *That always followed you around*
> *Well I'm gonna be as faithful as that puppy*
> *No I'll never let you down*
> *Cause it grows stronger, like a river flows*
> *And it gets bigger baby, and heaven knows*
> *And it gets sweeter baby, as it grows*
> *And do I love you my oh my*
> *Yeah, river deep mountain high*
> *Yeah, yeah, yeah*
> *If I lost you would I cry*
> *Oh how I love you baby, baby, baby, baby*
>
> *I love you baby like a flower loves the spring*
> *And I love you baby like a robin loves to sing*
> *And I love you baby like a schoolboy loves his pet*
> *And I love you baby river deep mountain high*
> *baby, baby, baby ... oh baby ... oh ... oh ...*
> *Do I love you my oh my*
> *Yeah, river deep mountain high*
> *Yeah, yeah, yeah*
> *If I lost you would I cry*
> *Oh how I love you baby, baby, baby, baby*

Test

Scoring: one point per correct answer unless otherwise indicated.

1
1 hilarious
2 furious
3 exhausted
4 brilliant/fascinating
5 terrified
6 thrilled
7 incredible/brilliant/amazing/fantastic
8 Awful/Dreadful/Terrible

2 (½ point each)
1 fell
2 was watching
3 was wearing
4 saw
5 Were you doing
6 phoned
7 didn't go
8 was raining

3 (½ point each)
1 Have you ever been
2 went
3 went
4 haven't seen
5 Have you seen
6 haven't seen
7 haven't received
8 posted

4
2 was
3 was travelling
4 decided
5 went
6 did
7 walked
8 were crossing
9 lost
10 tripped
11 fell
12 was swinging
13 was hanging
14 managed
15 have never been
16 was
17 haven't done

5
1 the biggest
2 the most dangerous
3 younger than
4 as important as / more important than
5 as clever as
6 more serious than / not as serious as
7 as early as
8 happier

Adrenalin Test

Name: _____   **Total:** _____ /40

1 Vocabulary – gradable and absolute adjectives
8 points

Complete the following dialogues using an appropriate absolute adjective.

A: Was the film funny?
B: Yeah, it was absolutely (1) _____ .

A: Was she angry?
B: Angry! She was (2) _____ .

A: Are you tired?
B: Yeah, I'm totally (3) _____ .

A: Is the book good?
B: Yes, it's absolutely (4) _____ .

A: Were you frightened?
B: Frightened! I was completely (5) _____ .

A: Were you pleased with your birthday present?
B: Yes, I was (6) _____ .

A: Did you have a good time?
B: It was great – absolutely (7) _____ .

A: What's your pizza like?
B: (8) _____ . I can't eat it!

2 Past simple and past continuous *4 points*

Put the verbs into the past simple or the past continuous.

I (1) _____ (fall) asleep while I (2) _____ (watch) television.

He (3) _____ (wear) a blue shirt when we (4) _____ (see) him.

_____ you (5) _____ (do) your homework when I (6) _____ (phone) you?

We (7) _____ (not/go) for a walk because it (8) _____ (rain).

3 Past simple and present perfect *4 points*

Put the verbs into either the past simple or the present perfect.

A: _____ you ever (1) _____ (be) to Peru?
B: Yes, I (2) _____ (go) there last year actually.

A: I (3) _____ (go) to the Van Gogh exhibition last week.
B: I (4) _____ (not/see) it yet – what's it like?

A: _____ you (5) _____ (see) Marta recently?
B: No, I (6) _____ (not/see) her for ages actually.

A: We (7) _____ (not/receive) your postcard yet.
B: That's strange – I (8) _____ (post) it last Friday.

4 Past simple, past continuous and present perfect
16 points

Choose the correct tense.

I think the most exciting and, as it turned out, the most dangerous thing I (1) ~~ever did~~/**have ever done** is trekking in Nepal. It (2) **has been/was** a few years ago and I (3) **travelled/was travelling** around Asia with a friend. We (4) **decided/were deciding** to leave the cities and the beaches behind us and do something different. First, we (5) **have gone/went** to a small town in the foothills of the Himalayas and from there we (6) **were doing/did** a two-week trek around the Annapurna Range. We (7) **have walked/walked** about twenty kilometres each day. One day, while we (8) **crossed/were crossing** a river way below us on a tiny bridge, I suddenly (9) **lost/was losing** my footing, (10) **tripped/was tripping** and nearly (11) **fell/was falling** over the edge. The bridge (12) **was swinging/swung** from side to side and I (13) **was hanging/have been hanging** on for what seemed like ages until my friend (14) **was managing/managed** to pull me back up. I (15) **was never/have never been** so scared in all my life! After that, the white-water rafting (16) **has been/was** plain sailing. But I (17) **haven't done/didn't do** that since either.

5 Comparatives and superlatives *8 points*

Complete the sentences using the adjectives in capital letters and any other necessary words.

1 Russia is _____ country in the world. BIG

2 Skydiving is _____ sport I have ever done. DANGEROUS

3 He is actually much _____ he looks. YOUNG

4 Taking part is _____ winning. IMPORTANT

5 He's not _____ he thinks he is. CLEVER

6 The problem is _____ we first thought. SERIOUS

7 Try to arrive _____ possible. EARLY

8 She's a lot _____ now he's here. HAPPY

5 Kids *Overview*

The topic in this unit is children. The grammar focus is defining relative clauses and *would* and *used to*.

Students examine the relationship between parents and children. They read seven definitions of a mother taken from children's points of view and they go on to write definitions of a father.

Students then listen to children describing things using relative clauses and practise using relative clauses in a game: *Definition Auction*.

Students practise stress timing using two popular English nursery rhymes.

Finally they read extracts about childhood memories from Roald Dahl's autobiography, *Boy*, and this is used to examine ways of talking about the past. Students are given the opportunity to listen to the end of extract from *Boy*.

Section	Aims	What the students are doing
Introduction page 42	*Conversation skills*: fluency work	Compiling and discussing lists to describe either the qualities of a good child or of a good parent. Then comparing these qualities.
A child's point of view page 42	*Grammar*: defining relative clauses	Reading children's definitions of a mother and writing a definition for a father.
	Listening skills: listening for detail	Listening to children defining various things.
Close up pages 43–44	*Grammar*: defining relative clauses;	Identifying relative clauses within sentences. Identifying relative pronouns.
		Practising relative clauses by completing definitions and writing definitions about educational systems.
	omitting relative pronouns	Identifying when to omit relative pronouns.
	Where, when & whose	Practising relative clauses by completing sentences.
Definition Auction page 45	*Grammar*: relative clauses	Playing a game, *Definition Auction*, to practise relative clauses.
Children's rhymes page 46	*Pronunciation*: stress timing	Practising stress timing by listening to nursery rhymes. Writing a nursery rhyme and marking stressed syllables.
First memory: The bicycle page 47–48	*Reading skills*: predicting; for gist;	Making predictions about an extract from Roald Dahl's autobiography, *Boy*, from an illustration. Reading the extract for gist.
	scanning	Scanning the extract to find differences between it and the illustration.
	Lexis: bicycles	Reviewing language to do with bicycles from the text.
Second memory: The Great Mouse Plot page 48	*Reading skills*: for gist;	Reading another extract from *Boy* for gist.
	for detail	Checking comprehension of the text by choosing the correct drawing.
Close up page 49	*would & used to*	Identifying ways of talking about the past using *would* and *used to* and the past simple.
	Conversation skills: fluency practice	Anecdote: talking about life at the age of eight.
	Listening skills: listening for gist	Optional: listening to the end of story from the second extract of *Boy*.

Kids *Teacher's notes*

Closed books. Tell students about your earliest memory. Encourage them to ask you questions about how old you were at the time and about the details of your memory. Ask students what their earliest memories are. Find out who can remember the furthest back and encourage them to give as many details as possible that they remember. Ask them what age their best childhood memories come from and whether they agree with the old saying that your schooldays are the best days of your life.

Open books. Students look at the illustrations. Ask how old they think the children are. Tell them to imagine that they can go back to being one of these ages. Which age would they choose and why?

1 Whole class. Students look at the age categories. Tell them the names of some children you know, say how old they are and how you know them. Then get students to write down the names of any children they know and put their names in the correct age category.

2 Pairwork. Students tell each other about the names they have written down. Encourage listening partners to ask questions about the children, for example, whose children they are and how their partner knows them. Go round and monitor, giving help with vocabulary if necessary.

3 Groupwork. Write on the board: Good child and Good parent. Elicit an example of the qualities that make a good child and a good parent. Write these under the appropriate headings.

Divide the class into two groups: Parents and Children with a 'secretary' in each. With a large class you could have more than one group for each. The Parents group discuss and list the qualities of a good child, the Children group do the same for a good parent.

Give students about ten minutes to do the activity, then the secretaries report to the class. Put the two groups together and allow them to compare what they have written. Ask the Children group if they agree with the Parents group and vice versa. Encourage them to give reasons.

A child's point of view (p 42)

Closed books. Write the following on the board:

You have to love your own because everyone else thinks it's a nuisance.

It's someone who tells you it won't hurt when he's hurting you.

Tell students these are definitions of things written by children. Get them to guess what they are (a baby and a doctor). Elicit examples of things students said or believed when they were children because of their limited experience of the world. Give a few examples of your own if possible, for example, you thought that electricity leaked into the room if you left a socket switched on without a plug in it.

1 Get individual students to read out the definitions to the class. Elicit or explain the meaning of any unknown vocabulary (*tucks you in* = puts you to bed and tucks the sheets and blankets tightly under the mattress so you feel safe and secure). Point out that these definitions were written by children and ask them to decide which one they like best. Have a show of hands to determine the class favourite.

2 Pairwork. Students write their own definitions of a father. Give them plenty of time to do this and go round offering help where needed.

3 🔲 **17 SB p 151**

Students look at the photos. Tell them they are going to hear the children in the photos defining some of the things from the list. Go through the list with the class, making sure they understand all the items.

Students listen to the recording and number the five items defined by the children in the correct order. Students compare their answers in pairs, then play the recording again. Check answers with the class.

> 1 dinosaur 2 God 3 iceberg
> 4 museum 5 robber

🔲 **17**

1
A: *Um, it's something that lived a l... a very long time ago. It looks very scary.*
B: *A thing that lived long time ago.*
C: *Um ... It's a big monster.*

2
D: *It's a man and, and um ... he lives in ... he lives up in space.*
E: *It's someone who um ... made the world and um ... he made the animals.*
F: *He's someone who lives ... who's died and he ... he, um ... looks down on people.*
G: *He's a man up in heaven.*
H: *A person that helps people, in heaven.*

3
I: *It's something that's er ... er, very cold and it's in ... it's a ... it's a ... it's a, um ... it's a stone.*
J: *It's something that crashes down on people and it's got ice.*
K: *It's a sort of big piece of, um ... ice that cracks off a bigger piece.*
L: *It's a big ice cube.*

4

M: *A place where ... where animals ... have been put up to show.*

N: *Somewhere where um ... they show you things that are very old.*

O: *It's somewhere where er, people will show things like dinosaurs and olden days things.*

P: *A place ... a place that um ... you see loads and loads of ... you see bones or things and pictures.*

Q: *It's in the country and you see dinosaur bones there.*

5

R: *It's a person who takes toys away.*

S: *It's someone that in the middle of the night ... and it's got um ... it's got a ... it's got um, a ba ... something around his face with, with, um ... round holes and he's ... he's got um ... a T-shirt that's got black and white and he robs things.*

T: *It's someone who steals things when you're asleep.*

U: *A person that steals things at night.*

4 Pairwork. Students choose other words from the list and try to define them as if to a child. Elicit some endings for some given objects. For example, give them the word *sandwich* and elicit *It's a sort of food; magazine – It's like a book; firefighter – It's a person who puts out fires; umbrella – It's something that you use when it's raining; library – It's a place where you go to borrow books; wedding – It's the celebration you have when two people get married.*

To start the activity off, choose one of the items from the list and elicit explanations. Write the ideas on the board.

Pairwork. Students write more explanations. Go round the class and help, where necessary. Take note of any particularly good explanations as you go round. Invite several pairs to read out their explanations without saying what it is they are explaining. Get the rest of the class to guess what they are talking about.

Optional activity

Each student writes on a piece of paper the name of an everyday thing or concept, not one of those in the Student's Book. Collect the pieces of paper and divide the class into two teams (or more if you have a very large class). Team members take turns to come to the front of the class to receive a piece of paper. They then have to return to their team and, without showing them the paper, explain the thing written on it. The team member who guesses correctly brings the paper back to the front of the class and receives another thing to explain to their team. The winners are the team who guess the most explanations.

Close up (p 43) (Workbook p 26, p 27, p 28, p 29)

Defining relative clauses

1 Write the first sentence on the board, then read it out to the class and ask them to identify the relative clause. Underline it.

Pairwork. Students look at the other sentences and underline the relative clauses. Check answers with the class. Elicit the answer to question b) from the class.

a)	1	that lived a long time ago
	2	that helps people
	3	that crashes down on people
	4	that steals things at night
b)	that	
c)	1 which 2 who 3 which 4 who	

2 Students look at the pictures and say what they are (a doorknocker, an elephant, a judge, a mother, a robber). Focus attention on the first joke and elicit which word should go in the blank. Students should be able to work out that it is *elephant*, if only because this is the only one that starts with a vowel. Then read the whole joke aloud to the class. See if anyone can explain why it is funny. (The joke hinges on the issue of politeness. If anyone you meet has a machine gun you will be polite to them, let alone an elephant. Therefore, for maximum politeness and to avoid trouble, he should be called 'sir'.)

Pairwork. Students try to complete the other jokes. Check answers with the whole class. See if anyone can explain why the jokes are funny. You might like to point out the use of relative clauses in these jokes.

2	mother (mini = small; mum = mother)
3	robber (12 months = the 12 months on a calendar and a 12-month prison sentence)
4	judge (*Justice Fingers* sounds like *just his fingers*, i.e. without thumbs. *Justice* is another word for judge.)
5	doorknocker (*Nobel* sounds like *no bell*, i.e. without a doorbell)

If you are teaching a monolingual class, try to translate the jokes with the whole class. If you have students of different nationalities, allow them to work together to see if they can translate the jokes into their own language.

Elicit feedback on a) whether the joke can be translated at all and b) whether it is funny.

Find out from students whether there are similar jokes in their language(s) and what type of jokes are common. For example, English has a lot of jokes involving elephants, a lot of jokes that begin *What do you call ... ?*, and a lot of jokes that involve a simple question and answer.

Optional activity

Ask students to think of a joke in their own language that would translate well into English. Allow them to work in pairs to do this if they speak the same language. Otherwise, you could set this for homework and ask students to come to the next class prepared to tell a joke in English to the others.

3 Give students a few minutes to try to complete the sentences by themselves. Encourage them to guess the answers if they don't know.

> *Possible answers*
>
> a) A professor is a person who is in charge of a university department.
>
> b) A secondary school is a school for pupils over the age of 11.
>
> c) Public schools are schools which you have to pay to attend.
>
> d) A degree is a qualification which you receive from a university.
>
> e) Undergraduates are people who are studying at university and do not have a degree.
>
> f) A student grant is money which the government pays to a student to allow him/her to study at university.

4 If your students are all from the same country, this exercise could be done in pairs. Otherwise they should work individually to produce sentences about the education systems of their countries. Get feedback with the whole class, asking selected students to read out their sentences.

Omitting relative pronouns (p 44)
(Workbook p 27)

Go through the first two example sentences with the class, making sure that everyone understands that both sentences are correct and mean the same, even though the relative pronoun has been omitted in the second one. Then read the third example sentence. Emphasise that the relative pronoun is necessary in this sentence and you cannot say *He's the man lives next door*. Elicit from students why the relative pronoun can be omitted in the first example but not here (we can only omit the relative pronoun when it is the object, not the subject, of the relative clause). Refer them to the Language reference section on page 46 if they are still unclear.

Focus attention on sentences a) to h). Write sentence a) on the board and ask students what the relative clause is, if the relative pronoun is the object or the subject of the clause and whether it is optional (the relative clause is *who you want to speak to*; the relative pronoun *who* is the object of the clause and it is optional). Cross it out on the board.

Pairwork. Students do the same with sentences b) to h). Encourage them to work in stages, identifying the relative clause, determining whether the relative pronoun is the object or subject and thus deciding if it is optional or not.

> The relative pronoun is only optional in sentences a), b), f) and g).

Refer students to the Language reference section on page 46 if they are still unclear of the rule for omitting the relative pronoun.

Where, when & whose (p 44) (Workbook p 26)

1 Establish that *where, when* and *whose* are also relative pronouns and can be used to make relative clauses. Complete the first sentence yourself as an example, then students complete the sentences for themselves. Make sure they understand that they should use a relative clause with *where* or *when*. Go round, offering help where necessary.

Pairwork. Students take turns to read a sentence to their partner and then give more details. Start them off by using an example of your own. Encourage students to use relative clauses when giving feedback.

2 Establish the sort of questions students will need to ask to get the information they need. For example, *What make is your car? When is your birthday?*

If space permits, do this as a mingling activity with students moving around asking questions until they have completed the table. You could also have a race to see who can complete their table first. If space is a problem, divide students into groups or ask individual students to tell the class the relevant information about themselves and then ask if anyone else has the same information (*My car's a Honda. Has anyone else got a Honda?*).

Definition Auction (p 45)

The board game provides further practice in the use of relative pronouns. Divide the class into teams and go through the rules of the game in the Student's Book. Make sure that students understand that they have to 'bid' (offer money to buy) for only those definitions that they think are true. Give the teams time to read through the definitions and decide which are true and which are false. Either you or a good student acts as the auctioneer, using the text in the Student's Book. The winning team is the one that successfully 'buys' the highest number of true definitions without overspending their budget. At the end of the game ensure that students are aware of the correct definitions.

> *Correct definitions*
>
> A midwife is a woman who delivers babies.
> A nappy is something a baby wears to keep clean.
> A mock exam is an exam which a student to practise for the real exam.
> A bully is a person who is unkind to other people.

Children's rhymes (p 46) (Workbook p 30)

Stress timing

English is a stress-timed language in that important words in a sentence are stressed and all the unstressed words are simply fitted in between the stresses, maintaining a fairly standard rhythm no matter how many of them there are. So, for example, the phrase *You and me and him and her* would take a native speaker the same time to say as the much longer phrase *You and then me and then him and then her*. In order to fit in the unstressed words within the rhythm, weak vowel sounds like the schwa /ə/ are often used. In this section, this is illustrated through nursery rhymes which maintain a simple rhythm into which phrases of varying length are fitted.

1 📼 **18**

Focus attention on the name of Humpty Dumpty. Ask if anyone can say who it is. (A children's nursery rhyme involving a fatal accident which happens to a character called Humpty Dumpty, usually portrayed as an egg. Humpty Dumpty sits on a wall. He then falls off and all the king's horses and men are unable to reassemble him.) Students look at the nursery rhyme. Establish that the boxes show the stressed syllables. Read the first line aloud to the class to demonstrate the difference between the stressed and unstressed syllables.

Students listen to the recording and follow the rhyme in their books.

2 Ask students to say the rhyme at the same speed as the recording. Repeat this as many times as necessary until they are able to keep in perfect time with the recording. Students say the rhyme again without the recording. Make sure they are still getting the stress right and that unstressed words are said quickly to maintain the correct rhythm.

> 📼 **18**
>
> *Humpty Dumpty sat on a wall*
> *Humpty Dumpty had a great fall*
> *All the king's horses and all the king's men*
> *Couldn't put Humpty together again*

3 📼 **19 SB p 151**

Focus students' attention on the Doctor Foster nursery rhyme and tell them that it is another traditional English nursery rhyme. Ask them to predict what it is about. (Doctor Foster walks to Gloucester in the rain. He steps in a very deep puddle of water which reaches his waist and he never goes there again.)

Note: You might want to point out that many traditional English nursery rhymes involve accidents, death, destruction and themes that might today be considered unsuitable for children. There are many theories about the origins of these rhymes: one is that they are a way of helping children to deal with unpleasant subjects by

presenting them in a fun way. Children rarely focus on the actual meaning, preferring the fun of the rhythm and the rhymes.

Go through the list of words from the nursery rhyme with the class. Make sure they understand them all and ask them to decide which of the words rhyme. Note: the pronunciation of *Gloucester* (a city in the west of England) is /ˈglɒstə(r)/; it rhymes with *Foster*. *Middle* here refers to the middle of Doctor Foster's body, ie his waist.

> again – rain
> Doctor – Foster – Gloucester
> middle – puddle (this is a half-rhyme)

📼 **19**

Doctor Foster went to Gloucester
In a shower of rain
He stepped in a puddle right up to his middle
And never went there again

Play the recording and ask students to write the rhyme out in the correct stress boxes in their books. Remind them that not all the words they need are in the list. Students compare their rhymes in pairs; then play the recording again. Check answers with the class and make sure that everyone has a correct version.

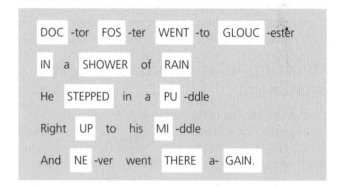

4 Students practise saying the rhyme at the same speed as the recording. Repeat this as many times as necessary until they are able to keep in perfect time with the recording. Students say the rhyme again without the recording. Make sure they are still getting the correct stress and rhythm.

5 Pairwork. This is quite a challenging activity, so give students plenty of time to work on their rhymes. Start by writing an example rhyme on the board:

I went to Rome

And then came back home.

I went out with a waiter

And came back later.

Go round offering help and encouragement. When students have finished, encourage them to read their rhymes to the class. You could display the finished rhymes on the classroom wall for everyone to read and enjoy.

First memory: The Bicycle (p 47)

Note: Roald Dahl is one of Britain's most famous and successful children's writers. One of his best-known books is *Charlie and the Chocolate Factory*, which was made into a popular film. He is also known for his tales of mystery and suspense, many of which have unusual and surprising endings – a twist at the end of the story.

Closed books. Ask students how old they were when they first learnt to read and what kind of stories they enjoyed when they were children. Did they prefer traditional stories or modern ones? Encourage them to give details of the books they read. Were there any particular writers whose work they enjoyed reading? If your class are all from the same country, find out if there is any one writer who was popular with most of the class. The writer whose work they are going to read in this section, Roald Dahl, has been translated into many different languages. Find out if your students have heard of him and what, if anything, they have read of his work.

1 Focus attention on the photo of Roald Dahl and read the introduction with the class. Elicit or explain that *monumental* means very big and that Dahl started writing after he received a severe head injury during the Second World War.

Pairwork. Students look at the illustration and discuss the questions.

> a) The year is 1923 when Roald Dahl was seven years old. (The clothes of the boys should give students some clue that this is an illustration from the past.)
>
> b) The boy on the bicycle is twelve and the others are seven.
>
> c) All the boys are wearing school uniform: caps, white shirts, ties, red and grey striped blazers, grey trousers, grey socks. The twelve-year-old has long trousers whereas the younger boys have short trousers.
>
> d) Possible answers
>
> The boys walk and cycle to school; most modern children go by car or take the bus.
>
> The boys have to wear an old-fashioned school uniform, a practice abandoned by many modern schools. Even those that still have a uniform seldom make children wear caps.
>
> The boy on the bicycle is wearing bicycle-clips to protect his trousers from the oil of the bicycle. Modern children would not bother with these.
>
> The two younger boys are holding conkers – the fruit of the horse chestnut tree. Children used to put these on strings and play conkers, a game in which you hit your conker against your opponent's and try to break it. Old-fashioned games like this are not so popular now. Modern children like to spend their time playing computer games and watching TV.

2 Explain that one of the younger boys in the picture is Roald Dahl at the age of seven. The text they are going to read is about one of his childhood memories. Tell students that they should read the text as quickly as possible in order to find only one piece of information – what Roald Dahl's greatest wish was at that moment. This is to encourage them to scan the text for the information required and not to spend time worrying about difficult words. It is sometimes a good idea to set the activity up as a race with the winner being the first person to find the information and raise their hand. This discourages them from getting stuck as soon as they encounter a word they don't know.

> Dahl's greatest wish was to have a bike like the older boy and to ride very fast down the hill without his hands on the handlebars.

3 Students read the passage again and find the four differences. This time, allow them plenty of time to read.

> The picture shows two seven-year-old boys walking home from school, but in the passage, Dahl says he walked home alone.
>
> The picture shows the boy on the bike with his hands on the handlebars. In the passage, Dahl describes him as riding with hands off the handlebars and crossed across his chest.
>
> The picture shows the boy on the bike with his feet off the pedals. In the passage Dahl says he was back-pedalling (with his feet on the pedals, pedalling backwards).
>
> In the picture the boy is about five yards away from him. In the passage it says he is twenty yards away. (One yard is 0.9 metres.)

Lexis (p 48)

1 Pairwork. Students find the words in the passage that match the underlined words. Check answers with the class.

> a) full speed
> b) flashed by
> c) stopped dead
> d) whizzing
> e) longing
> f) fabulous

2 Students underline all the words in the passage that are related to bicycles. Students compare their answers in pairs. Check answers with the class.

> Words students could have underlined: riding, bicycle, back-pedalling, free-wheeling mechanism, bike, handlebars, bicycle-clips, pedalling.

Second memory: The Great Mouse Plot (p 48)

1 🎦 20

Tell students that they are going to read and listen to the first part of Roald Dahl's second childhood memory. First students listen to the recording with books closed. Then, play the recording again while students follow the text on the page and find the answer to the question.

> The Sweet-shop owner was a horror

2 Pairwork. Students decide which of the three drawings best illustrates the boys' routine.

> Picture 2 shows the boys' routine

🎦 20

My second and only other memory of Llandaff Cathedral School is extremely bizarre. It happened a little over a year later, when I was just nine. By then I had made some friends and when I walked to school in the mornings I would start out alone but would pick up four other boys of my own age along the way. After school was over, the same four boys and I would set out together across the village green and through the village itself, heading for home. On the way to school and on the way back we always passed the sweet-shop. No we didn't, we never passed it. We always stopped. The sweet-shop in Llandaff in the year 1923 was the very centre of our lives. To us, it was what a bar is to a drunk, or a church is to a Bishop. Without it, there would have been little to live for. But it had one terrible drawback, this sweet-shop. The woman who owned it was a horror. We hated her and we had good reason for doing so.

Close up (p 49) (Workbook p 28)

Would & used to

1 Students complete the sentences without looking at the text on page 48, then look at the text to check their answers.

> a) would, would
> b) would

2 Students decide which of the three choices the use of *would* describes. Refer to the Language reference if necessary.

> The answer is a).

3 Groupwork. In small groups, students look at the sentences and discuss the three questions.

> 1 would + verb – sentences e, i
> 2 used to + verb – sentences a, b, e, g, h, i, j
> 3 Would is used to talk about regular or repeated past actions, often with a sense of nostalgia. *Used to* can be used to talk about regular or repeated past actions, and also past states or situations. *Used to* is used for negative and question forms.

Students discuss which of the sentences are true for them. You could have a quick vote on the questions. Refer to the Language reference if necessary.

Anecdote (p 49)

See Introduction, page 4, for more ideas on how to set up, monitor and repeat 'anecdotes'.

4 Pairwork. Students think about the questions and whether they apply to them. They discuss their childhood with their partners.

5 🎦 21 SB p 151

Students now listen to the second part of the story about Roald Dahl's childhood to find out why the boys hate Mrs Pratchett. You may need to explain that a *gobstopper* is a large, hard, round sweet in Britain. The name comes from *gob* (slang for mouth) and *stop* (to block). *For the high jump* means 'to be in trouble'.

🎦 21

Her name was Mrs Pratchett. She was a small skinny old hag with a moustache on her upper lip and a mouth as sour as a green gooseberry. She never smiled.

Her apron was grey and greasy. Her blouse had bits of breakfast all over it, toast-crumbs and tea stains and splotches of dried egg-yolk. It was her hands, however, that disturbed us most. They were disgusting. They were black with dirt and grime.

And do not forget that it was these hands and fingers that she would plunge into the sweet-jars when we asked for a pennyworth of Treacle Toffee or Wine Gums or Nut Clusters or whatever. There were precious few health laws in those days, and nobody, least of all Mrs Pratchett, ever thought of using a little shovel for getting sweets out as they do today.

The other thing we hated Mrs Pratchett for was her meanness. Unless you spent a whole sixpence all in one go, she wouldn't give you a bag. Instead you got your sweets twisted up in a small piece of newspaper which she tore off a pile of old *Daily Mirrors* lying on the counter.

So you can well understand that we had it in for Mrs Pratchett in a big way, but we didn't quite know what to do about it. Many schemes were put forward, but none of them was any good. None of them, that is, until suddenly, one memorable afternoon, we found the dead mouse.

My four friends and I had come across a loose floor-board at the back of the classroom, and when we prised it up with the blade of a pocket-knife, we discovered a big hollow space underneath. This, we decided, would be our secret hiding place for sweets and other small treasures such as conkers and monkey-nuts and birds' eggs.

Every afternoon, when the last lesson was over, the five of us would wait until the classroom had emptied, then we would lift up the floor-board and examine our secret hoard, perhaps adding to it or taking something away.

One day, when we lifted it up, we found a dead mouse lying among our treasures. It was an exciting discovery.

Thwaites took it out by its tail and waved it in front of our faces. 'What shall we do with it?' he cried.

'It stinks!' someone shouted. 'Throw it out of the window!'

'Hold on a tick,' I said. 'Don't throw it away.'

Thwaites hesitated. They all looked at me.

When writing about oneself, one must strive to be truthful. Truth is more important than modesty. I must tell you, therefore, that it was I and I alone who had the idea for the great and daring Mouse Plot. We all have our moments of brilliance and glory, and this was mine.

'Why don't we,' I said, 'slip it into one of Mrs Pratchett's jars of sweets? Then when she puts her dirty hand in to grab a handful, she'll grab a stinky dead mouse instead.'

The other four stared at me in wonder.

Then, as the sheer genius of the plot began to sink in, they all started grinning. They slapped me on the back. They cheered me and danced around the classroom. 'We'll do it today!' they cried. 'We'll do it on the way home. You had the idea,' they said to me, 'so you can be the one to put the mouse in the jar.'

Thwaites handed me the mouse. I put it into my trouser pocket. Then the five of us left the school, crossed the village green and headed for the sweet-shop. We were tremendously jazzed up. We felt like a gang of desperados setting out to rob a train or blow up the sheriff's office.

We were the victors now and Mrs Pratchett was the victim. She stood behind the counter, and her small malignant pig-eyes watched us suspiciously as we came forward.

'One Sherbet Sucker, please,' Thwaites said to her, holding out his penny.

I kept to the rear of the group, and when I saw Mrs Pratchett turn her head away for a couple of seconds to fish a Sherbert Sucker out of the box, I lifted the heavy glass lid of the Gobstopper jar and dropped the mouse in. Then I replaced the lid as silently as possible. My heart was thumping like mad and my hands had gone all sweaty.

As soon as we were outside, we broke into a run. 'Did you do it?' they shouted at me.

'Of course I did!' I said.

'Well done you!' they cried. 'What a super show!'

I felt like a hero. I was a hero. It was marvellous to be so popular.

The flush of triumph over the dead mouse was carried forward to the next morning as we met again to walk to school.

'Let's go in and see if it's still in the jar,' somebody said as we approached the sweet-shop.

'Don't,' Thwaites said firmly. 'It's too dangerous. Walk past as though nothing has happened.'

As we came level with the shop we saw a cardboard notice hanging on the door.

CLOSED.

We stopped and stared. We had never known the sweet-shop to be closed at this time in the morning, even on Sundays.

'What's happened?' we asked each other. 'What's going on?'

We pressed our faces against the window and looked inside. Mrs Pratchett was nowhere to be seen.

'Look!' I cried. 'The Gobstopper jar's gone! It's not on the shelf! There's a gap where it used to be!'

'It's on the floor!' someone said. 'It's smashed to bits and there's Gobstoppers everywhere!'

'There's the mouse!' someone else shouted.

We could see it all, the huge glass jar smashed to smithereens with the dead mouse lying in the wreckage and hundreds of many-coloured Gobstoppers littering the floor.

'She got such a shock when she grabbed hold of the mouse that she dropped everything,' somebody was saying.

'But why didn't she sweep it all up and open the shop?' I asked.

Nobody answered me.

After a while, Thwaites broke the silence. 'She must have got one heck of a shock,' he said. He paused. We all looked at him, wondering what wisdom the great medical authority was going to come out with next.

'Well now,' Thwaites went on, 'when an old person like Mrs Pratchett suddenly gets a very big shock, I suppose you know what happens next?'

'What?' we said. 'What happens?'

'You ask my father,' Thwaites said. 'He'll tell you.'

'You tell us,' we said.

'It gives her a heart attack,' Thwaites announced. 'Her heart stops beating and she's dead in five seconds.'

For a moment or two my own heart stopped beating. Thwaites pointed a finger at me and said darkly, 'I'm afraid you've killed her.'

'Me?' I cried. 'Why just me?'

'It was your idea,' he said. 'And what's more, you put the mouse in.'

All of a sudden, I was a murderer.

At exactly that point, we heard the school bell ringing in the distance and we had to gallop the rest of the way so as not to be late for prayers.

The Headmaster is the only teacher at Llandaff Cathedral School that I can remember, and for a reason you will soon discover, I can remember him very clearly indeed. His name was Mr Coombes.

Mr Coombes now proceeded to mumble through the same old prayers we had every day, but this morning, when the last amen had been spoken, he did not turn and lead his group rapidly out of the Hall as usual. He remained standing before us, and it was clear he had an announcement to make.

'The whole school is to go out and line up around the playground immediately,' he said. 'Leave your books behind. And no talking.'

Mr Coombes was looking grim. His hammy pink face had taken on that dangerous scowl which only appeared when he was extremely cross and somebody was for the high-jump. I sat there small and frightened among the rows and rows of other boys, and to me at that moment the Headmaster, with his black grown draped over his shoulders, was like a judge at a murder trial.

'He's after the killer,' Thwaites whispered to me.

I began to shiver.

As we made our way out into the playground my whole stomach began to feel as though it was slowly filling up with swirling water. I am only eight years old, I told myself. No little boy of eight has ever murdered anyone. It's not possible.

I half-expected to see two policemen come bounding out of the school to grab me by the arms and put handcuffs on my wrists.

A single door led out from the school on to the playground. Suddenly it swung open and through it, like the angel of death, strode Mr Coombes, huge and bulky in his tweed suit and black gown, and beside him, believe it or not, right beside him trotted the tiny figure of Mrs Pratchett herself!

Mrs Pratchett was alive!

The relief was tremendous.

Suddenly she let out a high-pitched yell and pointed a dirty finger straight at Thwaites. 'That's 'im!' she yelled. 'That's one of 'em! I'd know 'im a mile away, the scummy little bounder!'

The entire school turned to look at Thwaites. 'W- what have I done?' he stuttered, appealing to Mr Coombes.

'Shut up,' Mr Coombes said.

Mrs Pratchett's eyes flicked over and settled on my own face. I looked down and studied the black asphalt surface of the playground.

'Ere's another of 'em!' I heard her yelling. 'That one there!' She pointed at me now. 'You're quite sure?' Mr Coombes said.

'Of course I'm sure!' She cried. 'I never forget a face, least of all when it's as sly as that! 'Ee's one of 'em all right! There was five altogether. Now where's them other three?'

The other three, I knew very well, were coming up next.

'There they are!' she cried out, stabbing the air with her finger. ''Im … and 'im … and 'im! That's the five of 'em all right! We don't need to look no farther than this, 'Eadmaster! They're all 'ere, the nasty little pigs! You've got their names 'ave you?'

'I've got their names, Mrs Pratchett,' Mr Coombes told her. 'I'm very much obliged to you.'

Test

Scoring: one point per correct answer unless otherwise indicated.

1 1 who/that   2 (which/that)   3 (who/that)
4 (when)   5 which/that   6 (where)
7 whose   8 (which/that)

9 The film is about a boy who can travel in time.

10 Here is the card (that/which) we got for Diana's birthday.

11 Where is the photo that/which was on your desk?

12 I've bought the computer game (that/which) Pedro told us about.

2 One point for identification and one point for correction.
1 ✓
2 ✗ I had French lessons …
3 ✓
4 ✓
5 ✗ My best friend lived … /used to live
6 ✗ Did you live …
7 ✓

3 Jack and Jill

Went up the hill

To fetch a pail of water.

Jack fell down

And broke his crown

And Jill came tumbling after.

4 1 a baby   2 studies a lot   3 go to school
4 before the real exam   5 sucks it
6 an unkind person

5 Kids Test

Name: Total: _____ /40

1 Defining relative clauses *12 points*

Complete these sentences with *who, which, that, whose, where* or *when*. If the word can be left out, write it in brackets ( ).

1 The person _____ scores the most points is the winner.

2 This is the book _____ I was telling you about.

3 The boy _____ you met at the party phoned this morning.

4 Christmas is traditionally a time _____ families get together.

5 Where are the books _____ were on the table?

6 This is the exact spot _____ we first met.

7 That's the girl _____ party we went to.

8 The school _____ I went to is near here.

Write the two sentences as one using a relative clause.

9 The film is about a boy. He can travel in time.

_____

10 Here is the card. We got the card for Diana's birthday.

_____

11 Where is the photo? It was on your desk.

_____

12 I've bought the computer game. Pedro told us about the computer game.

_____

2 *Would* 10 points

Bianca is talking about her past. Three of the sentences are wrong. Mark them ✓ or ✗. Correct the sentences which are wrong.

1 I lived in France when I was a teenager. _____

2 I would have French lessons for two years. _____

3 I would often miss my French lessons. _____

4 We'd go to Spain at least once a year. _____

5 My best friend would live in Belgium when she was a child. _____

6 Would you live in a different country when you were little? _____

7 Did you enjoy school? _____

3 Stress timing *12 points*

Here is traditional nursery rhyme. In total there are fourteen stressed syllables. In the first line the stressed syllables have been marked. Put a line under the remaining twelve stressed syllables.

(*pail* = bucket   *crown* = part of the head *tumbling* = falling out of control)

Jack and Jill

Went up the hill

To fetch a pail of water.

Jack fell down

And broke his crown

And Jill came tumbling after.

4 Vocabulary – Childhood *6 points*

Answer the following questions.

1 Who wears a nappy and a bib? _____

2 What does a swot do a lot of? _____

3 What does a truant not do? _____

4 When do you take a mock exam? _____

5 What does a baby do with a dummy? _____

6 What is a bully? _____

Photocopiable

6 *News* Overview

The topic in this unit is news. The main grammatical focus is on the passives.

Students read a web-page about the intrusiveness of the paparazzi. They go on to discuss the relationship between celebrities and newspaper photographers.

Students practise using the passives by editing three short news stories. They listen to a radio news broadcast and to people giving personal news. They then practise empathising to personal news and finally they practise writing informal letters.

Section	Aims	What the students are doing
Introduction page 50	*Conversation skills:* fluency work	Talking about celebrities and celebrity scandal.
The hunters & the hunted pages 50–52	*Reading skills:* scanning	Scanning a web-page on the paparazzi for specific information.
	Lexis: collocations	Reviewing verb collocations from a web-page.
	Conversation skills: fluency work	Discussing fame and celebrity gossip.
Close up pages 52–53	*Grammar:* irregular verbs;	Reviewing irregular verbs.
	the passive voice	Identifying passive structures, how they are formed and when they are used.
		Practising the use of the passive voice by editing newspaper stories.
Headline news pages 54–55	*Reading & listening skills:* predicting;	Predicting radio broadcasts by matching photos to newspaper headlines.
	listening for detail;	Listening to the radio broadcast to check predictions and comprehension.
	performing	Making a radio broadcast based on newspaper headlines and photos.
Personal news page 56	*Reading & listening skills:* empathising;	Reading dialogues with people giving and reacting to personal news, and improving the dialogues by showing empathy.
	editing dialogues	Listening to an improved version of the dialogues, and comparing versions.
	Pronunciation: stress & intonation	Practising stress and intonation when showing empathy.
A letter from Berlin page 57	*Writing skills:* personal letter writing;	Completing a personal letter with the appropriate words and checking comprehension.
	paragraphing	Replying to the letter using given expressions to begin each paragraph.

6

News *Teacher's notes*

Closed books. Ask students *Have you ever seen anyone famous? Who did you see? Where were they? What were they doing? Were there lots of people around? Did anyone take photos? Did you take a photo? Did you speak to the famous person?*

Pairwork. Students look at the photographs and identify the people shown. Then they discuss the questions. If your students are from different countries, try to create pairs of different nationalities.

> Photo 1: Robert de Niro. American actor.
> Films include *The Deerhunter, The Awakening*.
>
> Photo 2: Jack Nicholson. American actor.
> Films include *One Flew over the Cuckoo's Nest, The Postman Always Rings Twice, The Shining As Good as it Gets*.
>
> Photo 3: Madonna. American singer and actor.

The hunters & the hunted (p 50)

Pairwork. Students discuss the possible connections between the two lists before they read the Internet page. Elicit or explain *paparazzo, scooter, black eye, pot-bellied pig*. Accept any reasonable connections, but don't confirm them at this stage. Students read the text and find the connections. To encourage scanning for information, you could make this a race, with the first pair to find all the connections raising their hands.

> The original paparazzo from the film *La Dolce Vita* rode around on a scooter.
>
> A photograph of a celebrity can be sold to a tabloid newspaper for nearly a million dollars.
>
> Tom Cruise was chased by paparazzi through the tunnel in Paris where Princess Diana was killed.
>
> Madonna was forced to drive at 130 kph to escape from paparazzi.
>
> Alec Baldwin hit a paparazzo and gave him a black eye when he photographed Baldwin and his wife returning home with their new baby.
>
> George Clooney has a pet Vietnamese pot-bellied pig which chased a paparazzo out of his garden.

Students read the text again and underline any words they don't know. Go through the underlined words with the class, encouraging students who do know the meanings to explain them to the rest.

Ask students what they think of the text. Do they agree with the writer or do they think that the lives of celebrities are 'public property'? Were Tom Cruise and Madonna really justified in putting their lives and the lives of others at risk in order to avoid being photographed, however unpleasant that might be? Was it the fault of the paparazzi? Get students to vote on how they would respond to the Internet text.

Lexis (p 52)

1 Whole class. Go through the instructions and make sure students understand that they can use items from the second column more than once.

Pairwork. Encourage students to make their collocations without looking at the text first. They then look at the text, check their answers and find any collocations they missed. Check answers with the class.

> *Suggested answers*
> a) give someone a black eye
> b) charge someone with assault
> c) follow someone's example
> d) go out of your way to do something
> e) invade someone's privacy
> f) leave someone alone
> g) make someone angry

2 Set a time limit, for example, three minutes for students to complete the sentences.

Check answers with the class.

> a) ... gave me a black eye.
> b) ... charged with assault.
> c) ... leave her alone.
> d) ... makes me angry ...
> e) ... going out of your way to ...
> f) ... followed his example.
> g) ... privacy has been invaded.

Discussion

Groupwork. Students discuss the statements in groups. Encourage them to give reasons for agreeing or disagreeing with each one.

Close up (p 52)

Irregular verbs (Workbook p 31)

1 The word *irregular* in the rubric should give students some clue as to how the words have been grouped. Students do the task individually. If, after a few minutes, some of them are unable to solve the puzzle, ask them what makes a verb 'irregular' and in what tense the irregularity is shown. Students first check their answers by referring to the table on page 147. Then check answers with the class. See if students can add any more verbs to the groups.

steal:	Group 2 (broke(n), spoke(n), chose(n), stole(n))
hit:	Group 3 (let, set, cost, hit)
know:	Group 4 (grew grown, flew flown, threw thrown, knew known)
begin:	Group 1 (swam swum, drank drunk, rang rung, began begun)
teach:	Group 5 (brought, fought, caught, taught)

2 Pairwork. Students test each other on the past tense of irregular verbs. One student says the infinitive of a verb and the other replies with the past tense and past participle, and then says another infinitive verb. Start the exercise by reading the example exchange with a student.

The passive voice (p 53)

(Workbook p 31, p 32, p 33)

1 Students complete the sentences with words from the box.

> a) the police; a judge
> b) paparazzi; a car crash
> c) his pet Vietnamese pot-bellied pig

2 Focus students' attention on the five sentences and elicit the difference between them and those in 1. Elicit the verb structure used.

> The verb structure used is the passive voice.

3 Pairwork. Students discuss the questions. Encourage them to look at the Language reference section on page 54. Check answers with the class.

> a) be + past participle
> b) c) (Clooney's pet Vietnamese pot-bellied pig)
> c) by
> d) 1 b) 2 a) 3 c)

4 Set a time limit of about 2–3 minutes for students to complete the stories. Explain that a 'wanted list' is a list of criminals the police still want to catch.

Check answers with the class.

1	was stolen
2	was handcuffed
3	was rescued
4	was killed
5	was sentenced
6	was arrested
7	was seriously injured

5 This can be done as a mingling activity if space permits. First elicit the questions students will need to ask to find out the information (*Have you ever been stopped and searched by customs? Have you ever been stopped for speeding?* etc). Establish that the correct reply is *Yes, I have* or *No, I haven't*. Emphasise that students do not have to answer questions they feel embarrassed about and can say *I'm sorry, I'd rather not say* (or can lie if they wish), but they should give the same answer to anyone who asks. Allow students to go round the class for about five minutes, asking each other questions and noting down the name of anyone who answers 'yes' to a question.

Students report back to the class on what they found out. Find out who got the highest number of 'yes' responses. If students who answered 'yes' are happy to give further details of the experience, they can be encouraged to do so.

In classes with limited space, get individual students to form the questions and ask them to the whole class or individual members of the class. Alternatively, get students to ask the questions in pairs and then report back to the class on any interesting replies. Alternatively, and if the class is not too big, it could be done as a *How many people ... ?* activity. Students go round the class, maybe in pairs or small groups, asking other students the questions and recording how many 'yes' and 'no' answers they get. Students, taking turns, then report back to the whole class, for example, *Three people in the class have appeared on TV.*

6 Groupwork. Divide the class into groups of three, each student taking an A, B or C role. Tell Student A to look at page 139 and Student B to look at page 141 and read their newspaper articles, while Student C reads the instructions on page 1430. Students A and B work together to decide on the best version of each story, using the active or passive forms of the verbs that are most appropriate. They dictate their versions to Student C, who writes them down. Have a few of the groups read their versions to the class. The class then decides on the best versions.

Headline news (p 54) (Workbook p 34, p 35)

Closed books. Pairwork. Students think of two stories that are in the news at the moment or have recently been in the news. They give brief details of the facts of the story to the rest of the class. Alternatively, you could cut some headlines out of a current newspaper, show them to students and ask if anyone can say what the story is about. If you are working in a non-English speaking country, use an English newspaper or translate the headlines from a local newspaper.

1 Open books. Groupwork. Students look at the photos and describe what they can see and what they think is happening. Read the newspaper headlines with the class. Point out that newspaper headlines are written in a shortened style, missing out unimportant words. This is done for impact.

Students match the headlines with the photos. Make sure they understand that some headlines do not have a photo. Check answers with the class.

> 1 b   2 d   3 e   4 g

Ask students which stories they would read first and why. In pairs/small groups, you could ask students to anticipate/invent the stories. Get them to think about the background as well as the details of the story. Students then tell their stories to each other. Students could then vote for their favourite version.

Optional activity

If you have time, you might like to give them the outlines of some current news stories and get them to write suitable newspaper headlines for them. If you have any English language newspapers at your disposal, look through them to find any examples of newspaper/headline language/words.

2 ▭ 22 SB p 152

Students listen to a radio news broadcast. Make sure they understand that it is from the same day as the newspaper headlines in 1 and that the stories are the same. Their task is to listen for the order that the stories occur in. Play the recording. Get feedback from the whole class.

> 1 e   2 b   3 d   4 g

▭ 22
(A1 = Announcer 1; A2 = Announcer 2)

A1: *And here are the news headlines. Following severe droughts in Africa, the President of the USA has announced that he is going to send food and provisions to the people of Somalia, who have lost their homes and livelihood.*

A2: *Robert Holmes, Minister for the Environment, has resigned. The Prime Minister has ordered an investigation into the mysterious disappearance of a large sum of money. A spokesman for the minister told us that he was out of the country and not available for comment.*

A1: *Schoolgirl Pauline Gates has not been allowed back into school after the summer holidays, because she has had her nose pierced. According to headmistress Jean Bradley, Pauline knew that piercing was against the school rules. The girl will be allowed back into school when she removes the offending ring.*

A2: *And finally, to end on a happier note, wedding bells are ringing for 81-year-old Max Williams, who won £16 million in the lottery last month. He is going to marry 22-year-old dancer, Sally Lister. The happy couple posed for photographers outside the millionaire's luxury home in Essex and Sally held out her hand to show off her £10,000 engagement ring for the cameras.*

3 ▭ 22 SB p 152

Go through the questions with the class so they know what information they are listening for. Encourage them to make brief notes as they listen. Play the recording. Elicit the answers from the class. If there are any questions they can't answer on the first listening, play the recording again as many times as necessary, making it clear which questions they are trying to answer.

> a) The President of the USA announced that he is going to send food and provisions to Somalia.
>
> b) There have been severe droughts in Africa and people have lost their homes and livelihood.
>
> c) Robert Holmes is Minister for the Environment.
>
> d) The Prime Minister ordered an investigation into the disappearance of a large sum of money.
>
> e) He is out of the country (abroad).
>
> f) She hasn't been allowed back to school because she has had her nose pierced.
>
> g) Pauline has to remove the ring in order to be allowed back into school.
>
> h) He is 81.
>
> i) He has £16 million.
>
> j) She is 22.
>
> k) It cost £10,000.

4 ▭ 22 SB p 152

Whole class. Read the text before you play the recording and see if students can tell you what the missing words are. They could write their ideas lightly in pencil. Students listen to the recording and fill in the missing words or correct their ideas.

> ... that he is going to send food and provisions to the people of Somalia who have lost their homes and livelihood.
>
> ... has resigned. ... has ordered an investigation ... out of the country ....
>
> ... not been allowed back into school after the summer holidays because she has had her nose pierced. ... Pauline knew that piercing was against the school rules. The girl will be allowed back into school when she removes the offending ring.
>
> ... 81-year-old ... £16 million ... 22-year-old ... £10,000 ...

5 Groupwork. Students write a radio news broadcast based on the three headlines and photographs to perform to the class. They should choose one member of the group to be the news broadcaster. If they wish, other members of the group can be reporters.

6 Get groups to take turns performing their radio broadcasts to the class. Encourage the rest of the class to listen quietly and to give positive feedback at the end of each broadcast.

Personal news (p 56)

Closed books. Ask if anyone has any personal news to tell, for example, a birthday, a wedding anniversary, passing a driving test, failing an exam, etc. When a student offers a piece of news, respond in an appropriate way with congratulations or commiserations. Get more students to offer pieces of news and encourage the rest of the class to respond appropriately.

1 Open books. Whole class. Read the conversation yourself, taking the part of Ken, and getting one of students to play Steve. Emphasise with your voice how dull and inadequate the response *Oh* to every statement is. Point out how difficult it is to keep a conversation going if your partner gives only a monosyllabic response.

Elicit ideas from the whole class on ways the conversation could be improved. Encourage them to think of additional things that Steve could say as well as Ken. Write the ideas on the board. Get students to act out the new versions.

2 ▭ 23 SB p 152

Students listen to the conversation and note the differences. Check answers with the class.

See bold items in tapescript.

▭ 23

(K = Ken; S= Steve)

K: *Hi, Steve. How are you?*

S: *Oh, not too bad. Actually, it's my wedding anniversary today.*

K: ***Oh, congratulations!***

S: *But um, I forgot and my wife was really upset.*

K: ***Oh, no. That's terrible.***

S: *But I just rang Le Petit Blanc and they actually had a table free, so we're going out for dinner.*

K: ***Excellent.***

S: *Anyway, I must go.*

K: *Er, yeah, me too. See you!*

3 Pairwork. Students decide what to put in the gaps, then practise the dialogues together.

Alternatively, play the first speaker in each dialogue yourself and choose a different student to play the second speaker each time. Draw their attention to the choices in the box. They will have to think on their feet to choose the appropriate response each time. Note: in dialogues B, G and H you will need to take the part of the second speaker so that the student gets the gap.

Ask the rest of the class each time if they think the correct response was chosen. This will ensure that they listen carefully to the dialogues. Point out if necessary that *Congratulations* is only used when the good news immediately concerns the other speaker. It would not be an appropriate response to a statement such as *Bill and Sue have just had a baby*. For statements such as this, *How wonderful!* or *That's great news!* would be more appropriate.

A	That's terrible!
B	Well done!
C	Lucky you!
D	Oh, I'm sorry to hear that.
E	You idiot!
F	Congratulations!
G	Oh, no!
H	Excellent!

4 🔲 **24 SB p 152**

Students listen to the recording and check their answers to 3.

🔲 **24**

a
A: Have you heard about Chris and Shirley?
B: No ... what about them?
A: They've split up.
B: That's terrible!

b
C: Hello. You're looking very pleased with yourself.
D: I am! I've just passed my driving test!
C: Well done! Can I have a lift?

c
E: Guess what. I've won a holiday to Florida.
F: Lucky you! Is it a holiday for two?
E: Yes, I'm taking my Mum.
F: Oh.

d
G: I've just had some bad news.
H: What's happened?
G: I've failed my final exams.
H: Oh, I'm sorry to hear that. Are you going to resit them?

e
I: Oh, no!
J: What's the matter?
I: I've left my bag on the bus.
J: You idiot! What are you going to do?
I: I suppose I'd better ring the bus company.

f
K: Have a glass of champagne!
L: Thank you. What are you celebrating?
K: My wife's just had a baby.
L: Congratulations! Boy or a girl?

g
M: You don't usually take the bus!
N: No – my car's broken down again.
M: Oh, no!

h
O: I didn't know you had a car.
P: My parents have bought a new car and they've given me their old one.
O: Excellent!

5 🔲 **25 SB p 153**

Whole class. Play the recording and tell students to pay attention to the intonation of the speakers. Point out that responses to positive news require a bright cheerful tone and responses to negative news require a lower, more sympathetic tone. Demonstrate the effect of the wrong tone by getting a student to tell you a piece of good news (respond with *Congratulations* in a depressed sounding voice) and then a piece of good news (respond with *Oh, I'm really sorry* in a cheerful tone).

Pairwork. Students practise the conversations. Go round checking that their pronunciation and intonation are correct.

🔲 **25**

That's terrible!

Well done!

Lucky you!

Oh, I'm sorry to hear that.

You idiot!

Congratulations!

Oh, no!

Excellent!

6 🔲 **26 SB p 153**

Whole class. Students listen to ten sentences and decide how they would respond. Stop the recording after each sentence. Students write down a response.

Play the recording again, stopping after each sentence and inviting several students to give their responses.

🔲 **26**

1 We got engaged last week.
2 My bicycle's been stolen again.
3 I've decided to move to Australia.
4 My husband's been taken into hospital.
5 My daughter's just had a baby.
6 I got off the bus, slipped and fell flat on my face.
7 I've won £1,000 on the National Lottery.
8 My car wouldn't start this morning.
9 When I got to the party, there was someone there wearing exactly the same dress as me.
10 I've just got my exam results and I've passed.

7 Pairwork. Students invent short conversations. Encourage them to use the responses/expressions from the previous exercises, for example:

You look happy.

I've just got my exam results – I passed them all.

Congratulations! Well done!

Get selected pairs to perform their conversations to the class.

A letter from Berlin (p 57)

1 Encourage students to read through the whole letter first, ignoring the gaps, so they get the sense of the whole thing. Students complete the letter, ideally without choosing words from the box. These are here to give help if they get stuck. Check answers with the class.

> 1 hear 2 sorry 3 but 4 pleased 5 Well
> 6 news 7 applied 8 loads 9 thing
> 10 By the way 11 heard 12 apparently
> 13 feel 14 embarrassing 15 Anyway
> 16 Apart 17 forward 18 soon 19 getting
> 20 what

2 Pairwork. Students discuss the relationships between Pia, Ian, Anna and Giorgio. They then answer the questions.

> Pia, Ian, Anna and Giorgio are all friends. Anna and Giorgio were planning to get married but have now called it off.

3 Students read the letter again and answer the questions with the names from 2.

> a) Pia
> b) Ian
> c) Pia's
> d) Ian
> e) Pia
> f) Anna and Giorgio
> g) Giorgio
> h) Anna's
> i) Pia
> j) Pia

4 Whole class. Go through the skeleton letter with the class and elicit some ideas for what Ian might say to Pia. Students write Ian's reply to Pia. This could be set as homework. Allow time in class for students to read and enjoy each other's letters.

Test

Scoring: one point per correct answer unless otherwise indicated.

1 1 matter 2 idiot 3 sorry, hear
   4 embarrassing 5 Congratulations

2 1 gave 2 charged 3 went 4 made
   5 leave

3 1 was attacked
   2 is being questioned
   3 was opened
   4 is estimated/has been estimated
   5 will be made/have been made/were made
   6 has been delayed
   7 is now hoped
   8 will be launched
   9 has been cancelled.
   10 is being repaired.
   11 is not included.
   12 was stolen.
   13 was fired.
   14 will be picked up.

4 ½ point each

Infinitive	Past simple	Past participle
begin	began	*begun*
bring	brought	brought
buy	bought	bought
cost	*cost*	cost
drink	*drank*	drunk
find	found	found
forget	forgot	forgotten
give	gave	*given*
go	went	gone
know	knew	*known*
put	*put*	put
set	set	set
sleep	slept	slept
take	took	taken
throw	threw	thrown
wear	*wore*	worn

6 News Test

Name: Total: _____ /40

1 Vocabulary – everyday expressions *5 points*

Complete the expressions by rearranging the mixed up words.

1   You look upset. What's the <u>tramet</u>?

2   You <u>diito</u>! I don't believe you did that!

3   Oh dear – I'm <u>rosyr</u> to <u>rhae</u> that.

4   How <u>seabargsmrin</u> ! I'd die if that happened to me.

5   Well done – <u>ogtrscatnnaulio</u> !

_____

_____

_____

_____

_____

2 Vocabulary – verb collocations *5 points*

Add the missing verbs.

1   She was so angry she _____ him a black eye.

2   Six people were _____ with assault.

3   He _____ out of his way to help them.

4   It _____ me very angry when she said that.

5   I offered to help him, but he told me to _____ him alone.

3 Passive *14 points*

Put the verbs into appropriate forms of the passive.

He (1) _____ (attack) as he left the building shortly after 8 o'clock last night.

The suspect (2) _____ (question) by detectives at the moment.

The new bridge (3) _____ (open) by the President last month.

It (4) _____ (estimate) that over a million people

(5) _____ (make) homeless by yesterday's earthquake.

The launch of the Space Shuttle (6) _____ (delay) yet

again. It (7) _____ (now/hope) that it

(8) _____ (launch) the day after tomorrow.

Rewrite the sentences so the meaning is the same. Begin with the words given and use the passive.

9   They have cancelled the concert.

The concert _____

10   Someone is repairing my car at the moment.

My car _____

11   The bill does not include service.

Service _____

12   Someone stole my bag at the party.

My bag _____

13   They fired him for stealing.

He _____

14   The coach will pick you up at 6.30.

You _____

4 Irregular verbs *16 points*

Complete the table.

Infinitive	Past simple	Past participle
		begun
bring		
buy		
	cost	
	drank	
find		
forget		
		given
go		
		known
	put	
set		
sleep		
take		
throw		
	wore	

Photocopiable

7 *Party* Overview

The topics in this unit are celebrations, festivals and parties. The grammar focus is on future forms.

Students read about a big Spanish festival and practise some new phrasal verbs. The focus on phrasal verbs is then continued with a game.

Students listen to a discussion on what makes a good party. This is followed by a questionnaire inviting them to discover how much they really enjoy parties, and then listen to the song *It's My Party*.

Students then practise inviting people to social events. They construct their own dialogues inviting people out, and write invitations and suitable replies.

Section	Aims	What the students are doing
Introduction pages 58–59	*Conversation skills:* fluency work	Talking about festivals.
	Reading skills: scanning	Scanning a text about a Spanish festival to find information.
	Lexis: phrasal verbs	Focusing on phrasal verbs from the text. Playing a game, *Call My Bluff*, to review phrasal verbs and to invent false definitions for them.
	Pronunciation: sounds	Identifying and practising short vowel sounds.
Close up page 60	*Grammar:* future forms: *will*, *(be) going to* & present continuous	Identifying future forms within a text and choosing the appropriate form. Practising future forms by completing sentences.
Invitations page 61	*Functions:* inviting; refusing; making excuses	Reviewing ways of inviting someone to go out, refusing an invitation and making excuses, and practising these functions by writing a dialogue.
Parties pages 62–63	*Conversation skills:* fluency	Talking about types of parties.
	Listening skills: listening for detail	Listening to a conversation about the ingredients of a good party. Comparing ingredients of a good party.
	Reading skills: for gist	Completing a questionnaire for pleasure on how much you enjoy parties.
	Lexis: collocations	Reviewing socialising expressions from the questionnaire.
Let's party! page 63	*Conversation skills:* fluency work	Anecdote: talking about a good party or a party that was a disaster.
		Organising a party as part of a competition.
It's my party page 64	*Listening skills:* predicting;	Listening to a song, *It's My Party*. Making predictions about the song by describing an illustration of it.
	listening for gist;	Listening to the song to identify the main characters in the illustration.
	listening for detail	Listening to the song to identify extra words in the lyrics that are not in the song.
Special occasions pages 65–66	*Writing skills:* using formal and informal language;	Distinguishing between formal and informal language used in letters of invitation and their replies.
	inviting, accepting and refusing	Writing letters of invitation and replies to letters of invitation.
	Lexis: greetings	Matching greeting cards with messages for special occasions.

7 *Party* *Teacher's notes*

Closed books. Write the word *party* in a small circle in the centre of the board. Invite students to call out all the words they know that are associated with the word *party*. As the words are called out, draw lines from the central circle and add the words in suitable places, gradually building up a spidergram. For example, if a student calls out *decorations*, put this word in and invite students to give examples of decorations – *balloons*, *streamers*, etc.

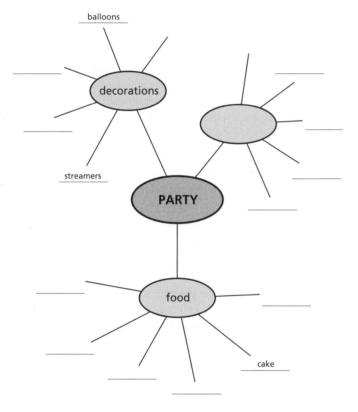

Show students how the words which are related have been grouped and after a few words have been added, invite them to say where in the diagram their new words should go. Encourage students to use spidergrams in their vocabulary notebooks when they note down new vocabulary. Grouping related words together helps students to remember them more easily.

1 **(Workbook p 39)**

Open books. Students look at the photograph. See if they can identify the country and the city in which this festival takes place (Valencia in Spain). Ask them to describe what they can see in the photograph.

Ask students for the names of some festivals they know or have heard about. Go through the list of questions with the class to give them some things to think about in relation to these festivals. If your students are from different countries, encourage them to tell the others a little about the festivals that take place in their own countries. If they are all from the same country, you could ask them to tell the class about festivals in other countries that they have experienced or which they know something about.

2 Students scan the text quickly for the answers to the questions. Scanning for information discourages them from getting stuck as soon as they come across a word they don't know. You could have a race to see which student or pair of students can find the answers first.

> a) Las Fallas
>
> b) Every year from 12th March to 19th March
>
> c) Eight days
>
> d) It started in the 18th century. People celebrated the end of winter by burning all their waste material, which was made into figures representing unpopular local characters.
>
> e) They build statues and burn them. They let off firecrackers. They have bands and parades. Children in traditional dress march into the city centre to decorate a statue of the Virgin Mary with flowers.
>
> f) At midnight on 19th March, there are lots of firecrackers and the statues are burned.

Check answers with the class, then give students time to read the text thoroughly. Answer any questions they have on difficult vocabulary. Note: *vibe* comes from *vibration* and is used to describe an atmosphere or feeling, usually a positive one.

Whole class. Students look at the photograph of the Glastonbury festival. Elicit their reactions to it. Ask what they can see, what the people are doing and if they would like to go to this festival.

Pairwork. Students discuss their own experiences of festivals, music festivals like Glastonbury or any others they have enjoyed.

Phrasal verbs (p 59) (Workbook p 38)

1 Whole class. Elicit the meaning of 'phrasal verb' and one or two examples: *get up, sit down, turn off,* etc. Students match the two halves of the sentences. Point out that the sentences contain verb and preposition partnerships and are split after the verbs. The phrasal verbs all come from the text, but are used here in different sentences. Check answers.

> a)   in the fun.
> b)   down in a fire in 1948.
> c)   up at six in the morning.
> d)   up the whole bay.
> e)   off in his hand and burnt him.
> f)   off at the airport.
> g)   down to some serious work.
> h)   on here? It's way past your bedtime.
> i)   up for the occasion.

Optional activity

When students have matched the two halves of the sentences, focus attention on the phrasal verbs and get them to go back through the Las Fallas text and underline them.

2 Students underline the phrasal verbs in the sentences they have matched in 1 and then match them with the meanings a–i.

> a)   burn down
> b)   dress up
> c)   go off
> d)   join in
> e)   go on
> f)   light up
> g)   see (someone) off
> h)   wake up
> i)   get down to

3 Pairwork. Students complete the paragraphs with the phrasal verbs from 2. Check answers with the whole class.

> **A** 1 woke up   2 went off   3 lit up
>   4 burnt down
> **B** 5 see (him) off   6 dress up   7 get down to
>   8 join in   9 going on

Optional activity

Get students to invent/write down their own sentences using these phrasal verbs. They could then turn them into gapped sentences for other students to complete.

4 Divide the class into three teams, A, B and C and tell them that they must only look at their team's page. Go through the rules of the game with the class: each team gets four true definitions of phrasal verbs. They write two false definitions for each one. The other teams decide which is the true definition. Explain that this is a television game in Britain called *Call my bluff.* To *bluff* is to try to deceive someone. Weaker classes can choose their false definitions from definitions for other words in the dictionary, but encourage students who are able to write their own to do so. Help the groups with the definitions and ensure that the other teams will not be able to detect the false definitions because of language errors.

When the teams read out their definitions, encourage them to jumble them up so that the true definition is not always in the same place. Teams take turns reading out their definitions. The other teams decide which is the true definition. Each team gets only one guess. If they guess correctly, they get a point. If neither team guesses correctly, the team reading out the definitions gets a point.

If you want to make the game more difficult, you could allow only one guess for each definition, ie from the team that calls out its guess first. If you do this, you could also deduct points for incorrect guesses to encourage teams to think carefully before they guess.

Pronunciation (p 59)

1 Focus attention on the phonetic symbols. Encourage students to guess the correct pronunciation of the symbols. Praise any correct answers but do not react negatively to wrong answers.

2 ▭ **27 SB p 153**
Pairwork. Write the phonetic symbols on the board in columns. Students decide which column each of the words should go in.

Call on individual students to pronounce each word in the list and tell you which column it goes into. When they choose correctly, write it on the board in the correct column. When you have finished all the words in the list, ask the class to read them aloud column by column.

Play the recording for students to check their answers.

/ɪ/	/e/	/ɒ/	/æ/	/ə/	/ʊ/	/ʌ/
busy	festival	holiday	band	around	full	fund
city	guest	modern	candle	different	good	public

27

1 / ɪ / – busy   city
2 / e / – festival   guest
3 / ɒ / – holiday   modern
4 / æ / – band   candle
5 / ɑ / – around   different
6 / ʊ / – full   good
7 / ʌ / – fund   public

3 Ask students to add more words to each column.

Optional activity

Get students in pairs or small groups to go round the classroom/school adding things they see to the list according to (one of) the vowel sound(s) they contain, for example *window* in the /ɪ/ column. You could give students a time limit or maybe get them to stop when they have added a certain number of items. You could do this as a competition, with the winners being the team with the most items added or the first to add ten/fifteen items.

Close up (p 60) (Workbook p 36, p 37)

Future forms

1 **28 SB p 153**

Whole class. Go through the instructions. Students listen to find out one thing only (why Sandy is unhappy).

If your students need more of a warm up, get them to suggest reasons why Sandy might be unhappy. Write any interesting suggestions on the board.

Play the recording. Check answers with the class.

> Sandy is unhappy because her boyfriend David said he would phone her today and he hasn't done so.

28

(Z = Zoë; S = Sandy)

Z: *Hi!*
S: *Oh, hello.*
Z: *You don't look very happy. What's the matter?*
S: *David hasn't rung.*
Z: *You only saw him yesterday.*
S: *Yes, and the last thing he said was 'I'll ring you tomorrow'.*
Z: *Well, tomorrow isn't finished yet.*
S: *No, but it's eight o'clock. What are you doing tonight? Do you fancy going for a drink?*
Z: *Um, I'd love to, but John's coming round and we're going for a meal.*
S: *Well, I'm not going to sit here waiting for the phone to ring. I know – I'll phone Becky.*

2 Students read the tapescript on page 153 and find three different structures which are used to refer to the future. Allow them to check their answers in pairs before checking with the whole class. Write the three forms on the board.

> *will*: I'll ring you tomorrow. I'll phone Becky.
>
> present continuous: What are you doing tonight? John's coming round and we're going for a meal.
>
> *going to*: I'm not going to sit here waiting for the phone to ring.

3 Whole class. Go through the instructions. Students decide when each form is used. Allow them to check in the Language reference section on page 61 before you check answers with the whole class.

> a) *will*
> b) *going to*
> c) present continuous

4 Pairwork. Encourage students to read the dialogue aloud as they make their decisions about the verbs. Reading aloud helps students decide what 'sounds right', which is a useful language learning tool. Check answers with the class and then ask two students to play Becky and Sandy and perform their conversation for the class.

> Sandy: Becky, are you doing anything tonight?
> Becky: Yes, I'm meeting Alex and Suzy ...
> Sandy: Where are you going?
> Sandy: Where are you meeting?
> Sandy: I'm going to the cinema with Becky.
> Sandy: I'm going to tell him to get lost.
> Zoë: I'll believe that when I see it.
> Zoë: I'll get her for you.
> David: I'm having dinner with my parents.
> Sandy: I'm going to the cinema anyway.
> David: I'll call you.
> Sandy: ... he's having dinner with his parents.
> Sandy: I'm definitely going to tell him to get lost!

5 **29 SB p 153**

Play the recording for students to check their answers. Encourage students to read the dialogue again in pairs, using similar intonation to the recording.

29

(B = Becky; S = Sandy; Z = Zoë; D = David)

B: *Hello?*
S: *Hi, Becky, it's Sandy.*
B: *Hiya.*

S: *Becky, are you doing anything tonight?*

B: *Yes. I'm meeting Alex and Suzy in about half an hour.*

S: *Where are you going?*

B: *To the cinema. Would you like to come with us?*

S: *Yes, I'd love to. Where are you meeting?*

B: *At their house, but we could meet you in front of the cinema in George Street at half past eight.*

S: *OK, thanks. See you later. ... I'm going to the cinema with Becky.*

Z: *Good idea.*

S: *And next time I see David, I'm going to tell him to get lost.*

Z: *Hmm. I'll believe that when I see it.*

...

Z: *Hello.*

D: *Is Sandy there please?*

Z: *Yeàh, hold on a moment – I'll get her for you. ... It's David.*

S: *Oh hello, David.*

D: *Look I'm really sorry I didn't call earlier, but I had to work late.*

S: *Oh, that's all right. I ... I forgot you were going to ring anyway.*

D: *Listen, I'm afraid I can't see you tonight, I'm having dinner with my parents.*

S: *It doesn't matter – I'm going to the cinema anyway.*

D: *Oh right. OK, well I'll call you.*

S: *When? I mean, all right. Bye.*

D: *Bye.*

...

Z: *You didn't tell him to get lost.*

S: *Well, he apologised – and he's having dinner with his parents. Anyway, I ... I must go. See you later.*

...

S: *Hi Alex. Hi Becky. Where's Suzy?*

B: *Oh, she changed her mind at the last minute. David phoned her and asked her to go for a meal at that new Japanese restaurant.*

S: *What?! I'm definitely going to tell him to get lost!*

6 Pairwork. Students complete the sentences. Go round helping where necessary and make sure students can explain their choices. Ask some pairs to read their mini-dialogues out to the class.

Invitations (p 61) (Workbook p 36, p 37)

1 Pairwork. Students look back to the tapescripts of Sandy's conversations in the previous section and find items a) to d). Check answers with the whole class.

> a) What are you doing tonight? Are you doing anything tonight?
>
> b) Do you fancy going for a drink? Would you like to come with us?
>
> c) I'd love to, but ... , I'm afraid I can't see you tonight ...
>
> d) I'm having dinner with my parents.

2 Whole class. Go through the instructions and make sure students understand the contents of the dialogue they have to write and that they can use ideas from the tapescript of Sandy's conversations.

Pairwork. Students write their dialogues. Go round, offering help, praising and correcting where needed.

3 Pairwork. Students read their dialogues aloud, taking turns to be Alex and Jo. Invite several pairs to perform their dialogues to the class. You could then get some of the stronger students to improvise dialogues.

4 Pairwork. This exercise also involves developing a dialogue about making invitations, but this time students are free to construct the dialogue in their own way. If your students need guidance, have a brainstorming session of possible excuses for not accepting an invitation. Write some of their ideas on the board.

Parties (p 62) (Workbook p 36)

Closed books. Pairwork. Students take turns to talk about the last party they went to. First elicit a few questions that their partner could ask and write these on the board. For example,

What kind of party was it?
How many people were there?
What did you eat and drink?
Did you dance?
What did you wear?

1 Open books. Whole class. Students look at the photo and describe what they can see and what they think is happening. (The photo shows a masked ball during the Venice Carnival.) Go through the list of parties with the class and elicit words they associate with each one. Ask if anyone has been to one of these parties recently. If so, encourage them to tell the class what happened.

Notes: Hallowe'en (All Hallows Eve) is the 31st October. It is believed to be the time when the dead can return to the world. Children dress up in scary costumes (witches, ghosts, vampires, etc), have parties and go round to local houses saying 'trick or treat'. If people give them treats (usually sweets), they will go away. If they refuse, the children may play a trick on them. The custom of 'trick or treat' is more common in the United States but gained in popularity in Britain after the release of the film *ET* in which it was shown.

The 21st birthday is traditionally regarded in Britain and the United States as the time when a child becomes an adult and people often hold special 'coming of age' parties. However, recently it has become more normal to regard someone as an adult when they reach 18. Most of the rights of an adult (the right to marry, drink alcohol, drive a car, etc) are gained at 18 or earlier.

2 Groupwork. Students think of as many different kinds of parties as they can. Give them three or four minutes to produce a list. If your students are of different nationalities/religions, encourage them to compare types of parties/celebrations in each country. Find out which group has the longest list and get them to read it out to the class. Encourage other students to add any ideas that have not been mentioned.

3 Students write their lists individually at first. Give them five or six minutes to do this.

Pairwork. Students compare their lists and agree on the three most important ingredients. Write the three ingredients from each pair on the board. Finally, have a show of hands to determine the three most important. Make sure students keep a record of their lists as they will need them for the next section. Variation: as different parties have different ingredients, you could assign different kinds of parties to different groups for discussion, for example, *What makes a good wedding / eighteenth birthday party?*

4 ▭ **30 SB p 153**
Students listen to three people talking about what makes a good party and make notes about the ideas mentioned. They compare what Alyson, Geoff and Rachel said with the lists they made in the last section. Ask students whether they agree with Alyson, Geoff and Rachel or not.

▭ **30**
(R = Rachel; A = Alyson; G = Geoff)

R: *What do you think makes a good party then?*

A: *Um … I think the place is really important. It should be big enough but not too big.*

G: *Yes, it needs to be quite crowded to make an atmosphere … and dark.*

R: *Oh, I don't like it when you can't see who you're talking to.*

G: *No … no, I mean soft lighting. I like it when there are some decorations too. You know, a few balloons and things, just to make it special.*

A: *What, like a children's party?*

G: *Yeah, I suppose so – or candles and things on the wall.*

R: *Candles make a nice atmosphere, but you have to be careful the house doesn't catch fire.*

G: *W … well, you can get those candle-holders. But the most important thing is the food and drink.*

A: *Oh, yes. There must be lots of drink and enough food. It's terrible when there isn't enough food.*

R: *What sort of food do you think is good for parties?*

A: *Um, the sort of thing you can eat with your fingers. I mean, you don't want to have loads of washing-up at the end of the party.*

R: *Actually, I think the music is the most important thing. Loud, but not too loud, and the sort of music you can dance to.*

G: *I think the best thing is to prepare party tapes with all the best dance tracks, then you don't have to worry about it.*

A: *But what about people? That's quite important, isn't it?*

G: *Um, yes, you do need people for a party!*

A: *No, I … I mean the right people. You need some party animals who get up and start the dancing.*

R: *And you need a mix of men and women. I went to a party recently where there were five women for every man.*

G: *Sounds all right to me.*

A: *Oh, shut up. So what do we think are the three most important things?*

R: *Food and drink, music and the right mix of people.*

G: *Right.*

5 Whole class. Before students look at the questionnaire, ask what they think the terms *party animal* and *party pooper* mean. (A *party animal* is a very outgoing person who loves parties and a *party pooper* is someone who doesn't have much fun at parties, perhaps feeling more comfortable in smaller quieter groups.) Emphasise that this questionnaire is just for fun and not meant as a criticism of people who don't enjoy parties much.

Pairwork. Students answer the questionnaire, add up their scores and read the *What it means* section on page 142. Ask students if they agree with the results of the questionnaire.

Optional activity

Give students a few minutes in small groups to write two or three more questions for the questionnaire. Make it clear that these questions should have a sentence to set the situation, followed by the beginning of the question and then three multiple choice answers designed to reveal whether someone is a party animal, a party pooper or somewhere in between. Allow the groups to exchange their questions with other groups and read a few of the best ones aloud to the class.

Lexis (p 63)

1 Students complete the sentences individually. Encourage them not to look back at the questionnaire until they have tried to do this from memory.

Students compare their answers in pairs and check with the questionnaire. Check answers with the whole class.

a) *'you only live once, so make sure you have a good time'*.

b) *When I want to refuse an invitation, I sometimes say that I've got a previous engagement ...*

c) *I'm not very good at going up to strangers and introducing myself.*

d) *I usually end up enjoying myself.*

e) *I really enjoy an evening at home on my own.*

2 Pairwork. Students discuss whether the sentences are true for them.

Let's party! (p 63)

Anecdote

See Introduction, page 4, for more ideas on how to set up, monitor and repeat 'anecdotes'.

1 Students make notes on the questions individually.

2 Pairwork. Students take turns to tell each other about their parties.

3 Groupwork. Appoint a secretary in each group to take notes and report back to the class. Make sure students understand that they are taking part in a competition. The competitive element may spur them on to make more effort in their party planning. Give students plenty of time to discuss and decide on the items in the list. They will probably need at least 15 minutes for this. Go round offering help and encouragement.

4 Whole class. Students vote on which party they are going to attend. The parties all take place on the same day so they can't go to more than one. They also can't go to their own party. Each group presents the details of their party to the class and tries to convince the others to come.

It's my party ... (p 64)

Note: the song *It's my party and I'll cry if I want to* was a hit in the 1960s for Lesley Gore.

1 Whole class. Read the title and ask students if they have ever heard the song. Students look at the picture and say what they think it is about. Don't confirm any answers at this stage.

2 📼 **31 SB p 153**
Play the recording. Students listen to find out if they guessed correctly.

> The song is about a disastrous birthday party. It is sung by a teenage girl and it is her party. Some time during the party one of her friends (Judy) leaves with Johnny, who is supposed to be the singer's boyfriend. When they come back into the party, Judy is wearing Johnny's ring and it is clear that he

is now Judy's boyfriend. The singer is miserable and says she has every reason to cry because everything has gone wrong. 'I'll cry if I want to' suggests a rather childish response to a friend's attempt to stop her crying.

Note: the singer is American. It is common in the United States for a teenage girl to wear her boyfriend's ring as a sign that they are going out together. It does not imply that the couple are engaged or married.

📼 **31**

It's My Party by Lesley Gore

It's my party and I'll cry if I want to,
Cry if I want to, cry if I want to.
You would cry too if it happened to you.

Nobody knows where my Johnny has gone,
But Judy left the same time.
Why was he holding her hand,
When he's supposed to be mine?

It's my party ...

Play all my records, keep dancing all night,
But leave me alone for a while,
'Til Johnny's dancing with me,
I've got no reason to smile.

It's my party ...

Judy and Johnny just walked thru' the door,
Like a queen with her king.
Oh, what a birthday surprise,
Judy's wearing his ring.

It's my party ...

Students identify the people in the picture and say what the relationship between them is.

> The party hostess is the girl crying on the right.
>
> Judy and Johnny are the couple leaving the room.
>
> Judy is a guest at the party, formerly a friend of the hostess.
>
> Johnny was the hostess's boyfriend, but he is now Judy's boyfriend.

3 Play the song again as students read the lyrics. Make sure they understand that there is one extra word or part of a word in each line. They cross these out as they listen.

Verse 1
Line 1: really   Line 2: at   Line 3: still   Line 4: all

Verse 2
Line 1: of   Line 2: just   Line 3: back
Line 4: more

Verse 3
Line 1: in   Line 2: walking   Line 3: party
Line 4: ear-

Optional activity

Tell students that the song *It's my party and I'll cry if I want to* was followed by another hit for Lesley Gore called *It's Judy's turn to cry*. In this song, she tells how Johnny comes back to her, making her happy again and making Judy cry.

Pairwork. Students discuss what happens next in the story and write a short account of it. To give them ideas, ask questions such as:

Does Lesley decide that Johnny isn't worth having after all?

Does Johnny go off with another girl?

Special occasions (p 65) (Workbook p 40)

Writing

1 Pairwork. Students read the letters and match the invitations and the replies. Check answers with the class.

> 2–4; 5–3; 6–1

2 Whole class. Elicit endings for the first two expressions from the class, then get them to complete the others individually. Go round offering help where necessary. Check answers with the class, getting several different endings for each one. Students then look back at the letters to compare their answers with the original texts.

> a) ... celebrate our 30th wedding anniversary ...
> b) ... if you could come to dinner next Saturday.
> c) ... can make it.
> d) ... bringing David with you?
> e) ... I won't be able to join you ...
> f) ... to seeing you.
> g) ... to come.
> h) ... come.
> i) ... to come down here ...
> j) ... I'm afraid I've got exams ...

3 Students go through their completed sentences and label them I, A or R as appropriate. They then decide which are the most formal and underline them. Allow students to compare their answers with a partner before checking with the whole class.

> (Formal expressions have (F) after them)
>
> **I**
> a) We would like you to join us for a small party to ... (F)
> b) This is just a short note to ask you if you could ... (F)
> c) I do hope you ...
> d) How about ...
> h) Please try to ...
> i) I was wondering if you'd like ...
>
> **A**
> f) I'm really looking forward ... (F)
> g) Thanks for the invitation to dinner. I'd love ...
>
> **R**
> e) Thank you for your kind invitation to your wedding anniversary. Unfortunately ... (F)
> j) Thank you for inviting me down for the weekend, but ...

4 Pairwork. Students write invitations to another pair and reply to the invitation they receive. Go round offering help where needed.

5 Pairwork. Students work in pairs to match the greetings cards to the messages. Check answers with the class. Elicit whether any of these cards would be sent in student's countries.

> 1–b engagement announcement   2–g birthday
> 3–j success in driving test   4–h moving house
> 5–i colleague leaving work   6–e illness
> 7–c death   8–f thanks   9–d birth of new baby
> 10–a wedding day

Test

> Scoring: one point per correct answer unless otherwise indicated.
>
> **1** 1 off   2 up   3 on   4 up   5 up   6 in   7 off
> 8 down   9 down   10 after
>
> **2** 1   /ɪ / busy, invite, music
> 2   /æ/ candle, band, hat
> 3   /e / guest, present, dress
> 4   /ʌ / fun, cup, come
> 5   /ʊ / book, full, good
> 6   /ɒ / song, holiday, strong
>
> **3** (2 points each)
> 1   'll go   2 'm meeting   3 'll pay
> 4   'm going to get   5 'll get
> 6   're going to see/'re seeing   7 's coming
> 8   'm going to wash   9 'm not doing
> 10   'll cook   11 Are you going/Are you going to go
> 12   're going

Name: _____   **Total:** _____ /40

---

1 Vocabulary – phrasal verbs *10 points*

Complete the sentences by adding the missing particles.

Thomas leaves for India tomorrow. We're all going to the airport to see him (1) _____ .

The fireworks lit (2) _____ the whole sky.

That was Pilar on the phone. She wants to know what's going (3) _____ this afternoon.

Do you think we need to get dressed (4) _____ for the party?

The children usually wake me (5) _____ long before the alarm clock does.

Don't sit there on your own. Come on and join (6) _____ the fun!

A bomb went (7) _____ in the shopping centre at the weekend.

Their house burnt (8) _____ while they were on holiday.

I think you should get (9) _____ to your homework now.

She really takes (10) _____ her mother, doesn't she?

2 Pronunciation – short vowel sounds *6 points*

Put the words into the six groups below according to the underlined vowel sound.

b<u>u</u>sy c<u>a</u>ndle g<u>ue</u>st f<u>u</u>n b<u>oo</u>k m<u>u</u>sic h<u>o</u>liday s<u>o</u>ng
<u>i</u>nvite pr<u>e</u>sent b<u>a</u>nd dr<u>e</u>ss f<u>u</u>ll c<u>u</u>p h<u>a</u>t c<u>o</u>me g<u>oo</u>d
str<u>o</u>ng

1   /ɪ/
2   /æ/
3   /e/
4   /ʌ/
5   /ʊ/
6   /ɒ/

3 Talking about the future *24 points*

Put the verbs into an appropriate future form.

Tom: Did you remember to get the stamps?

Anna: Oh, sorry, I forgot. I (1) _____ (go) back and get them.

Francine: Do you fancy a drink this evening?

Alain: I'd love to, but I (2) _____ (meet) Veronique at eight.

Akiko: Could you possibly lend me $20?

Ken: Sure.

Akiko: Thanks, I (3) _____ (pay) you back later this evening.

Ahmed: I (4) _____ (get) some bread. Do you want anything from the shops?

Fatima: Yeah, we need some milk.

Ahmed: OK, I (5) _____ (get) some. Anything else?

Marina: We (6) _____ (see) the new James Bond film tonight. Do you want to come?

Enrico: I can't. Claudia (7) _____ (come) over for dinner.

Silvia: Why are you putting those old clothes on?

José: I (8) _____ (wash) the car.

Rebecca: Have you got any plans for this evening?

Tracy: No, I (9) _____ (not/do) anything at all.

Rebecca: Well, why don't you come over to my place. I (10) _____ (cook) us dinner if you like.

Tracy: Sounds great. Thanks.

Heinz: (11) _____ you _____ (go) on holiday this summer?

Laura: Yeah, to Greece. We (12) _____ (go) with Kristina and Petra.

8 *Review 1* *Teacher's notes*

Test yourself (p 67)

Questions

1. How did Jane Couch make history in November 1998?
2. Who wrote the book *Boy*?
3. When does Las Fallas take place in Valencia, Spain?
4. Which song did Elton John sing at Princess Diana's funeral?
5. Why did burglar Frank Gort get an extra year on his prison sentence?
6. How many words are there in *The Little Book of Calm*?
7. Where did Australians Joel Emerson and Lisa Bunyan first meet?

Answers

1. She won the first official female boxing match.
2. Roald Dahl.
3. From March 12th to March 19th.
4. *Candle in the Wind* (renamed *Goodbye England's Rose*).
5. He broke down in tears when he was sentenced to seven years in jail because it was his unlucky number. The judge increased the sentence to eight years.
6. 1,000.
7. At their wedding.

Once in a blue moon (p 67)

Adverbs of frequency

Possible answers
b) How often do you cook?
c) How often do you use a computer?
d) How often do you travel by plane?
e) How often do you go shopping?
f) How often do you go to a nightclub?

Friends (p 68)

Listening

 32 SB p 153

Sue – Sindy   Juan – Hans   Elisa – Enrico
Key words
Sue: met at university; studied music; travelled for a year; friends since university; three or four times a week; both outgoing and energetic; band

Juan: studying; no time to feel homesick; plane; lots to talk about; wish we could see each other more often

Elisa: India, just after university, didn't get on at first, travelled together, similar interest; same music; going to gigs; friends for three or four years

Enrico: similar interests; particularly music; see bands; go out a lot; travel; met in Asia; four years ago

Sindy: a few years; get on well; see each other a lot, both play in a band; go to pubs; friends' houses; chat; like parties

Hans; met at airport, check-in; study; away from home; travelled before going home; three or four times a year

32

Sue

We met at university – we both studied music actually and I suppose we hit it off straightaway. Afterwards, I went away travelling for a year or so, and we lost touch for a while, but really we've been friends since we were students. We see each other, say, three or four times a week I guess. We're both very outgoing and energetic, which I suppose is why we get on so well in the band ...

Juan

It was an amazing coincidence really. Not only to meet like that, but to get on so well and have so much in common. We helped each other with our studying as well. And there was no time at all to feel homesick or anything. From the moment we got on the plane we had lots to talk about. And when we finished, we had a brilliant time seeing the place and, well, it was just one big party 'till it was time to come back home. I wish we could see each other more often these days.

Elisa

It was in India, just after university. I'd been there for a few months at the time. At first, we didn't get on too well, but we kept bumping into each other, as you do when you're travelling, so we, um, well, we ended up travelling together. We found we had similar interests ... you know, we like the same music and like going to gigs and we had similar outlooks and so on. I suppose we've been friends for about, well, three or four years now.

Enrico

We've got similar interests, particularly music. We like to see as many bands as we can. We like going out a lot. We, er, don't get to travel as much as we used to, but we're planning to go back to Asia together for a few weeks next year. That's where we met in the first place actually, about four years ago.

Sindy

We've known each other for a few years now and we still get on well, most of the time anyway! We see each other a lot. Of course we're together twice a week when the band rehearses and we often go to pubs or to friends' houses and just, sort of, hang out and chat really. Yeah, we both love a good party!

Hans

We first met in the, er, airport actually. We just bumped into each other at the check-in. It turned out we were both going to the same place to study and we ended up living in rooms on the same corridor in the hall. It was pretty amazing really! We got on from the word go. It just happened naturally, you know, two people away from home and all that. We did almost everything together and then when the course was over we travelled around the country for a month or so, before coming home. Now, I guess we only see each other three or four times a year or so.

Fancy going out? (p 68)

Future forms

1 Are you doing   2 'm going to see/'m seeing a film
3 are you going to see/are you seeing   4 're meeting
5 'll try/'re going to try   6 'll come   7 're meeting
8 'll give   9 Shall I call   10 'll see

Sound & vision (p 68)

Pronunciation

2   The only sound not in the picture is /uː/.

Keep in touch (p 69)

Tense review

1 'm having   2 've been   3 is   4 is getting
5 've met   6 've become/'m becoming
7 Do you remember 8 met   9 is studying
10 tells/told   11 is coming/is going to come
12 's spending/'s going to spend/'ll spend
13 hope   14 remembers
15 Do you miss/Are you missing   16 was
17 wanted   18 feel/'m feeling   19 Have you seen
20 was working   21 saw   22 is   23 Tell
24 'm thinking/'ll think   25 've got
26 'll finish   27 'll write

Do you know Paris? (p 69)

Sentence stress

1   1   live
       2   Paris
       3   really, Whereabouts
       4   know
       5   Quite, friend
       6   right, centre, Champs Elysées
       7   Nice, street
       8   Marbeuf, know
       9   think, opposite, café
      10   right
      11   friend, François, corner

📼 33

(V = Val; T = Tony)

V: *Where do you live?*

T: *In Paris.*

V: *Oh, really? Whereabouts?*

T: *Do you know Paris?*

V: *Quite well. I've got a friend there.*

T: *Oh, right. Um, I'm right in the centre. Near the Champs Elysées.*

V: *Nice! Which street?*

T: *Rue Marbeuf. Do you know it?*

V: *I think so. Is it just opposite that big café?*

T: *Yeah, that's right.*

V: *Yeah, my friend lives in rue François, just round the corner.*

Did you know ... ? (p 70)

Passive

a) 35,000 million bananas are harvested in Brazil every year.

b) 3,500 km^2 of the world's forest is destroyed every week.

c) The World Cup will be held/is being held/is going to be held/was held in Japan and South Korea in 2002.

d) 25,000 litres of petrol are used in the USA every second.

e) 300 babies are born in the world every minute.

f) Sliced bread was invented in 1928.

g) Great Britain has been ruled by the House of Windsor since 1910.

h) Halley's comet will next be seen in 2061.

i) 20 people in India are killed by falling coconuts every year.

j) 13,000 tonnes of fish are eaten in Japan every day.

People & places (p 70)

Relative clauses

1 b) who/that   c) which/that   d) who/that
   e) who/that   f) which/that   g) whose   h) where
   i) which/that   j) where   k) who/that
   l) who/that   m) where

2 a) Venice   b) Gandhi   c) Liverpool   d) Curie
   e) Gagarin   f) Brazil   g) Madonna   h) Mecca
   i) Olympus   j) Dallas   k) Victoria   l) Amundsen
   m) Macedonia

Far, far away (p 71)

Adjectives

1 exciting   exasperating   fascinating   captivated
   amazing   highest   charming   busiest   exhausted
   relaxed

2 Possible answers

   1 amazing   2 wonderful   3 excellent   4 delicious
   5 relaxed   6 more exciting   7 crowded
   8 interesting   9 captivating   10 most fascinating
   11 charming   12 irritating   13 exasperating

A letter to a friend (p 71)

General revision

It's great to hear that you are having a good time in Australia and I'm glad the school and the course are good.

So, when is Miguel coming to Australia?

Maybe I will visit you at the same time!

Does he look like him?

Write soon and tell me all about him.

We especially missed you last weekend.

Juliette had a party for her birthday.

Everybody was there and I spent most of the evening dancing.

Remember the people who we met last month at the Superhead concert?

Well, Juliette invited them to the party ...

We had an absolutely fantastic time.

Stefan and I really hit if off.

In fact, I'm going to see him again tomorrow. He rang me ...

I'm so excited.

Marcella says hello to you.

Her exam was yesterday.

I haven't spoken to her since then ...

Mum, Dad, Thomas and I are spending a few days next week with my grandparents in Hamburg.

As you know, we usually go there twice a year.

I'm always glad when it's time to come home!

And this year it'll be harder than ever to be away!

Mid Course Test

1
1 do you live
2 do you do
3 did you start
4 do you work
5 Do you enjoy
6 Do you have/Have you got
7 do you like reading
8 Are you reading
9 do you go
10 did you last go
11 Did you have
12 are you next going
13 Are you going
14 Have you been
15 Who discovered ...
16 When did humans first land ...
17 In which city is the White House?/Which city is the White house in?
18 What do Americans celebrate ...
19 What does the word 'garbage' mean?
20 How many states are there in the USA?

2
1 Have you ever been   2 went   3 think
4 've lost   5 Have you seen   6 were
7 Have you looked
8 Do you know   9 is   10 is doing
11 Are you doing   12 'm going
13 Have you forgotten   14 told
15 'm going/'m going to go   16 Do you want
17 'll stay   18 'm expecting
19 Have you seen   20 was driving
21 haven't spoken
22 Did you see   23 left/was leaving   24 arrived
25 have you done   26 fell   27 was doing
28 have you lived   29 had just come back
30 fell

3   1 since   2 for   3 since   4 since

4
1 I've never been ...   2 He is generally ...
3 I play golf from time to time.
4 We hardly ever eat ...
5 The rooms are usually cleaned twice a week.
6 We normally visit our grandparents every other week.

5   1 who/that   2 which/that   3 when   4 whose
5 where
Correct words
6 both   7 both   8 whose   9 where
10 whose   11 both   12 both   13 who/that
14 (which/that)   15 (which/that)   16 (which/that)
17 where   18 (which/that)   19 who/that
20 which/that

6   1 used to   2 would/used to   3 used to
4 used to/would

7   1 was born   2 was opened   3 has been burgled
4 was dismissed   5 is being repaired
6 are made   7 has been beaten
8 wasn't/hasn't been invited

8   1 Are you doing   2 'm going
3 'll go   4 Will you get   5 shall we meet
6 'm working   7 'm going to make
8 'm going to tell

9   1 boring   2 absolutely terrified   3 fascinating
4 the biggest   5 interested   6 embarrassing
7 really bad   8 much easier

10   1 up   2 up   3 in   4 off   5 up   6 off
7 down   8 after   9 on   10 on

11   1 apart   2 blue   3 off   4 crush   5 sight
6 two   7 minded   8 fashioned   9 big
10 breath   11 far   12 swot   13 black
14 with   15 hear   16 in   17 went   18 boring
19 housewarming   20 happy

12   hat   Which   Claudia
blue   Cindy   red   bedroom
My   brother's   table

Mid Course Test

Name: **Total:** _____ /150

---

1 Questions *20 points*

Look at the answers and complete the questions.

1   Where _____ ? I live in Paris.

2   What _____ ? I'm a teacher.

3   When _____ teaching? I started teaching in 1998.

4   Where _____ ? I work in a language school, near the city centre.

5   _____ your job? Yes, I enjoy my job very much.

6   _____ any hobbies? Yes, reading and travelling when I can.

7   What kind of books _____ ? I like reading historical novels mainly.

8   _____ a book at the moment? Yes, I'm reading *Captain Corelli's Mandolin* by Louis de Bernières.

9   How often _____ abroad? I usually go abroad three or four times a year.

10   When _____ last _____ away? I last went away two months ago – to Thailand.

11   _____ a good time? Yes, I had a great time.

12   When _____ next _____ away? I'm next going away in a month's time – to Morocco for a few weeks.

13   _____ alone? No, I'm going with a friend.

14   _____ there before? I haven't, but my friend went there a few years ago.

The following questions have mistakes in them.
Correct them.

15   Who did discover America?

   _____

16   When did humans first landed on the moon?

   _____

17   In which city the White House is?

   _____

18   What do celebrate Americans on the 4th July?

   _____

19   What means the word 'garbage'?

   _____

20   How many states there are in the USA?

   _____

2 General tenses and verb forms *30 points*

Put the verbs into the most appropriate form.

Tom: (1) _____ you ever _____ (be) to the USA?

Angie: Yes, I (2) _____ (go) there last year actually.

Anna: Oh no! I (3) _____ (think) I (4) _____ (lose) my keys! (5) _____ you _____ (see) them anywhere?

Benny: Well, they (6) _____ (be) by the phone earlier this morning, (7) _____ you _____ (look) there?

Petra: (8) _____ you _____ (know) where Antonio is?

Gerta: Yes, he (9) _____ (be) in his bedroom. He (10) _____ (do) his homework.

Jon: (11) _____ you _____ (do) anything this evening?

Linda: Yes, I (12) _____ (go) for a drink with Sue. (13) _____ you _____ (forget)? I (14) _____ (tell) you about it this morning.

Amit: I (15) _____ (go) for a walk. (16) _____ you _____ (want) to come?

Ajay: No, thanks. I (17) _____ (stay) here. I (18) _____ (expect) a phone call.

Pittara: (19) _____ you _____ (see) Sasa recently?

Peach: Yes, this morning actually while I (20) _____ (drive) to work. But, I (21) _____ (not/speak) to her for weeks.

Pascale: (22) _____ you _____ (see) him at the party last night?

François: Yes, but he (23) _____ (leave) when we (24) _____ (arrive).

Photocopiable

Julio: What (25) _____ you _____ (do) to your arm?

Ying: Oh, I (26) _____ (fall) off the ladder while I (27) _____ (do) some decorating the other day.

Henri: How long (28) _____ (live) here?

Marta: Just over ten years now. I (29) _____ (just come back) from travelling in South America and I (30) _____ (fall) in love with the place straight away.

3 Since and for *4 points*

Add *since* or *for* to the sentences.

1 I've known them _____ I was at school.

2 We've lived here _____ almost ten years.

3 They've been here _____ ten o'clock.

4 He's worked for the BBC _____ 1998.

4 Adverbs of frequency *8 points*

Put the adverbs into an appropriate place in the sentences.

1 I've been to Russia. (never)

_____

2 He is on time. (generally)

_____

3 I play golf. (from time to time)

_____

4 We eat in restaurants. (hardly ever)

_____

5 The rooms are cleaned. (usually, twice a week)

_____

6 We visit our grandparents. (normally, every other week)

_____

5 Defining relative clauses *20 points*

The words in bold are wrong. Cross them out and write the correct words.

1 A vegetarian is someone **which** doesn't eat meat.

2 Holi is a Hindu festival **where** celebrates the beginning of spring.

3 Traditionally, Christmas is a time **whose** families get together.

4 A widower is a man **who** wife has died.

5 A boarding school is a school **when** children live as well as study.

In some of the following sentences both underlined words are possible. Cross out any words which are not possible.

6 The man that/who phoned earlier is here.

7 That's the dog that/which bit me.

8 This is the man that/whose camera you found.

9 The church where/that we got married is near here.

10 There's the girl whose/that party we went to.

11 Have you seen the magazine that/which I bought this morning?

12 The film is about a boy who/that lives on the streets of India.

Add an appropriate word only if it is necessary.

13 There's the man _____ took your bag.

14 Here's the book _____ I was telling you about.

15 Can you see the birthday card _____ Alex gave me?

16 This is the school _____ I went to.

17 The bar _____ we first met is near here I think.

18 The hotel _____ we stayed in was wonderful.

19 Carmen was the only person _____ helped me.

20 Where is the picture _____ was on the wall just here?

6 Used to and would *4 points*

Complete the sentences using *used to* or *would*. In some sentences both are possible.

1 I _____ smoke, but I gave up 5 years ago.

2 As a child I _____ often miss school, especially when we had maths.

3 I think she _____ live in Australia.

4 He _____ always be the first to arrive at parties.

7 Passive *8 points*

Put the verbs into an appropriate form of the passive. In some sentences there is more than one possibility.

1 I _____ (born) in 1987.

2 The new factory _____ (open) by the Queen last Friday.

3 Our house _____ (burgle) twice already this month.

4 He _____ (dismiss) after he admitted stealing the money.

5 My car _____ (repair) at the moment.

6 Clothes _____ (make) in this factory.

7 Real Madrid _____ (beat) twice this year by Manchester United.

8 She's a little upset because she _____ (not/invite) to the party.

8 Talking about the future *8 points*

Choose the most appropriate form.

Freda: (1) **Will you do/Are you doing** anything tonight?

Francine: Yes, I (2) **'ll go/'m going** to the cinema with Alain.

Mohammed: There's no milk. Oh well, I suppose I (3) **'m going to go/'ll go** and get some.

Saqulain: (4) **Are you getting/Will you get** some bread as well?

Cloë: What time (5) **shall we meet/will we meet**?

Boris: What about seven thirty. I (6) **'m working/'m going to work** until seven.

Emily: I think it's time you had a haircut.

Sue: Yes, I know. I (7) **'m making/ 'm going to make** an appointment this afternoon actually.

Sung: Have you told him yet?

Pittara: No, I (8) **'m telling/ 'm going to tell** him this evening.

9 Adjectives *8 points*

Each sentence contains one mistake. Find it and correct it.

1 Don't bother going to see the film – it's really bored.

2 I was very terrified when I saw it!

3 The museum is absolutely fascinated.

4 He lives in the most biggest house I've ever seen.

5 Are you interesting in Greek mythology?

6 The photos were so embarrassed!

7 I'm going home – this party is completely bad.

8 This one is much more easy than that one.

10 Phrasal verbs *10 points*

Add an appropriate preposition.

1 Did everyone dress _____ in costumes for the party?

2 What time did you wake _____ this morning?

3 Everyone's having fun. Let's join _____ .

4 Sorry I'm late. I went to the airport to see Andy _____ .

5 The explosion lit _____ the whole sky.

6 The bomb went _____ and killed 20 people.

7 It was awful. The flames were huge and the house burnt _____ in minutes.

8 He takes _____ his mother much more than his father, don't you think?

9 I wonder what's going _____ next door. They're making a lot of noise.

10 We got _____ with each other from the moment we met.

11 General vocabulary *20 points*

Choose the correct word.

1 We were friends for years, but we drifted **away/apart** when we left school.

2 We go there once in a **blue/red** moon.

3 I generally find it easy to switch **off/out** from work when I'm at home.

4 I once had a **crash/crush** on Leonardo DiCaprio.

5 Do you believe in love at first **sight/seeing**?

6 Don't trust him – he's **two/double**-faced.

7 She's so absent- **headed/minded**. She's always losing things.

8 Why do want to buy that? It's a bit old-**fashionable/fashioned**!

9 He's always been **large/big**-headed!

10 The views really took my **breath/words** away.

11 This one is by **far/long** the best.

12 He never stops working – he's a real **swot/swat**.

13 Have you seen Gabrielle? Someone's given her a **blue/black** eye.

14 I'm having dinner **with/at** John tonight.

15 That's terrible. I'm really sorry to **hear/know** that.

16 Don't sit on your own. Come and join **on/in**!

17 The bomb **blew/went** off at exactly half past nine.

18 That film was really **bored/boring**. What a waste of money!

19 Are you going to Victor and Lenka's **housewarming/housewelcoming** party next week?

20 It's your birthday? Oh, many **pleasant/happy** returns.

12 Pronunciation *10 points*

<u>Underline</u> the strongest stress in each sentence of the dialogue. The first one has been done as an example.

A: What's the <u>matter</u>?
B: I can't find my hat.
A: Which hat?
B: The one I got from Claudia.
A: The blue one?
B: That was from Cindy. The red one.
A: It's in the bedroom.
B: My bedroom?
A: No, your brother's bedroom. On the table.

9 *Soap* Overview

This unit is based on one episode of a fictitious American TV soap series, *Pacific Heights*. The main grammatical focus is on reported speech and *will* for the future.

Students read a TV guide in which they are introduced to the characters of the soap, and they revise family vocabulary and vocabulary used to describe people. Students then read and listen to Scene 1 of *Pacific Heights*, and look at phrasal verbs and everyday expressions from the script. They go on to listen to Scenes 2–4 and write their own TV preview for the episode after next.

Section	Aims	What the students are doing
Introduction page 72	*Lexis*: family relationships	Reviewing vocabulary to do with family relationships.
Pacific Heights pages 72–74	*Reading skills*: scanning	Scanning a script from a TV soap opera, *Pacific Heights*, for information and to introduce the main characters.
	Lexis: relationships;	Focusing on vocabulary to do with family relationships connected with the script.
	describing people	Reviewing vocabulary to do with describing people's appearance.
	say/tell:	Distinguishing between *say* and *tell* within a TV review of *Pacific Heights*.
Pacific Heights: Scene 1 pages 74–75	*Reading & listening skills*: skimming and listening for gist	Reading and listening to Scene 1 for information about the characters and their actions, and to describe how the characters feel about each other.
	Lexis: phrasal verbs; everyday expressions	Focusing on phrasal verbs and everyday expressions from the script.
	Speaking skills: performing	Acting out a part from Scene 1 of *Pacific Heights*.
Close up page 76	*Grammar*: reported speech	Learning about backshifting in reported speech. Practising reported speech.
Pacific Heights: Scene 2–4 pages 77–78	*Reading skills*: scanning	Focusing on vocabulary to do with relationships in *Pacific Heights* within the text.
	Listening skills: listening for detail	Checking listening comprehension by identifying the correct order of Scenes 2–4 from the illustrations of the scenes.
	Lexis: everyday expressions;	Focusing on everyday expressions from Scenes 2–4 of *Pacific Heights*.
	summarising	Completing a summary of Scenes 2–4.
Pacific Heights: The next episode page 79	*Writing skills*: giving information	Making predictions about what will happen in the next episode of *Pacific Heights* from a TV preview. Writing a TV preview for the episode after that.
Close up page 80	*Grammar*: *will* for prediction; *will* + continuous, *will* + perfect	Identifying the three future *will* tenses for prediction. Practising the tenses by making predictions about the future.

Soap

9 *Soap* *Teacher's notes*

Closed books. Whole class. Elicit the meaning of *soap opera* (televison or radio drama of everyday life). Elicit the names of the longest running soaps in the students' country or countries and ask why they think soap operas are so popular.

Groupwork. Students choose a popular television soap which they watch. They discuss what is happening in the soap and report the story to the rest of the class. When each group has reported the story, encourage them to say what they think will happen next.

1 Workbook (p 44)

Open books. Students revise common words for family relationships and learn some new ones by making word combinations. Check answers with the class.

> *Possible answers*
>
> mother-in-law   single mother   step-mother
> grandmother   great grandmother   ex-wife
> ex-husband   father-in-law   single father
> step-father   grandfather   great grandfather
> daughter-in-law   step-daughter   second daughter
> first daughter   only daughter   granddaughter
> great granddaughter   great uncle   brother-in-law
> step-brother   half-brother   son-in-law   step-son
> second son   first son   only son   grandson
> great grandson   great aunt   great nephew
> great niece   sister-in-law   step-sister   half-sister
> single parent   first cousin   second cousin
> first husband   second husband   first wife
> second wife   only child   first child   second child
> step-child

2 Encourage students to think of their own family and decide how many of the words in 1 could apply to them.

3 Draw a diagram on the board of your own family. Point to people in the diagram and tell students what relation you are to them. Students draw their own family diagrams. Encourage them to include people illustrating as many of the words in 1 as they can.

4 Go through the instructions one by one, getting students to mark their spidergrams appropriately.

5 Pairwork. Students compare their diagrams and take turns talking about the relatives they have put in them. Go round offering help and encouragement. Students should give as many details as possible.

Pacific Heights (p 72)

1 Pairwork. Students look at the photos on page 73. Before they read the text, they discuss what they think the characters are like. They then read the background information about the characters and complete the family tree with names. (See answer at the bottom of this page.) Encourage them to scan the text for the information needed rather than spend time on any parts they don't understand.

2 Pairwork. Students discuss who Annick, Katy and John are and what their relationship is to Daniel. They will need to read the text more carefully this time. Check answers with the whole class.

> Annick is the daughter of a French distributor that Max is trying to do a deal with. She is Daniel's fiancée.
>
> Katy is Daniel's ex-girlfriend.
>
> John is Daniel's best friend and now Katy's boyfriend.

Lexis (p 73)

1 Whole class. Students look at the completed Dalton family tree and answer the questions. This can be done with students raising their hands as they find the answers.

> a) Edith   b) Phil   c) Daniel   d) Katy
> e) Annick   f) Sarah   g) Penny

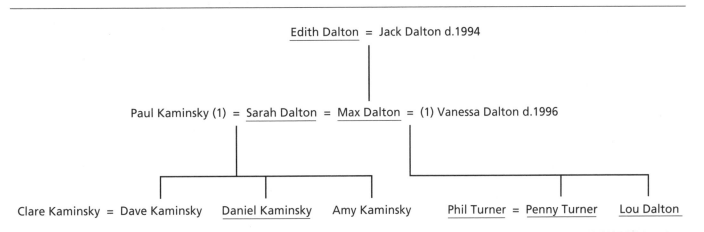

2 Pairwork. Students first write questions individually, then work in pairs to ask and answer them.

3 Give students a few minutes to correct the mistakes in the sentences, then check answers with the class.

> a) At the age of 52 ...
> b) Lou is 21./Lou is 21 years old.
> c) Katy has big blue eyes.
> d) ... in their mid twenties.
> e) Sarah's curly red hair ...
> f) ... she is 78.
> g) ... Edith is in her late seventies ...
> h) Daniel is Dave's 27-year-old brother.
> i) Daniel is more outgoing than Dave.
> j) Most men (of) his age ...

4 Students complete the sentences with the names of their own family or friends, or famous people, and appropriate information. Allow them to compare their answers in pairs or groups before eliciting feedback from the class.

say/tell (p 74) (Workbook p 47)

Whole class. Write these sentences on the board:

I told him about the soap opera.

I said that the soap opera was on Mondays.

Elicit the difference between *said* and *told* (we *say* something, but we *tell* someone). Get students to call out more sentences using *say* and *tell*.

1 Pairwork. Students complete the text with *said* and *told*. Check answers with the class.

> 1 said   2 told   3 told   4 told   5 said

2 Pairwork. Students decide who said each of the sentences. Check answers with the class.

> a) Katy
> b) Daniel
> c) The doctor
> d) Penny

3 Students should now be able to do this quite easily.

> You tell somebody.
> You say something.

Pacific Heights: Scene 1 (p 74)

1 34

Ensure students understand that they are reading and listening for four important events or pieces of information, one in each part. Play the recording. Students read the tapescript as they listen. With weaker classes, you could stop the recording after each part and give students time to discuss in pairs and write down what the important thing is.

> Part 1:   Daniel is having second thoughts about marrying Annick now he has learnt that Katy, his ex-girlfriend, is no longer going out with John.
>
> Part 2:   Daniel left the room when Sarah told him that Annick looked gorgeous in her wedding dress.
>
> Part 3:   Max became angry when Edith told him and Sarah that Daniel was having doubts about marrying Annick.
>
> Part 4:   Max and Lou had an argument and Lou told Max she had seen Daniel and Katy together.

> 📼 34
> **Scene 1**
> Part 1
> (D = Daniel; E = Edith)
> D: *Hi, Grandma.*
> E: *Hello, dear. How's it going?*
> D: *Oh, don't ask.*
> E: *Are you still thinking about Katy?*
> D: *Yes. I can't get her off my mind. I don't know what to do.*
> E: *I thought you'd got over her.*
> D: *I had ... until I saw her again. When she told me she'd broken up with John, all the old feelings came back.*
> E: *But Daniel, what about Annick and the wedding?*
> D: *I know. I thought I loved Annick. When I asked her to marry me I meant it – but now I'm not sure how I feel.*
> E: *Look, why don't you go away for a few days and think about it. How about going to stay with Dave and Clare – they'd love to see you.*
> D: *But I thought Dave was in Mexico.*
> E: *Oh yes, he is, isn't he? Well, Clare's there – you could talk it through with her.*
> D: *Yes, that's not a bad idea. I'll go and see her tomorrow.*

Part 2

(M = Max; E = Edith; S = Sarah; D = Daniel)

M: *What a day! The traffic was worse than ever.*

E: *Sit down, both of you. Do you want juice?*

S: *Oh, thank you, Edith. I'm worn out.*

D: *Why, have you had a busy day?*

S: *Yes, I've been shopping with Annick. She asked me to help her choose her wedding dress.*

E: *Did you have any luck?*

S: *Yes, finally. You should see her, Daniel. She looks gorgeous.*

D: *Oh ... good. I ... I've got to go out. See you later.*

Part 3

(S = Sarah; E = Edith; M = Max)

S: *What did I say?*

E: *Listen, there's something you should know.*

M: *What's the matter? Mom, are you all right?*

E: *Yes, I'm fine, dear. It's Daniel – he says he's having doubts about Annick.*

M: *What! What does he mean?*

E: *He's seen Katy again.*

M: *Katy? I thought she was married to somebody else. Anyway, it's too late to cancel the wedding now.*

S: *Oh, but Max, if Daniel's still in love with Katy ...*

M: *I don't care who he's in love with, the wedding is going ahead.*

Part 4

(P = Penny; M = Max; E = Edith; L = Lou)

P: *Oh, dear. What's going on here?*

M: *Er, nothing – everything's fine.*

E: *Juice, dear?*

P: *Oh, yes, please. We've had a terrible day – we've been shopping to get Lou a bridesmaid's dress and she says she won't wear a dress.*

L: *Well, I hate dresses – it's not fair. Why can't I wear a suit?*

S: *Because you're a bridesmaid and bridesmaids don't wear suits – it's only for one day.*

L: *Why don't you mind your own business?*

P: *Lou!*

M: *How dare you speak to Sarah like that – I think you'd better apologize young lady!*

L: *Don't call me young lady!*

M: *Say you're sorry right now, or I'll ...*

E: *Max, calm down. Remember what the doctor told you.*

L: *It doesn't look as if there's going to be a wedding anyway – I've just seen Daniel with Katy, and he had his arm around her.*

M: *What! Wait till I get my hands on that boy.*

E: *Max, he's not a boy, he's a man. It's his life. Leave him alone.*

M: *Leave him alone. I'll leave him alone if he messes this up for me. I'll never speak to him again. Annick's father is about to sign the biggest contract we've ever had and you tell me to leave him alone.*

S: *Max, wait ...*

2 Whole class. Elicit ideas about why Daniel, Max and Lou are worried about the wedding. Ask students what they think. Should Daniel marry Annick if he is still in love with Katy? Should Max be more concerned with his step-son's happiness than his business deal? Should Lou be allowed to wear what she wants at the wedding or is she just being selfish?

Daniel:	He's having second thoughts. He thinks he is still in love with Katy and now she is free again, he's not sure he wants to marry Annick.
Lou:	She is going to be a bridesmaid. She hates dresses and wants to wear a suit, but she has been told she has to wear a dress for the wedding.
Max:	Annick's father is about to sign a very big contract with his company. If Daniel doesn't marry Annick, her father will be very angry and may call off the deal.

3 Pairwork. Students discuss the relationships between the characters. Students use the circular diagram to show the relationships between the characters by drawing lines between those who are in love, those who are related by birth, etc. Go round offering help and encouragement.

Lexis (p 75)

1 Pairwork. Students look through the tapescript to find the corresponding phrasal verbs. You could do this as a race, with the first pair to finish raising their hands. Check answers with the class, asking them to give the infinitive form of the verbs as well as the form that occurs in the script.

a)	get over (I thought you'd got over her)	
b)	break up with (she told me she'd broken up with John)	
c)	talk it through (you could talk it through with her)	
d)	go ahead (the wedding is going ahead)	
e)	go on (What's going on here?)	
f)	mess up (I'll leave him alone if he messes this up for me)	

2 Pairwork. Students decide which phrasal verb is suitable for each dialogue. Check answers with the class.

> *Possible answers*
> a) Sure, let's talk it through.
> b) No, she broke up with him last week.
> c) No, I've got over it.
> d) I'm afraid I messed it up.
> e) What's going on?
> f) They said it was going ahead.

3 Pairwork. Students decide what the missing words are. Encourage them to do this first without looking back at the tapescript. They can then check their answers. This could also be done as a race with the first student to finish raising his or her hand. Check answers with the class.

> a) It's not fair!
> b) I don't care.
> c) How dare you!
> d) What a day!
> e) I'm worn out.
> f) Leave him alone.
> g) What's the matter?
> h) Mind your own business.

4 Pairwork. Give pairs of students plenty of time to work out their dialogues. Go round offering help and encouragement. Allow students to write their dialogues down, but encourage them to perform them without reading from their scripts. Get several pairs to perform their dialogues for the class.

5 Pairwork or groupwork. Pairs or groups decide on a part of the scene and each student chooses one of the characters to play. Students should work individually, then consult with their partner or the rest of the group. They practise their roles alone and with their partner or group. Get the groups to perform their part from Scene 1 for the rest of the class. Encourage the audience to watch attentively and to show their appreciation at the end of each part.

Close up (p 76) (Workbook p 44, p 45)

Reported speech

1 Whole class. Go through the examples. Make sure that students understand that 'I'm having second thoughts' is direct speech using the present continuous and that 'He told Edith that he was having second thoughts' is reported speech using the past continuous. Write another present continuous sentence on the board, for example, *I'm doing my homework* and elicit how this would be reported (*He said he was doing his homework*).

Students look at the list of structures. Explain that in backshifting, the corresponding past tense is used so that a continuous tense remains continuous but shifts back to the past. Make sure that students also notice that in reported speech appropriate adjustments have to be made to pronouns. In the first example *I* becomes *he* in the reported speech.

Do the first one with the whole class, getting students to call out examples of direct speech using the present simple and their reported speech equivalents, using the past simple. There are several examples they can find in *Pacific Heights* or students can make up their own.

Groupwork. Students invent examples of reported speech for the other structures. Go round offering help and encouragement. Check answers with the class. Go through the Language reference section with them if they are still having problems with reported speech.

> *Possible answers*
> a) 'I don't know what to do.' He told her he didn't know what to do.
> b) 'I have split up with John.' She said that she had split up with John.
> c) 'We had a terrible day.' She said that they had had a terrible day.
> d) 'I'll never speak to him again.' He said he would never speak to him again.
> e) 'I can't get you off my mind.' He told her he couldn't get her off his mind.
> f) 'You must take it easy for a while.' The doctor told him that he had to take it easy for a while.
> g) 'Daniel is going to see Katy tonight.' She told him that Daniel was going to see Katy that night.

2 Remind students that the imperative form is the same as the infinitive, but without *to*. When we report an imperative we add *to* back in. When we report a negative imperative we add *not* before *to*.

> He told her to go away.
> He told her not to do that.

3 Students make their lists of people and the things that were said individually.

Pairwork. Students discuss their lists. Go round making sure that they are using reported speech properly to report their conversations.

4 Whole class. Go through the instructions. Go round the class and check students' questions as they work. If space allows, students mingle around the class, asking and answering their questions. If space is a problem, this could be done in groups.

5 Pairwork. Students talk about the information they have found out and the difference between actual and predicted answers, using reported speech.

Pacific heights: Scenes 2–4 (p 77)

(Workbook p 47)

Closed books. Ask students what they remember of the story of *Pacific Heights* so far. Get each student in turn to tell you one piece of information about the characters or one event in the story.

1   Students fill in the gaps. Allow them to compare their answers in pairs before checking with the class.

> a)   Daniel is engaged to Annick.
>
> b)   Max is married to Sarah.
>
> c)   Katy broke Daniel's heart.
>
> d)   Phil is Max's business partner.
>
> e)   Lou has a difficult relationship with Sarah.
>
> f)   Everybody confides in Edith.
>
> g)   Katy has recently split up with John.

2   Students read about the characters in Scenes 2–4 and fill in the gaps. Check answers with the class.

> a)   Phil is married to Penny. Dave is married to Clare.
>
> b)   Becky is Charlie's girlfriend. Amy is Mark's girlfriend.
>
> c)   Ella and Mara are identical twins.
>
> d)   Dave's wife likes younger men.
>
> e)   Amy and Mark are involved with an Animal Rights group.

3   Pairwork. Students look at the gaps in 1 and 2 and see if they can complete them with names of their own family and friends. They then discuss them with a partner.

Listening (p 78)

1   🔲 35 SB p 154

Whole class. Explain that film directors use sketches to help them plan their films. Students look at the pictures and decide which characters they can see in each one.

Play the recording. Pairwork. Students listen to Scenes 2–4 and put the pictures in the correct order. Check answers with the class.

> Picture A – Scene 4
>
> Picture B – Scene 2
>
> Picture C – Scene 3

2   Play the recording again. Students note down the answers to the questions. Give students time to compare their answers with a partner before checking.

> a)   Charlie's surfboard is at home.
>
> b)   They want to go travelling, but their parents won't let them.
>
> c)   Her boyfriend Charlie is having an affair with Clare.
>
> d)   She wants to take part in the demonstration but her parents will be very angry if she does.

🔲 **35**

Scene 2

(P = Penny; E = Ella; Ph = Phil; M = Mara)

P: *So what have you been up to today?*

E: *We've been to the travel agent's to get some brochures.*

Ph: *I thought we'd talked about that.*

M: *But Dad ...*

Ph: *Look, I've told you once and I'll tell you again – you are not going travelling on your own. You're too young.*

E: *But Becky's parents let her go travelling last year.*

Ph: *Yes, but she went with her brother.*

M: *Well, let's ask Charlie. Where is he, by the way?*

P: *Oh, he's taking part in a big surfing competition out of town.*

Ph: *But his surfboard's here.*

P: *Oh, that's strange. I must have made a mistake.*

M: *Come on, Ella ... let's go round to Becky's.*

P: *Er, don't be late for dinner.*

Scene 3

(M = Mara; E = Ella)

M: *I think I know where Charlie is.*

E: *Where?*

M: *He's gone to see Clare. I'm sure there's something going on.*

E: *Oh, between Charlie and Clare?*

M: *Yes.*

E: *But Clare's married to Uncle Dave.*

M: *So? Lots of married people have affairs.*

E: *Well, I don't think it's right. Anyway, how do you know?*

M: *Well, I heard him talking to her on the phone yesterday. He asked her if Dave had left for America and then he said he couldn't wait to be in her arms again!*

E: *Oh, what a creep. Poor Becky.*

M: *Oh, don't worry, she'll get over it. But listen, I've got an idea.*

E: *If it's about Charlie coming travelling with us, forget it. He's already said he doesn't want to.*

M: *Yes, but if we catch him with Clare, we can blackmail·him to come travelling with us.*

E: *Oh, yes. I see what you mean. But don't you think we should tell Becky about him and Clare.*

M: *No, stupid. If we tell her, we won't be able to blackmail him. Come on, let's make a plan.*

Scene 4
(A = Amy; M = Mark)

A: *I don't know what to do. If I don't take part in the demonstration I'll have to leave the group.*

M: *Just think about those poor little animals. Have you any idea what they do to them?*

A: *I know, but it's my step-father's company.*

M: *Well, it serves him right for experimenting on animals.*

A: *Are they going to do any damage?*

M: *No, it's a peaceful demonstration, that's all. Anyway, it's up to you.*

A: *Um, OK, I'll come, but my mom will kill me if she finds out.*

Lexis (p 78) (Workbook p 47)

1 Students should first try to do this without looking back at the tapescript. Allow them to compare their answers in pairs before checking with the class. Make sure students understand all the expressions. You can test their understanding by asking them to think of more sentences using the expressions or to suggest situations in which they might be used.

> a) What have you been up to?
> b) It's up to you.
> c) I see what you mean.
> d) I must have made a mistake.
> e) I've told you once and I'll tell you again.
> f) She'll get over it.
> g) It serves him right.
> h) Have you any idea what they do to them?

2 Students match the expressions in 1 to the sentences.

> 1 d 2 c 3 a 4 h 5 e 6 b 7 g 8 f

3 🔲 **35 SB p 154**

Students listen to Scenes 2–4 again and put the expressions in the order they hear them. Allow students to compare their answers in pairs, then check with the whole class.

> a) What have you been up to? 1
> b) It's up to you. 8
> c) I see what you mean. 5
> d) I must have made a mistake. 3
> e) I've told you once and I'll tell you again. 2
> f) She'll get over it. 4
> g) It serves him right. 7
> h) Have you any idea what they do to them? 6

Closed books. Students could make up/improvise some short exchanges to practise the expressions, for example, *Where shall we go? It's up to you.*

4 Pairwork. Students write a summary using the frame in their books. Go round offering help and encouragement. Remind them that they need to use reported speech and that they can look back at the Grammar reference on page 76 if they need reminding of this. Get several pairs to read their summaries to the rest of the class.

> Ella and Mara told their parents they had been to the travel agent's to get some brochures. But Penny and Phil told them that they were too young to go travelling on their own. Meanwhile, Charlie arranged to go and spend the weekend with Clare while Dave was away in America. He told his parents he was taking part in a surfing competition. Mara told Ella that Charlie was at Clare's and that they could blackmail him into going travelling with them. Amy said that she was worried about taking part in the animal rights demonstration at her step-father's company. But Mark told her that it would be a peaceful demonstration but that it was up to her whether she went or not.

Pacific Heights: The next episode (p 79) (Workbook p 47)

1 Groupwork. Students try to predict what will happen next in *Pacific Heights*. Go through the announcement first with the whole class; the questions will give them some ideas of what to talk about and will remind them of what has gone before. Allow plenty of time for discussion and go round monitoring and offering help where necessary.

2 Groupwork. In the same groups, students prepare an announcement for the episode after next, using the one in 1 as a model. Their announcements should be a mixture of information about things that happen in the episode and tantalising questions which the reader will want to find the answers to by watching the programme.

3 Groupwork. Pass the announcements around the groups so that each group gets a chance to read them all. Students should discuss how the other predictions differ from their own and which one they like best.

Close up (p 80) (Workbook p 45)

will for prediction

1 Whole class. Read the introduction, the predictions and the questions. Ensure that students understand *nuclear family* (a family that consists of a father, mother and children; nothing to do with nuclear power).

Pairwork. Students discuss the questions.

2 Whole class. Elicit the names of the underlined structures.

> *will be* = future simple
> *will be living* = future continuous
> *will have become* = future perfect

3 Pairwork. Students match the symbols to the structures and write explanations of their answers. Check answers with the class.

> 1 = future simple (a single action which will happen in the future)
>
> 2 = future continuous (an action in the future which will continue for some time. It starts before and continues after a certain point in time)
>
> 3 = future perfect (an action in the future viewed from a point even further in the future when it has already been completed)

4 Pairwork. Students discuss their own futures. Direct them to the Language toolbox for some useful expressions to talk about the future.

will + continuous; *will* + perfect (p 80)

1 Students look at the diagram and complete the sentences using *will be (doing)* or *will have (done)*. Check answers with the class.

> a) At six o'clock she will be having a shower.
>
> b) At seven o'clock she will have had a shower and she will be eating breakfast.
>
> c) At eight she will be driving to London.
>
> d) At nine thirty she will be visiting the new de Kooning exhibition.
>
> e) At eleven thirty she will have left the de Kooning exhibition and she will be talking to Roland Hoff.
>
> f) At twelve thirty she will have finished with Roland Hoff and she will be having lunch with Dani.
>
> g) At two she will have had lunch and she will be meeting her accountant.
>
> h) At five thirty she will be driving back to Oxford.

2 Give students sufficient time to write similar sentences about what they will be doing tomorrow.

3 Give students time to write their predictions. Students then compare and discuss their predictions with a partner.

Test

> Scoring: one point per correct answer unless otherwise indicated.
>
> **1**
> 1 business
> 2 matter
> 3 care
> 4 up
> 5 over
> 6 up
> 7 dare
> 8 idea
> 9 serves
> 10 mean
>
> **2** (1½ points each)
> 1 he was a teacher
> 2 he's nearly ready
> 3 (that) she didn't know his name
> 4 (that) he's got a new girlfriend
> 5 (that) they'd be there soon
> 6 where I lived
> 7 if I had ever been to Spain
> 8 she was living in Vienna (then)
>
> **3**
> 1 will be having
> 2 will be driving
> 3 will have had
> 4 will be playing
> 5 will have had
> 6 will have gone
> 7 will live/will be living
> 8 will be
> 9 will live/will have lived
> 10 will have visited
> 11 will have
> 12 will be living
>
> **4**
> 1 do
> 2 actor
> 3 theatre, films
> 4 Both, television
> 5 famous
> 6 three Oscars

9 *Soap* Test

Name: _____   **Total:** _____ /40

---

1 Vocabulary – everyday expressions *10 points*

Complete the expressions by adding a word from the box.
Use all the words.

> serves   idea   dare   matter   business   care
> up   up   over   mean

I'm not telling you. Mind your own (1) _____!

What's the (2) _____? Are you OK?

I don't (3) _____ where we go. It's (4) _____ to you.

It's very sad but she'll get (5) _____ it.

What are you (6) _____ to? Come on, tell me.

How (7) _____ you! I've never been so insulted in all
my life.

Have you any (8) _____ what her name is?

You shouldn't have drunk so much. It (9) _____ you
right!

I see what you (10) _____ . It's not as easy as it looks.

2 Reporting *12 points*

Report the following beginning, with the words given.

1   'I'm a teacher.'

    He said _____

2   'I'm nearly ready.'

    He says _____

3   'I don't know his name.'

    She told them _____

4   'He's got a new girlfriend.'

    Carlos tells me _____

5   'We'll be there soon.'

    He said _____

6   'Where do you live?'

    She asked me _____

7   'Have you ever been to Spain?'

    She asked me _____

8   'I think she's living in Vienna at the moment.'

    He thought _____

3 will *12 points*

Look at what Belinda will be doing tomorrow.

8am–8.30	have breakfast
9am	drive to work
9.30am	arrive at work
10am–11.30am	visit the new offices
1pm–2.30pm	have lunch
3pm–4pm	play tennis
4pm	drive home
8.30pm–9.30pm	have dinner
11pm	go to bed

Complete the sentences using *will be doing* or *will have
done*.

1   At 8.15, she _____ breakfast.

2   At 9.15, she _____ to work.

3   At 2.45, she _____ lunch.

4   At 3.30, she _____ tennis.

5   At 10.00, she _____ dinner.

6   At midnight, she _____ to bed.

Here are some predictions about the future. Put the verbs
into an appropriate form using *will*.

7   In 2020, a third of all Britons _____ (live) alone.

8   China _____ (be) the major world power in 2100.

9   By 2050, a human _____ (live) to be 150.

10 Aliens _____ (visit) the Earth by 2100.

11 This time next year, the USA _____ (have) a
woman president.

12 By 2500, humans _____ (live) on Mars.

4 Pronunciation *6 points*

Underline the stressed syllable(s) in each sentence of the
following dialogue.

1   Hans: What do you do?   (1 stress)

2   Luisa: I'm an actor.   (1 stress)

3   Hans: In the theatre or films?   (2 stresses)

4   Luisa: Both, and on television.   (2 stresses)

5   Hans: Are you famous?   (1 stress)

6   Luisa: Well, I've got three Oscars!   (2 stresses)

Photocopiable

10 *Time* Overview

The topics in this unit are time management and work. The main grammatical focus is on modals for obligation, prohibition and permission.

The unit begins with students looking at sayings about time and comparing English sayings with sayings in their own language.

Students listen to a radio discussion on time management skills. They go on to practise dates, prepositions and time expressions, before reading an article giving advice on managing time.

Finally students listen to three people discussing office cultures in their workplace and then practise writing business letters.

Section	Aims	What the students are doing
Introduction page 82	*Lexis*: sayings	Comparing sayings about 'Time'.
Punctuality pages 83–85	*Conversation skills*: fluency work	Talking about punctuality to generate interest in the topic.
	Listening skills: listening for detail	Completing a questionnaire on time management and comparing it with the answers given by a time management consultant in a radio broadcast.
	Pronunciation: sounds	Distinguishing between /θ/ and /ð/, and /s/ and /z/. Practising the sounds.
	Lexis: prepositions; time expressions	Reviewing dates and prepositions. Identifying vocabulary to do with festivals and time expressions. Practising the time expressions.
Things to do pages 86–87	*Reading skills*: scanning	Scanning an article about making lists for information.
	Lexis: collocations	Reviewing collocations from text and forming new collocations.
Close up page 88	*Grammar*: modals of obligation	Identifying modals of obligation. Practising using these modals by describing priorities in the near future and talking about rules and regulations at work.
Office cultures page 89	*Listening skills*: predicting; listening for detail	Looking at photos of people in their workplace and making predictions about companies they work for. Listening to check predictions and for specific information.
To whom it may concern pages 90–91	*Lexis*: business expressions	Focusing on language used in business letters and its function. Completing a business letter using appropriate words and phrases.
	Writing skills: making improvements – appropriacy	Reading a letter of application in reply to an advertisement and improving it by using more appropriate language.

1 Open books. Whole class. Read the three English translations of the three proverbs. Ask students whether they agree with them or not. Elicit one or two proverbs or sayings about time in the students' language and write them on the board. Help students to translate them into English.

Groupwork. Students think of three more expressions about time, translate them into English and discuss whether or not they agree with them.

2 Groupwork. Students read the expressions in the book and compare them with the ones they have just discussed. They decide what they mean and which ones they like best.

Optional activity

Many proverbs in English are characterised by the obvious nature of their message; the meaning of others is hidden in obscure imagery. An English magazine once ran a competition for fake proverbs which sound profound, but on closer inspection turn out to be banal or meaningless. Students might enjoy reading a few examples before they invent their own.

He digs deepest who deepest digs.

Seek not cherry blossom on the plum tree.

Do not wear earmuffs in the land of the rattlesnake.

A bald man does not fear grey hair.

Gloves make a poor present for the man with no hands.

Punctuality (p 83)

Whole class. Students look at the cartoon. Elicit what is happening. Ask students what things in life it is important to be on time for.

Note: in some cultures it is acceptable, even expected, for a bride to be late for her wedding.

Groupwork. Students discuss the questions. In a), when they have discussed how punctual they are, they could put the events in order according to how important they think it is to be on time for them.

Listening (p 83) (Workbook p 51)

1 Whole class. Go through the questions and deal with any difficult vocabulary. Elicit or explain the meaning of *to kill time* (to use up spare time while you are waiting for something to happen) and elicit things students do to kill time, for example, if they arrive early at an airport or station. Students answer the questions individually and then compare their answers in pairs.

2 📼 **36 SB p 154**

Students listen to two people answering the questions and make notes on their answers.

Pairwork. Students discuss Roberta and Paul's answers and say whether they agree with them or not.

1   For a formal meeting in Britain you should arrive on time, for less formal meetings you can arrive a few minutes late. In other countries attitudes might be different.

2   You should tell your friend how long you'll wait.

3   You should arrange appointments to discuss important matters later.

4   Try to do the unpleasant task first.

5   A hard-working person is not necessarily a productive person.

📼 **36**

(PR = Paul Roesch; RW = Roberta Wilson)

PR: *That was Sonny Best with 'Midnight in Vermont'. Now, do you make the best of your time? In the studio today, we've got Roberta Wilson, who's a time management consultant. Good morning, Roberta.*

RW: *Good morning, Paul.*

PR: *Roberta, what exactly do time management consultants do?*

RW: *Well, Paul, it's all about helping people to organise their work in an effective way; maximum efficiency, minimum stress.*

PR: *Hah, sounds like something I need. Er, who are your clients?*

RW: *Um, mainly business people, but I've also worked with politicians, civil servants and university lecturers.*

PR: *Um, quite a range, then. And what sort of things help people to organise their time? I suppose punctuality is important?*

RW: *Um, yes and no. It's easier to finish a meeting on time if it starts on time. But in international contexts, you do have to aware of cultural differences.*

PR: *For example?*

RW: *Well, in Britain big, formal meetings usually start on time, but less formal meetings often begin a few minutes late. In Germany, on the other hand, people expect all meetings to begin on time. In some countries, er, for example, in*

Latin America, there's a more ... relaxed attitude. So, you do have to adapt to circumstances.

PR: When in Rome ...

RW: Er, to some extent, yes.

PR: Um, it sounds like even if you manage your own time very well, you still can't control what other people do.

RW: Well, you can set limits. If you're meeting a friend who always arrives late, you can say 'Well, I'm going to wait for 15 minutes. If they aren't there by then, I'll leave.'

PR: Hmm. I've got one friend who's always late. I don't think I'd ever see her if I did that.

RW: Hah, but people who are always late are the ones you need to set limits with. If they know that you won't wait, then, perhaps they'll make an effort.

PR: Isn't that rather harsh?

RW: No, not really. Someone who constantly turns up late is putting a low value on your time. Let them know you've got other things to do. And I'm not suggesting you do that with everyone – just the persistent latecomers. Though, again, different cultures do have different viewpoints on what constitutes serious lateness.

PR: What about interruptions? I often come into the studio with something important I need to do. Then the phone rings or someone comes to see me ... Before I know it, the day's over and I haven't done what I planned.

RW: Um, you need to defend your time. If you're working on something important and someone drops in to see you, get your diary out. Politely tell them you're busy and make an appointment for another time. If it isn't important anyway, they'll just go away. If it is, they'll make an appointment and you can deal with it properly.

PR: That sounds practical.

RW: Um, again, you do have to be careful. In some cultures, particularly Latin ones, this technique can upset people. But here in the United States, almost no one will be offended.

PR: Hmm. So, does everything depend on culture?

RW: No. Attitudes to time are one of the big differences between cultures. But how you organise your own work is up to you. And there are lots of techniques here. For example, imagine you've got two important things to do. One of them is pleasant and the other isn't. Always try to do the unpleasant task first. That way, the pleasant task is a reward for finishing. If you do it the other way round, you'll tend to slow down the pleasant task because you don't want to do the unpleasant one.

PR: Hah, hah. I'll remember that. Finally, what, for you, is a hard-working person?

RW: Oh, I'm not very interested in hard-working people. You can spend twelve hours a day at the office without doing very much. I'm interested in productive – and happy – people.

PR: And on that note, I have to say we've run out of time. Thank you Roberta and over to Jasmine Dahar with the news ...

3 Whole class. Remind students that Roberta thinks 'Waiting for someone who's late is a waste of time'. Elicit one or two other things students think are a waste of time.

Pairwork. Students make a list of at least three time-wasting activities.

Pronunciation (p 84)

1 Pairwork. Students read the words in the box aloud and decide which phonetic symbols the underlined sounds match. Check answers with the class.

/s/: Saturday   weeks   first   second
/z/: hours   Tuesday   weekends   Wednesday
/θ/: thirty   Thursday   month   third
/ð/: there   weather   that   these

2 🔲 **37 SB p 155**

Students listen to the recording and check their answers. Students could add more words to each category, things they can see in the classroom or through the windows. It could be a competition to add the most in, say, five or ten minutes.

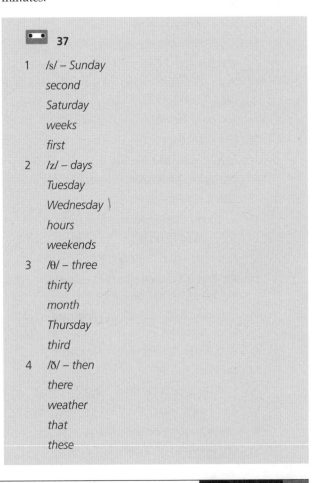

🔲 **37**

1 /s/ – Sunday
second
Saturday
weeks
first

2 /z/ – days
Tuesday
Wednesday
hours
weekends

3 /θ/ – three
thirty
month
Thursday
third

4 /ð/ – then
there
weather
that
these

Dates (p 84) (Workbook p 49)

1 Pairwork. Students work individually to choose five important dates and then take turns dictating them to their partner. Each student checks what their partner has written and explains why the dates are important. The partner should ask questions to elicit further details.

2 ▭▭ **38 SB p155**

Students listen to the recording and make a note of the dates Julie mentions and the reasons why they are important to her.

20th February 1997 – cat's birthday

24th May 1972 – birthday

5th November 1999 – bonfire night

31st July 1991 – left college, got job in Habitat Superstore

15th July next year – going on a world trip

▭▭ **38**

(J = Julie; M = Martin)

M: *OK, so what dates did you get?*

J: *I've got 20th February 1997.*

M: *OK, I'll write that down ... '97.*

J: *Um, 24th May 1972.*

M: *OK.*

J: *Then I've got 5th November, 1999.*

M: *OK.*

J: *Then there's 31st July, 1991.*

M: *... '91. OK, and the last one?*

J: *The last one ... I've got 15th July next year.*

M: *Right. OK, well, let's go for the oldest one. 24th May '72. What's that?*

J: *That's my birthday.*

M: *Hah, hah, hah.*

J: *Hah ... and I'm a Gemini.*

M: *Oh, right. OK. Er, 20th February '97?*

J: *That is my cat's birthday.*

M: *... I don't even know my cat's ...*

J: *She's called 'Sparkle'.*

M: *Hah, hah, hah. 31st July '91?*

J: *Ah. This is the date that I left college and I got my first job in Habitat Superstore.*

M: *Hah, hah. Right, OK. Er, 5th November ... 5th November. '99.*

J: *Well, that's bonfire night, of course.*

M: *Oh, right.*

J: *Yeah. A huge party takes place.*

M: *And finally, what's this 15th July next year?*

J: *Well, I'm going on a world trip.*

M: *Oh, where are you going?*

J: *I'm going to Australia, Sri Lanka, to India, the Far East, then to America ... . All over the place.*

M: *Oh, lucky you. It sounds great.*

Optional activity

Write a date that is important to you on the board. Students have 20 guesses to find out why it is important. This will give practice in nouns such as birthday, wedding anniversary, etc, and also the structure *the day when you passed your driving test*, etc. The student who guesses correctly can then write another important date on the board, or students could continue the game in pairs.

Prepositions (p 84) (Workbook p 52)

1 Elicit when we use *on, in* or *at*. We use *on* with the names of days and dates and in the expression *on time*. We use *in* with months, years, seasons, periods of the day – the morning, the afternoon, etc, periods of history and in expressions like *in time*. We use *at* with times and expressions like *at the weekend, at night, at the moment, at Christmas*.

Note the difference between *on time* and *in time*. We use *on time* to mean not early or late (*The plane left on time*). We use *in time* to mean with sufficient time to do something (*We arrived at the airport in time to have lunch before catching the plane*).

Students complete the sentences with *on, in* or *at*. Check answers with the class. Students could then write some gapped sentences of their own for other students to complete.

---

a) in   b) at   c) on   d) in   e) at   f) in   g) in
h) in   i) in, on   j) in   k) at   l) on   m) on
n) at   o) at

---

2 Pairwork. Students decide if the statements in 1 are true for them, then turn them into questions and ask their partner. They should ask follow-up questions to find out as much information as possible as in the example.

Time expressions (p 85)

1 Whole class. Students look at the planner. Go through the instructions carefully and elicit the meaning of *Boxing Day* (the day after Christmas Day) and *fortnight* (two weeks). Students follow the instructions carefully, crossing out, underlining, circling and bracketing the days specified. Using today's date, ask students questions, for example, *What day/date is the day after tomorrow/a week yesterday?* Students can then ask each other.

Pairwork. Students compare their planners to see how many days remain. They should find that eight days – the 2nd, 3rd, 14th, 15th, 20th, 21st, 28th and 30th – are unmarked. Each pair writes similar instructions for marking these days and exchanges them with another pair. They follow the instructions they have received and see if all the days are then marked.

2 Pairwork. Students use the expressions in 1 to discuss some of the things they've done recently and their plans for the future.

3 Whole class. Read the expressions in the box, which are all used to give rough estimates of time. There is no hard and fast rule about how these are used; it depends on the speaker's perspective and the circumstances. *Just gone two* to a person who is not in a hurry might be almost five past two to someone else who is more anxious about the time. Elicit that *just gone* and *just after* mean much the same thing as do *about, almost, around* and *XX-ish*. *XX-ish* is generally used to refer to whole hours, for example, *ten-ish, eight-ish*. Explain that when we give approximate times, we usually refer backwards or forwards to the nearest five- or ten-minute division of the clock, so 2.01 might be *just gone two* and 2.04 could be *almost five past two*.

Ask a student to tell you what the time is now using one of these expressions (choose a time to ask this when it isn't exactly 3 o'clock, etc). Students look at the clocks and decide how to describe them, using the expressions in the box.

> *Possible answers*
>
> 1 just before ten, almost ten o'clock, tenish
> 2 around twelve o'clock, just gone twelve, just after twelve, almost twelve
> 3 almost quarter past two, about 2.15
> 4 just gone half past three, just after half past three
> 5 just before half past four, around half past four, 4.30
> 6 around a quarter to ten, just before a quarter to ten
> 7 just gone a quarter past ten
> 8 about a quarter to twelve
> 9 almost ten past ten, about ten past ten

4 Pairwork. Students use the expressions in 3 to talk about six things they have done so far today.

Things to do (p 86)

Whole class. Look at the six lists and discuss the three questions. Start the discussion by telling students whether you are a listmaker or not and the kind of things you have on your lists. You could also ask students to speculate on what kind of people made the lists on this page, before they read the article. They should look at the content of the lists and their presentation to determine what sort of people they are: male/female, job, character, organised/disorganised, etc.

1 Whole class. Students read the article and write the names of the people next to the lists. Check answers with the class.

> 1 Jacqueline Maddocks   2 Kate Rollins
> 5 Barbara Vanilli   6 James Oliver

2 Pairwork. Discourage students from looking back at the text as they discuss it using the prompts.

Whole class. Get feedback on the discussions and then allow students to look at the text again.

Collocation (p 87)

1 Whole class. Elicit that a collocation is a combination of words that frequently occur together. Students fill in the gaps using words from the article on list-making. Check answers with the class.

> a) immediate   b) standard   c) high-powered
> d) chief   e) electronic

2 Pairwork. Students ask and answer the completed questions.

Optional activity

Elicit further example sentences using the collocations in 1.

3 Students make further collocations using the new words and the nouns from 1. Check answers with the class.

> distant future   normal practice   low-paid job
> senior executive   personal organiser

Pairwork. Students think of other possible collocations. They may need to use a dictionary to find some of them. Check answers with the class.

> *Possible answers*
>
> not too distant future   good practice   bad practice
> social organiser   well-paid jobs   junior executive
> top executive

Close up (p 88) (Workbook p 49, p 50)

must & should

1 Whole class. Remind students that in the article they read about list-making, James Oliver talked about his 'Time Management Matrix'. Ask what they can remember about this.

Pairwork. Students discuss where they would put the sentence beginnings. Check answers with the class.

> a) I   b) III   c) II   d) IV

2 Students match the sentence beginnings in 2 with the sentence endings. Check answers with the class.

> a) – 3   I must do it today or there'll be trouble tomorrow.
> b) – 2   I should do it today but if I run out of time I can leave it until first thing tomorrow.

c) – 4   I must do it soon, so I'll do it next week.

d) – 2   I should do it soon, so I'll see if I've got
time next week.

3 Students work individually to write a 'things to do' list categorised according to the matrix in 1.

Pairwork. Students discuss their lists and their priorities.

4 Pairwork. Students match the four sets of verbs and phrases to the headings.

A   obligation

B   prohibition

C   no obligation

D   permission

5 Students work individually to write a list of the rules and regulations in their place of work or study. In pairs or small groups, they discuss their lists and find similarities and differences.

Office cultures (p 89) (Workbook p 50)

1 Groupwork. Students look at the photos on page 89 and discuss the questions.

2 ▭ **39 SB p 155**

Students listen to the recording and check their guesses.

▭ **39**

1

We're supposed to start work at nine, but I often come in later because I have to take my children to school first, but then I stay a bit later. Of course, if I've got an early meeting or if I've got to be in court first thing in the morning, my wife has to take the kids to school. We're supposed to work a 40-hour week, but I think most people actually work more than that. We're supposed to dress smartly, particularly if we have contact with clients, so I always wear a suit and tie to work. Female lawyers aren't allowed to wear trousers or even dark tights. They have to wear knee-length skirts – no minis. The secretaries can wear tailored trousers, but no jeans. A weekly dress-down day has been introduced recently – it's an idea from America where everybody comes into work in casual dress on a Friday. Personally, I have no desire to come into work wearing jeans and a T-shirt. I like to make a difference between work and home, and I can wear casual clothes at home. I think people should dress smartly for work – it gives a good impression. Smoking, eating and drinking are strictly forbidden in the office. There's a non-smoking cafeteria downstairs, and smokers have to go outside. Personally, I think smoking ought to be banned in all public places.

2

As you can see, it's a really busy office and we have to work long hours. Everybody works different hours because people are coming in and out all the time. We can have a drink at our desks but we're not allowed to bring food into the offices. There's a canteen downstairs. We're supposed to have a break every two hours, but when you're working to a deadline, you can't afford to take time for a break. Sometimes I work right through my lunch hour – it's mad really. In fact, you have to be mad to work here. Hah. We're not supposed to smoke in the office but some of the reporters and journalists do when they're working late. You know they've been smoking because the place smells horrible in the morning. As far as dress is concerned, it depends. The editors and senior staff dress smartly. I think our senior editor has two suits and about twenty identical striped shirts because I've never seen him wearing anything else. The younger men are a bit more fashion-conscious and they don't have to wear suits. The women can wear trousers or skirts, but we can't wear jeans. Smart-casual clothes are OK.

3

As you can imagine, people who work here are pretty fashion-conscious. They can wear whatever they like, but people usually choose to dress smartly for work. They're the sort of people who enjoy dressing up and they're quite competitive. Most people wear black – it's a bit like wearing a uniform, really! Black polo-neck pullovers, black bootleg trousers, black leather jackets and boots – and that's just the girls. Hah. The men tend to be more imaginative with their colours. They wear nice brightly coloured shirts ... and then colour their hair to match! Personally, I go for a more elegant look – suits and high heels.
Unfortunately, most of the young models who come to the agency are smokers – but they're not allowed to smoke in the building, In fact, they can't smoke anywhere near the building. It gives such a bad impression when you see people smoking in the entrance.
The agency is open from ten o'clock in the morning but the staff arrive any time after eight. They have to work a nine-hour day, but the starting and finishing times are flexible.
Coffee is available whenever you want it, but food isn't allowed in the office. Nobody here eats anyway!

3 ▭ **39 SB p 155**

Whole class. Go through the information. Elicit the meaning of 'working hours are flexible' (= in some offices you can start and finish work at whatever time you like as long as your working day is a fixed number of hours). Students listen to the recording again and take notes of any different information. Point out that nearly all offices are now non-smoking.

Pairwork. Students use their notes to correct the information.

> **Office 1**
>
> Working hours are not flexible.
> True
> You cannot smoke in the cafeteria.
> You are not allowed to have your lunch at your desk.
>
> **Office 2**
>
> You are not allowed to smoke in the office.
> You can have a drink at your desk.
> You are supposed to take a break every two hours.
> You cannot wear jeans.
>
> **Office 3**
>
> True
> You're supposed to start work at ten o'clock.
> True
> Coffee is available whenever you want it.

4 Groupwork. Students discuss whether they would like to work in one of these offices. Encourage them to give reasons and to decide which office would be the best and which the worst for them. Students can choose which two or three rules/regulations are the most important/appealing for them.

To whom it may concern (p 90)

(Workbook p 53)

1 Whole class. Ask students if they understand the title. Explain that it is the way we start a formal letter when we do not know the name or title of the person who will read the letter. Elicit that business letters and personal letters differ in the style and formality of the language used. Read all the choices for beginnings and endings. Students choose the correct ones for use in a business letter. Check answers with the class.

> Dear Sir or Madam,   Yours faithfully
> Dear Mr Maggs,   Yours sincerely/Best wishes

2 Students complete the sentences using words from the box. Check answers with the class.

> a) 16th May
> b) grateful
> c) enclose
> d) Unfortunately
> e) pleased
> f) complain
> g) hearing
> h) confirm
> i) response
> j) apply

3 Students match the phrases from 2 to the list of functions. Check answers with the class.

> asking for information b)
> applying for a job j)
> beginning a letter a), i)
> closing a letter g)
> giving bad news d)
> giving good news e)
> complaining f)
> saying that you are sending something with the letter c)
> asking for confirmation h)

4 Pairwork. Students read and discuss the letter and the job advertisement. They decide whether the writer would be considered a suitable candidate or not. Check answers with the class.

> The letter contains several errors, and is too informal. Whether or not this would disqualify the writer as a candidate for the job is a matter of personal opinion.

5 Whole class. Elicit some of the mistakes made in the letter and ways in which it could be improved.

Pairwork. Students rewrite and improve the letter using some of the phrases in 1 and 2.

6 Students turn to page 141, look at the corrected letter and compare it with theirs.

Students write their own application letter for the job, using Tony's letter as a model.

Test

> **1** 1 in 2 on 3 on 4 in 5 at 6 in
> 7 at, in 8 on/in 9 at 10 at 11 on 12 in
> 13 on
>
> **2** Students' own answers
>
> **3** /s/ police, choice, see, answer
> /z/ music, Thursday, choose, zero,
> /θ/ breath, think, month, three
> /ð/ there, mother, that, breathe
>
> **4** 1 have to 2 must/have to
> 3 don't have to 4 mustn't 5 had to
> 6 must 7 correct 8 not correct – must/should
> 9 correct 10 not correct – mustn't
> 11 not correct – shouldn't
> 12 not correct – must 13 correct
> 14 not correct – must

10 Time Test

Name: **Total:** _____ /40

---

1 Prepositions *14 points*

Complete the sentences by adding an appropriate preposition.

1 She was born _____ 1988.

2 Her birthday is _____ 15th May.

3 I last saw them _____ New Year's Day.

4 I never work _____ the evening.

5 I saw them _____ the weekend.

6 We're hoping to go away for a few weeks _____ the summer.

7 It gets dark _____ around 3 o'clock _____ winter.

8 The bus is just about to leave. I hope he gets here _____ time.

9 What are you doing _____ the moment?

10 I seem to work best _____ night.

11 You've arrived late twice this week. I expect you _____ time tomorrow.

12 We're going there _____ October.

13 I'm going to see them _____ Wednesday afternoon.

2 Write today's date here: _____ *8 points*

What is/was the date ...

1 the day after tomorrow? _____

2 a week tomorrow? _____

3 the day before yesterday? _____

4 a fortnight today? _____

5 in four days' time? _____

6 the Friday after next? _____

7 a week yesterday? _____

8 three weeks today? _____

3 Pronunciation – /s/, /z/, /θ/ and /ð/ *4 points*

Put the following words into four groups according to the underlined sounds.

police	breath	music	there	Thursday	choice
mother	that	choose	zero	think	see
answer	month	three	breathe		

/s/	/z/	/θ/	/ð/
_____	_____	_____	_____
_____	_____	_____	_____
_____	_____	_____	_____
_____	_____	_____	_____

4 Modal verbs – obligation, prohibition and permission *14 points*

Complete the following with *must, mustn't, have to* or *don't have to*. Sometimes there is more than one possibility.

1 I can't make it to your party I'm afraid. I _____ go out to dinner with some clients.

2 I _____ go now or I'll miss my bus.

3 In some countries you _____ wear a helmet on a motorbike, whereas in others it's obligatory.

4 The water here is very polluted. You _____ drink it.

5 Sorry I'm late. I _____ pick up the children from school.

6 I haven't seen Paola for ages. I _____ get in touch with her soon.

Decide whether the following sentences are correct or not. If not, use a more appropriate modal verb.

7 You really should go to the Louvre when you're in Paris.

8 I really have to tidy up, but I'm too tired.

9 You can leave if you've finished.

10 You don't have to do that. It's against the law here.

11 He mustn't be driving so fast on this road.

12 You can have a passport if you want to travel to the USA.

13 She shouldn't stay up so late. She'll be tired in the morning.

14 You can arrive before 6.30. Otherwise you'll not be allowed into the theatre.

11 *Journey* Overview

The topics in this unit are travel and holidays. The main grammatical focus is on modals for speculating and deducing; *would* for unreal situations and on the past perfect.

Students read an excerpt from the travel book, *The Beach* and talk about their own travelling experiences.

Students listen to a traveller describing to a friend two places he'd visited on a world trip and practise speculating and deducing by identifying the photos he mentions in the recording. They go on to practise writing postcards and to describe their dream weekend.

Students then read about a motorbike trip across the States and describe a journey they have been on.

Finally they practise writing a story in the past perfect and learn how to make their story more vivid and detailed by using adverbs.

Section	Aims	What the students are doing
Introduction page 92	*Reading skills*: skimming	Skimming an excerpt from a novel, *The Beach*, for gist.
	Conversation skills: fluency work	Talking about reasons for travelling to generate interest in the topic.
	Lexis: countries & expressions of location	Reviewing vocabulary of countries and expressions to describe locations of places.
Conrad's round-the-world trip page 93	*Listening skills*: listening for detail	Looking at photos of holiday destinations to generate interest in the recording. Listening to a traveller describing his travel photos to a friend and guessing which of the two photos he is talking about.
Close up page 94	*Grammar*: speculating & deducing	Identifying words and expressions to do with speculating and deducing from the recording in Conrad's round-the-world trip. Finding the correct endings of grammatically correct sentences that make no sense so that they make sense.
Wish you were here page 95	*Lexis*: collocations	Completing sentences in postcards by choosing the correct collocation.
	Writing skills: describing places	Writing postcards from two of the other places Conrad visited on his round-the-world trip.
	Listening skills: listening for detail	Listening to people describing a dream weekend as a model for the following activity. Identifying questions they answered.
	Conversation skills: fluency work	Anecdote: talking about a dream weekend.
Close up page 96	*Grammar*: *would* for unreal situations	Identifying real and unreal conditionals. Practising unreal conditionals by describing an imaginary place.
Coast to coast page 97	*Reading skills*: skimming; scanning; predicting	Skimming text for gist. Scanning text for specific information. Predicting the conclusion of the story.
	Conversation skills: fluency work	Anecdote: talking about a journey.
Close up page 98	*Grammar*: past perfect	Identifying the difference between past simple and past perfect structures. Practising the past perfect by completing sentences.
Tell us a story page 99	*Reading & writing skills*: using the past perfect in narratives; making narratives more interesting	Understanding the significance of words and phrases within a text. Adding adverbs of attitude, manner and time to improve the text. Writing a story using a story skeleton and including past perfect structures, and adverbs of attitude, manner and time to make the narrative more interesting.

1 Students skim read the text to find the answer to the question. Point out that the difficult vocabulary in the text is glossed in the margin. Check answers with the class.

> To escape from an uncomfortable situation with his ex-girlfriend.

2 Pairwork. Students discuss the reasons for travelling and say whether they have ever travelled for any of them or whether they might in the future. They then think of other reasons for travelling.

3 **(Workbook p 54)**
Whole class. Choose a place beginning with A, for example, Australia and ask if anyone has been there. If not, try Austria, Amsterdam, Algiers, etc. When a student says they have been there, write the place name on the board and the student's name next to it. That student then thinks of a place beginning with B and asks if anyone has been there, continuing with more B place names until the answer is yes. The student then writes the name on the board. The next student asks about a C place name and so on through the alphabet. For difficult letters, you may need to prompt or ask students to volunteer the names of places they have been to using those letters. You may have students who have been to Xian, Xuzhou, Zanzibar, Zambia, Zagreb or Zaire. If not, pass over these letters once one or two questions have been asked. Leave the list on the board as students will need it in the next activity. To save time, get students to shout out places for each letter as you go through the alphabet.

4 Students use the expressions to pinpoint five of the places in the class list and the place where they live.

Conrad's round-the-world trip (p 93)

1 Students look at Conrad's holiday photos and say where they think they were taken and if any of them could have been taken in their own country or countries. Can they identify any of them precisely? Don't confirm answers at this stage.

2 ▭ **40 SB p 155**
Students listen to Conrad and his friend. They decide which two photos they are talking about. Play the recording. Check answers with the class.

> They are talking about photos 5 and 1.

▭ **40**
(F = Friend; C = Conrad)

F: *It must be very strange to be back home after such a long time.*

C: *Yes it is. I ... I mean, it's lovely to see everybody and I really appreciate my bed.*

F: *Let's have a look at these photos then.*

C: *Well, they're all mixed up at the moment. I've got to sort them out.*

F: *Um, this looks nice. Where is it?*

C: *Where do you think it is?*

F: *Ah, well ... it must be somewhere really hot. It looks like paradise. I suppose it could be Thailand or Bali, or it could even be India.*

C: *No. I'll give you a clue. It's an island in the Pacific Ocean.*

F: *Hawaii.*

C: *No, I didn't go to Hawaii.*

F: *Oh, right ... I thought you'd been everywhere! It's probably Fiji then.*

C: *That's right. Oh, it was lovely. This man wanted me to marry his daughter. She was beautiful.*

F: *Oh, a Fijian wedding ... that would've been fun.*

C: *Yeah, that's what I thought. But I don't think my mum would've been very pleased. Hah. Anyway, what about this one?*

F: *Ah, this is a bit different. Well, must be Switzerland or somewhere in the French Alps?*

C: *Nope.*

F: *Who's the girl by the way?*

C: *Oh, yes ... that's, er, what's-her-name. She's Argentinian.*

F: *Oh, was she travelling around Europe then?*

C: *No. In this picture, she wasn't far from home.*

F: *Well, it can't be Argentina, can it? Maybe it's Chile?*

C: *No, it is the southern part of Argentina ... Patagonia.*

F: *Oh ...*

C: *They call it the Switzerland of the southern hemisphere.*

F: *Really? That's amazing. It really does look like Switzerland. So anyway, did you meet a girl in every country you visited?*

3 Pairwork. Students look at the map showing the route of Conrad's journey and discuss where they think the remaining photos were taken.

> Photo 2: Spain (Basque area)
>
> Photo 3: Italy (Lake Como)
>
> Photo 4: India (New Delhi)
>
> Photo 6: Jordan (Petra)

Close up (p 94)

Speculating & deducing (Workbook p 54)

1 🔘 **40 SB p 155**

Students listen to the recording again and complete the sentences. Allow them to compare their answers in pairs before checking with the class.

> First picture: It must be somewhere really hot.
>
> I suppose it could be Thailand or Bali.
>
> It's probably Fiji then.
>
> Second picture: It must be Switzerland or somewhere in the French Alps.
>
> It can't be Argentina.
>
> Maybe it's Chile.

2 Students put the expressions into the three categories. Check answers with the class.

> a) It must be ...   It can't be ...
>
> b) It's probably ...
>
> c) I suppose it could be ...   Maybe it's ...

3 Students add the expressions to the categories. Check answers with the class.

> All three expressions go in category c).

4 Pairwork. Students discuss the questions. If they are obviously having difficulty with this, go through the Language reference section below with them and then ask them to complete the activities.

> a) It must be ...
>
> ... it could be ...
>
> It can't be ...
>
> It might be ...
>
> It may be ...
>
> b) It can't be Carmen; ...
>
> It must be John; ...

5 Pairwork. Students rearrange the sentences. Check answers with the class.

> a) They can't be short of money. They go skiing every year.
>
> b) You've been driving all day. You must be absolutely exhausted.
>
> c) That hotel must be doing well. It's always got the 'No Vacancies' sign up.
>
> d) I must be getting old. I can't remember anything about last night.
>
> e) A new car? On my salary?! You must be joking.
>
> f) The new restaurant can't be very good. It's never got anybody in it.
>
> g) You must be Sarah's husband. I've heard such a lot about you.
>
> h) Great news about your engagement. You must be delighted.

Optional activity

Pairwork. Students look at the corrected pairs of sentences in the previous activity again. They replace one sentence in each pair with a new sentence of their own. They can then jumble them up again and give them to a new pair to solve.

Wish you were here (p 95) (Workbook p 57)

Optional activity

Ask all students to stand up. Choose one student but do not reveal who it is. Then give the class a piece of information about the student, for example, *The person has got brown hair.* Students who think/know it can't be them sit down with a chorus of *It can't be me*, and those who think it could be them remain standing with a chorus of *It could/might be me.* Continue until only one student is left standing. The final chorus will be *It must be X.*

1 Students look at the postcards and complete them with words from the box. Encourage them to read all the postcards through first, ignoring the gaps, so they get a general idea of the content. They could then guess what goes in the gaps before looking at the words in the box. Check answers with the class.

> 1 fascinating   2 jams   3 spicy   4 touristy
> 5 friendly   6 gorgeous   7 overlooking
> 8 breathtaking   9 peaks   10 paradise
> 11 Sandy   12 clear   13 palm   14 breaking

2 Students guess which places he sent the postcards from. Encourage them to use the language for speculating and deducing which they have just learnt. Check answers with the class.

Postcard 1: India
Postcard 2: Italy
Postcard 3: Fiji

3 Students use Conrad's postcards as a model to write two more from places that Conrad visited.

Anecdote (p 95)

See Introduction, page 4, for more ideas on how to set up, monitor and repeat 'anecdotes'.

4 Open books. Whole class. Focus attention on the cartoon and tell the class whether this would be your idea of a dream weekend. Give them some more details of what your perfect weekend would consist of (use the list for ideas). Encourage students to ask you questions about your weekend.

▭▭ 41 SB p 155

Students listen and note down their guesses at each pause. Allow them to compare notes with a partner before checking answers with the class.

Speaker 1 wants to go to Kyoto in Japan.
Speaker 2 wants to go to Paris in France.
Speaker 3 wants to go to a Greek island.

▭▭ 41
Liz
(I = Interviewer; L = Liz)

I: So, who would your ideal companion be?

L: My friend, Anna, who's doing a course in Oriental studies.

I: Ahah, and how would you get around?

L: We'd probably use one of those very fast bullet trains to get there, and then go by taxi or on foot.

I: And what would you wear?

L: It depends on the time of year. I'd want to go there in spring for the cherry blossom, so probably just jeans and a sweatshirt. I'd make sure I had a clean pair of socks and some slip-on shoes because I think you have to take them off when you visit the temples.

…

I: What would you buy?

L: Nothing touristy. I might buy an electronic gadget like a calculator. They are supposed to be cheaper there.

I: Er, and what would you eat and drink?

L: I'd look for western food and probably end up eating at McDonald's. I can't stand raw fish, and I don't like rice much either.

I: Hm. What essential items would you take with you?

L: My camera would be essential – the temples, the … the shrines and the gardens. They're all supposed to be stunning.

…

I: Who would you most like to meet there?

L: I'd like to meet a geisha who speaks English and ask her lots of questions.

I: What sights would you want to see?

L: I'd visit the Golden Temple and the 'Ryoan-ji' temple I think it is, where they've got that amazing Zen rock garden.

…

I: Er, who would you send a postcard to?

L: My ex-boyfriend to show him what a good time I'm having without him.

I: Hah. What would spoil your perfect weekend?

L: Bumping into somebody from work. Although I don't think it's likely on the other side of the world in Kyoto!

Cristina
(I = Interviewer; C = Cristina)

I: Who would your ideal companion be?

C: My mum and her cheque book.

I: And how would you get around?

C: On foot or on the underground.

I: What would you wear?

C: I'd wear all the new clothes my mum's going to buy for me there.

I: And what would you buy?

C: Apart from clothes, maybe a painting from one of the artists who sell their stuff along the river.

…

I: What would you eat and drink?

C: I'd sit and drink lots of lovely coffee and watch the world go by.

I: Um, and what essential items would you take with you?

C: Sunglasses. Not for the sun, but because they look cool.

I: Who would you most like to meet there?

C: Jean Paul Gaultier – I love him.

I: What sights would you want to see?

C: Well, I've been to all the obvious places, so I'd just like to hang out in the Latin Quarter.

…

I: Who would you send a postcard to?

C: My dad.

I: What would spoil your perfect weekend?

C: If the shops were shut. Paris is a beautiful city, but for me the main attraction is the shopping.

Rick

(I = Interviewer; R = Rick)

I: *Who would your ideal companion be?*

R: *Er, definitely not my wife. She can't stand the sun. Um, probably my brother because I don't see him very often.*

I: *Um, how would you get around?*

R: *On foot. I'll only be going from the hotel to the beach.*

I: *What would you wear?*

R: *As little as possible.*

I: *And what would you buy?*

R: *I'd probably buy some souvenirs for my wife and children at the airport.*

I: *What would you eat and drink?*

R: *Um, what's that special dish? ... um, moussaka?*
...

I: *Right. Who would you most like to meet there?*

R: *Oh, nobody at all. I like peace and quiet.*

I: *And what essential items would you take with you?*

R: *Um, a couple of good books and plenty of suntan lotion.*

I: *Er, what sights would you want to visit?*

R: *The beach in the daytime and a taverna at night.*
...

I: *Er, who would you send a postcard to?*

R: *Nobody. Writing a postcard would be too much like hard work.*

I: *Hm. And what would spoil your perfect weekend?*

R: *Rain. Oh, also, if the island was full of other English people. Greece is a popular destination for English people.*

5 Students look at the picture and the list in 4, and think about their own dream weekends. They should prepare to tell a partner about it. Go round and help with language as necessary.

6 Pairwork. Students tell their partners about their weekends and decide if they would be good travelling companions.

Close up (p 96) (Workbook p 55)

would for unreal situations

1 Students look at the four questions and underline the auxiliary verbs. Check answers with the class.

> a) did   b) are   c) will   d) would

2 Students match the endings with the questions in 1. Check answers with the class.

> a) yesterday
> b) at the moment
> c) when you finish university
> d) if you won the lottery

3 Pairwork. Students look at the completed questions and decide which ones refer to real situations. Check answers with the class and refer them to the Language reference section down the page for more information about *would*.

> a, b and c

4 Students practise using *would* in imaginary situations.

Pairwork. Students choose a place from the list and discuss the questions.

Encourage pairs to talk about their imaginary visit to the class.

Coast to coast (p 97)

1 Students read the text quickly to find out what problems Nick Campbell had. Check answers with the class.

> His motorbike broke down three times.

2 Groupwork. Students read the text again and discuss the questions. The first three questions only require students to scan the text for the answers. The fourth question requires more thought and discussion. Encourage them to think of several reasons why the mechanic said what he did.

> a) $600
> b) $3,000
> c) $2,400
> d) Possible answers
>
> Maybe the motorbike was a rare model and worth a lot more than $3,000.
>
> Perhaps he thought the motorbike had been featured in a famous film and so was worth a lot of money.
>
> Perhaps there was something on the bike like the badge that was worth more than the bike itself.
>
> Maybe he saw that the problem with the bike was very minor and could easily be fixed, making it much more valuable.

3 Groupwork. Students look at page 142 to find the real reason and discuss the questions.

Note: students should be familiar with Elvis, but may not know that James Dean was a famous film star who died young.

Anecdote (p 97) (Workbook p 56, p 58)

See Introduction, page 4, for more ideas on how to set up, monitor and repeat 'anecdotes'.

4 Pairwork. Students first think about the questions individually, perhaps making notes on them.

5 Students tell the story of their journey to a partner and listen to their partner's story.

Close up (p 98) (Workbook p 55)

Past perfect

1/2 Students look at the illustration which shows Nick's route across the USA. Ask where he is at the beginning of the story and what happened in each of the cities. Encourage them to answer without looking back at the story if possible.

> At the beginning of the story he is just outside Atlanta.
>
> Miami: He bought the motorbike.
>
> Atlanta: He broke down 5 km outside the city and pushed the motorbike into town to get it fixed. The mechanic offered to buy it.
>
> Kansas: The motorbike broke down for the second time. He thought about selling the motorbike, but decided to carry on.
>
> Denver: The motorbike broke down for the third time and he sold it to the mechanic.

3 Pairwork. Students look back at the text to find the tenses used to describe each event.

> a) Events before the beginning of the story are described using the past perfect. Events after that are described in the past simple:
>
> Past perfect examples:
>
> … he'd bought from a back-street garage …
>
> For years he had dreamt …
>
> … he'd finally decided …
>
> He'd given up his job, sold his car and set off …
>
> Past simple examples:
>
> Nick Campbell sat …
>
> He pushed the bike …
>
> The young mechanic told him …
>
> The man asked if the bike was for sale.

Whole class. Elicit how the past perfect is formed and establish that it is the same for all persons.

> b) *had* + past participle

Pairwork. Students discuss which is the best explanation.

> c) To look back at a past event from another, more recent, point in the past.

4 Students finish the sentences. Ask several students to read their answers to the class.

5 Students work with a partner to write another set of sentences, using the past perfect in each sentence. Go round and check that the tense is is being used properly. Ask a few pairs to read their sentences to the class.

Tell us a story (p 99)

1 Students read the story about the mid-air drama and try to explain the significance of the words and phrases.

> a) microwave – because the pilot couldn't get the machine to work, both pilots were out of the cockpit at the same time.
>
> b) anti-terrorist lock – a lock that cannot be opened without a special key, so the pilots could not get back into the cockpit.
>
> c) Swiss army knife – a knife with many different blades which is supposed to be able to do anything so should be able to open the door. If they managed to open the door with it, it means that the anti-terrorist lock didn't work very well.
>
> d) Indian Ocean – as the Indian Ocean is to the east of Nairobi and they were flying east, it means that they had flown over Nairobi and were heading away from it.

2 Students work in teams. They should look at each sentence in the story in turn and try to add in as many of the adverbs as possible. This gives the story more atmosphere and dramatic effect.

3 Pairwork. Students discuss the three questions.

4 Groupwork. Divide the class into small groups. Each group chooses one of the skeleton stories on the right, or tell them they can invent their own story if they want to. The groups look at each line of the skeleton in turn and begin to add in details to fill out the skeleton. You will need to give them some time to do this.

When they have finished their stories, tell students to add in the adverbs as indicated in the Student's Book. Groups should then reread their stories until they are happy with them.

5 Groups hand their stories to another group to read until each group has read all the stories. Each group decides which is the best story (they cannot vote for their own). The whole class then comes together to decide on the best story.

Test

1
1. must
2. can't
3. can't
4. might/may
5. can't
6. must
7. can't
8. might/could/may
9. can't
10. must
11. might not/may not
12. can't

2
1. was
2. was
3. came
4. had travelled
5. had never been
6. had saved
7. sat
8. had made
9. started
10. had just finished
11. had decided
12. got on
13. ended up

3 (1/2 point each)
1. I wonder what it would feel like ...
2. ... I'd take up skiing.
3. I wouldn't do that ...
4. What would you do ...
5. If I won the lottery ...
6. Would you do the same as me?

4 (2 points each)
1. touristy
2. overlooking
3. sandy
4. friendly
5. breathtaking
6. paradise

11 Journey Test

Name: **Total:** _____ /40

1 Modal verbs – deduction *12 points*

Complete the sentences by adding *must, can't, might (not), could (not)* or *may (not)*.

1   You haven't stopped working for hours. You _____ be exhausted.

2   She looks much older than him. They _____ be twins.

3   She doesn't know where the bathroom is. She _____ live here.

4   They look like tourists themselves, but they _____ be able to show us the way.

5   He _____ still be hungry – he's just eaten a huge lunch.

6   He drives a Ferrari. He _____ be rich.

7   He can't speak Spanish. He _____ be from Mexico.

8   Well, it _____ be her, but I'm not sure.

9   This _____ be the right road. It doesn't look familiar at all.

10 Well, he _____ like his job. He's worked here for over 20 years.

11 I think she's seen the film before so she _____ want to see it again.

12 It _____ be him. He wasn't here at the time.

2 Past simple or past perfect *13 points*

Put the verbs into the past simple or the past perfect.

The first time (1) _____ (be) just after university. You know, the usual backpacker sort of thing. I (2) _____ (be) away for just over a year, although I (3) _____ (come) back home for a couple of weeks to go to a friend's wedding. I (4) _____ (travel) a little before then, but only for a few weeks at a time and I (5) _____ (never/be) outside Europe. Anyway, finally, when I (6) _____ (save) up enough money I set off. I remember, as I (7) _____ (sit) on the plane before take-off, wondering if I (8) _____ (make) the right decision – you know, maybe I should've got a job and started a career and so on. Anyway, thirty minutes into the flight I

(9) _____ (start) talking to this guy sitting next to me. He too (10) _____ (just/finish) university and (11) _____ (decide) to see a bit of the world before settling down. Anyway, to cut a long story short, we (12) _____ (get on) really well and we (13) _____ (end up) travelling together – for the whole year. In fact, we're just on our way to the airport to pick up our son, Kim. He's just coming back from a year in South America.

3 *would* *3 points*

Correct the sentences.

1   I wonder what it would feels like to stand on the top of Everest.

2   If I were younger, I'd to take up skiing.

3   I don't would do that! It's dangerous.

4   What do you would do in my situation?

5   If I would win the lottery, I'd travel round the world.

6   Would you to do the same as me?

4 Vocabulary – describing places *12 points*

Rearrange the mixed-up words.

> Dear Milena,
>
> Here we are in Karvala, a small coastal town in the south-west. Unfortunately, it's a bit more (1) yostruti _____ than we'd imagined, but we have managed to get away from the crowds a bit. We're staying in a tiny hut on the cliff top (2) vongeloriko _____ a beautiful, (3) dnsay _____ beach. The locals are (4) rlfinedy _____ and the views are simply (5) treihktagban _____ I'm in (6) sepadari!
>
> Love, Astrid xxx

Basics *Overview*

The topics in this unit are restaurants, food and sleep. The main grammatical focus is on countable and uncountable nouns and quantifiers.

The unit begins with students talking about eating habits. They then listen to a conversation in a restaurant between a couple on their first date. Students look at appropriacy of language within the context of restaurants, and then talk about enjoyable or unenjoyable meals they've had in a restaurant.

Students study vocabulary related to food and use it to help them design a meal. They then listen to a radio interview in which a man talks about unusual food he has eaten.

Finally students read a report on sleep and then practise writing reports.

Section	Aims	What the students are doing
Introduction page 100	*Conversation skills*: fluency work	Talking about eating habits to generate interest in the topic.
First date page 100	*Listening skills*: predicting; listening for detail	Making predictions about what can go wrong on a first date. Listening to a conversation between a couple on their first date and describing how the two speakers feel. Listening to the next part of the conversation to find out what went wrong on the date. Listening to the whole conversation again to complete the script with an appropriate quantifier.
Close up page 101	*Grammar*: quantity; countable & uncountable nouns	Categorising quantifiers. Distinguishing between countable and uncountable nouns. Classifying words into countable and uncountable nouns.
Eating out pages 102–103	*Lexis*: restaurants; appropriacy	Reviewing language to do with restaurants. Rewriting a dialogue using appropriate register.
	Conversation skills: fluency work	Anecdote: talking about a meal in a restaurant.
What's for dinner? page 104	*Lexis*: food	Reviewing vocabulary to do with food.
	Conversation skills: fluency work	Designing a meal for a special occasion.
Incredible edibles page 105	*Lexis*: taste & texture	Describing tastes and textures of food.
	Listening skills: predicting; for detail	Making predictions about the taste and texture of the food mentioned in a recording from an illustration. Listening to check predictions.
Bedtime pages 106–107	*Reading skills*: scanning	Completing a questionnaire and comparing answers. Scanning a survey report for facts and figures.
	Writing skills: paragraphing	Writing a report on sleeping habits.

12 *Basics* *Teacher's notes*

1 Open books. Whole class. Read through the statements and check difficult vocabulary (to skip a meal is to miss it). Students decide who they will work with and then work individually to decide whether the statements are true for their partner.

2 Pairwork. Students ask and answer questions to find out if they guessed correctly.

Get feedback from the class and encourage students to report any surprising or interesting things they learnt about their partners.

First date (p 100)

1 Closed books. Whole class. Brainstorm the kind of things that can go wrong on a first date. If students are a bit slow in suggesting ideas, put forward a few of your own, for example, you or your date could be late, you might hate each other on sight, you might find your old boyfriend/girlfriend sitting at the next table in a restaurant, etc. Write students' ideas on the board.

2 ⊙ **42 SB p 156**
Open books. Students look at the picture. Elicit what it shows (two people on a first date in a restaurant) and how the people feel (awkward, nervous, apprehensive). Students listen to the recording and decide how the people feel.

> *Possible answers*
> Embarrassed (because there aren't many vegetarian dishes and they like different kinds of water)
> Awkward (because they don't know each other very well)

> ⊙ **42**
> (M = Matthew; D = Dawn; W = Waiter)
> M: *Well, here we are at last. Hah. Do you like it?*
> D: *Yes, it's very nice. The music's not too loud. I hate it when they have loud music in restaurants.*
> M: *Me too.*
> D: *Hah.*
> W: *Good evening. Er, are you ready to order?*
> M: *Oh, no. We haven't looked at the menu yet. Could we have something to drink first?*
> W: *Certainly. Er, what would you like?*

> M: *Um, would you like some wine?*
> D: *Oh, yes, that would be nice. Um, red, please.*
> M: *Two glasses of red wine, please, and er, could we have a few olives with that?*
> W: *Of course. I'll be back to take your order in a moment.*
> M: *Right, right, we'd better look at the menu. What sort of thing do you like?*
> D: *Er, well, um, I don't eat meat or fish, so anything without meat or fish, I suppose. Hah …*
> M: *Oh dear … I didn't know you were vegetarian. I don't think there are any vegetarian dishes on the menu.*
> D: *Oh. Oh, yes, there are. Look, there are loads of things. Um, well, they do omelettes anyway. I'll have a cheese omelette and salad.*
> M: *Are you sure?*
> D: *Yes, that's fine. I love omelettes.*
> M: *OK. Um, do you mind if I have meat?*
> D: *No, o … of course not. That's up to you.*
> W: *Are you ready to order now?*
> M: *Yes, um, we'll have a cheese omelette and salad and, er, steak and chips, please.*
> W: *How would you like your steak done, sir?*
> M: *Medium rare, please. And could we have some French bread and a bottle of mineral water, please?*
> W: *Still or sparkling?*
> D/M: *Still./Sparkling.*
> D: *Oh, that's all right, I don't mind.*
> M: *No, no, it's OK, er, let's have still. Still, please.*
> W: *Anything else?*
> M: *No, that's all for now, thank you.*

3 ⊙ **43 SB p 156**
Students listen to the next part of the conversation and say what went wrong. You might like to point out the waiter's use of the colloquial *Who's the omelette?* meaning *Who is having the omelette?* rather than *Who is the omelette?*

> The man knocked a glass of wine over the woman's skirt.

43

(M = Matthew; D = Dawn; W = Waiter)

M: *So, how long have you been living in London?*

D: *Er, a couple of years. How about you?*

M: *Only a few months. I moved down here for the job.*

D: *Ah.*

M: *There's no work where I come from.*

W: *Your bread, sir, madam. Er, water. Er, can I get you anything else?*

M: *No, I'm fine, thank you. How about you?*

D: *I'm fine too, thanks.*

M: *And, er, where do you come from originally?*

D: *Oh, er, from a little village just outside Oxford. Um, there was nothing to do there so I moved to London.*

M: *And do you like living ... Oh no – I'm terribly sorry. Oh, dear, did it go on your skirt?*

D: *Er, just a little. It's OK.*

M: *Waiter, waiter! Er, can you bring a cloth ... Er, I've spilt some wine.*

D: *It's OK, honestly. Hardly any of it went on my skirt. Just a drop.*

M: *I'm really sorry. I'll pay for the dry cleaning.*

W: *A cloth, sir.*

M: *Thank you. Here, there, let me wipe it up.*

D: *No, it's fine really. Don't touch me!*

W: *Who is the omelette?*

---

4   42 & 43 SB p 156

Students listen to the conversation again and complete the blanks. Check answers with the class.

a) some   b) a few   c) any   d) loads   e) some
f) a little   g) some   h) any

Close up (p 101) (Workbook p 59, p 60)

Quantity

1 Pairwork. Students go back over their answers to 4 and classify the quantifiers used. You might like to put a list of these quantifiers on the board first (*some, a few, any, loads of, a little*). Check answers with the class.

countable: a few *olives*
uncountable: a little
both: some, any, loads
wine ← veg dishes
people
water

---

2 Pairwork. Students add the quantifiers in the box to the categories. Check answers with the class.

countable:	several, very few, not many, a couple of
uncountable:	not much, very little
both:	a lot of, lots of

3 Pairwork. Students work together to choose and cross out the incorrect word in each sentence. Check answers with the class. Refer students to the section on quantifiers in the Language reference section on page 102 if they are still having trouble.

a) some   b) a few   c) A little   d) little
e) a little   f) any   g) some   h) anything

Countable & uncountable nouns (p 101)

1 Whole class. Students look at the two groups of nouns and decide which are countable and which are uncountable.

Countable:	car, mobile phone, computer, job, fridge, passport, washing machine,
Uncountable:	meat, love, travel, pasta, music, money, humour, rice, nicotine, oxygen

2 Groupwork. Students discuss how important the things are in their lives and then work individually to add one word to each sentence.

3 Pairwork. Students complete the grammar rules by writing C or U in the gaps. They then give two or three examples of each. Check answers with the class.

a)   C Possible examples: apples, oranges, bananas

b)   C Possible examples: book – books, tooth – teeth, potato – potatoes

c)   U Possible examples: milk, beef, salt

4 Pairwork. Students discuss the words and decide if they are countable, uncountable or both. Check answers with the class. Encourage students to make sentences showing how some words can be countable or uncountable, depending on the meaning, for example, *Glass is a useful material. There were two glasses of water on the table.*

C: sandwich, pea, oyster
U: bread, food, salt
C/U: Coca-Cola, glass, lamb

5 Students complete the sentences using the nouns they put in the C/U category in 4. Check answers with the class.

> a) The glasses are in the cupboard over the sink.
>
> b) Coca-Cola is sold all over the world.
>
> c) In spring there are lambs in all the fields around here.
>
> d) Would you like another slice of lamb?
>
> e) I'm thirsty – I think I'll have a Coca-Cola.
>
> f) Glass is one of the hardest materials there is.

6 Students decide if the nouns are countable or uncountable. Check answers with the class. Refer students to the grammar rules in 3 if they are still unsure. Encourage them to call out sentences using each word. Establish that *jeans* and *scissors* are uncountable plural forms and take a plural verb. *News* is an uncountable plural noun which takes a singular verb.

> C: people
>
> U: news, jeans, scissors

7 Students choose the correct words in the sentences. Check answers with the class.

> a) are   b) was   c) Those; look   d) they're

Eating out (p 102)

Point out the joke in the margin box. Ask if anyone can explain it. (The waiter's question means *Who is having the fish?* not *Who is the fish?*, but the customer really is a fish.) They should remember the colloquial question *Who's the omelette?* from the earlier listening exercise.

1 Pairwork. Students discuss and match the questions with the responses.

Check answers with the class. Elicit or explain that 'house red' means a bottle of the cheapest red wine available in a particular restaurant, not usually listed by name, and that 'under "Clinton" ' means that the reservation was made in the name of Clinton.

> a) Over here.
>
> b) A bottle of house red, please.
>
> c) Yes, under 'Clinton'.
>
> d) Yes, thanks.
>
> e) No, that's everything.
>
> f) 'Non', please.
>
> g) Just some olive oil, please.

2 Pairwork. Students discuss the choices and decide which they would say.

Check answers with the class.

Note: some of these expressions are colloquial and your students may not know them. Encourage them to work out the most likely answers and make it clear that they will not be penalised in any way for getting them wrong!

> a) What can I get you?
>
> b) Nothing to start with, thanks.
>
> c) Just a drop, thanks.
>
> d) I'm all right, thanks.
>
> e) Don't wait for me.

3 Choose two confident students who are likely to realise quickly what is wrong with the conversation and read it aloud to the class with you taking the part of the waiter and the students the customers. Use a rather abrupt tone to emphasise the point that this is not the polite style of speech one would expect in the circumstances. Elicit what students notice about the conversation.

> The conversation is grammatically correct but both the waiter and the customers would be considered impolite, if not rude, in most English-speaking cultures.

4 Whole class. Before students rewrite the conversation, elicit from the class some ways in which it could be improved. Point out that waiters usually refer to customers as 'sir' and 'madam' and are more likely to say 'Would you mind sitting over there by the window?' than the abrupt imperative 'Go and sit'. Customers in restaurants usually say 'please' when they want something and 'I would like' or 'I'll have' rather than 'I want'. Go through the instructions for the four parts of the task with students before putting them in groups of three.

Groupwork. Students discuss ways of improving the conversation by rewriting it with more appropriate language. They then write their own section where something goes wrong. Go round offering help and encouragement where necessary. Groups practise their conversations before performing them for the class.

> *Possible answer*
>
> Waiter: Do you have a reservation, sir?
>
> Man: Yes, we've booked a table for two. The name is Jones.
>
> Waiter: Thank you, sir. Would you like to sit at this table by the window?
>
> ...
>
> Waiter: Are you ready to order?
>
> Woman: We haven't decided yet. Could you give us a few more minutes? And could we have some drinks, please?

Waiter:	Certainly, madam. What would you like?
Woman:	Two gin and tonics, please.
Waiter:	Certainly, madam.
	…
Woman:	Excuse me.
Waiter:	Yes, madam?
Woman:	I'd like the tomato salad and then the lamb, please?
Waiter:	Certainly, madam. And for you, sir?
Man:	I won't have a starter. I'll just have the grilled salmon steak, please.
Waiter:	What would you like with it?
Man:	A side salad. Oh, and we'd like a bottle of house red and some mineral water, please.
Waiter:	Certainly, sir.
	…
Waiter:	Was everything all right?
Man:	Yes, it was fine.
Waiter:	Would you like some coffee now?
Woman:	Yes, please. Two black coffees. And could we have the bill, please?
Waiter:	Yes, of course.

Anecdote (p 103)

See Introduction, page 4, for more ideas on how to set up, monitor and repeat 'anecdotes'.

5 Pairwork. Students read the list of questions and decide what they are going to talk about, what they will say about each question and what language they will need. Give them a few minutes to prepare and go round answering any questions and giving help with vocabulary where necessary.

6 Pairwork. Students take turns telling their partner about their experience, giving as much detail as possible. Alternatively, students ask each other the questions.

What's for dinner? (p 104) (Workbook p 62)

1 Whole class. Students look at the photo and identify the food shown in it. As they call out the names, write them on a spidergram on the board. Put the word FOOD in the middle with lines out to FRUIT, VEGETABLES, MEAT and DAIRY PRODUCTS. As students identify the items in the photo, get them to say which category they should go in. When students have named all the food items in the photo, encourage them to call out further food names to put on the spidergram.

Optional activity

Students look at the picture for one minute then close their books. Either alone or in pairs, they write down as many of the foods as they can remember. The winner is the student/pair with the most correctly remembered. Students then do the spidergram activity.

2 Pairwork. Students discuss the various food items listed and classify them according to their 'colour' (red = meat, blue = fish and seafood, etc). They check any words they don't know in their dictionaries. Check answers with the class. Point out that peppers, tomatoes, olives and aubergines are fruit, but are generally thought of as vegetables.

> Stressed syllables are underlined.
>
> meat (red): bacon, sausages, turkey, veal
>
> fish and seafood (blue): cod, hake, lobster, mussels, prawns, salmon, sardines, trout, tuna
>
> vegetables (green): aubergines, beans, cauliflower, celery, courgettes, cucumbers, garlic, leeks, lettuces, mushrooms, olives, onions, peppers, spinach, tomatoes
>
> fruit (orange): figs, grapefruit, limes, melons, oranges, peaches, plums, raspberries, strawberries

3 Pairwork. Students ask and answer questions about the types of food they prefer. Encourage them to be specific about their likes and dislikes, for example, soft rather than hard cheeses, particular types of meat: beef, lamb, pork, chicken, etc.

4 Groupwork. Read through the instructions and the situations with the class. Students choose one of the situations and discuss suitable foods. They then design a menu for the meal. Groups take turns to read their menus, without saying which situation they chose. The rest of the class guess the situation.

Incredible edibles (p 105) (Workbook p 61)

Closed books. Whole class. Tell the class about the most unusual thing you have ever eaten. Describe the texture and the taste and say whether you enjoyed it and whether you would eat it again. Ask if anyone else has eaten this thing and whether anyone would consider eating it.

1 Open books. Students read the words to describe taste and texture and the names of the different kinds of food. They check the meaning of any unknown words in their dictionaries and write sentences using the taste and texture words to describe the different kinds of food. Check answers with the class.

Optional activity

Groupwork. Each student thinks of a kind of food and describes it to the rest of the group in terms of taste and texture, but without naming the food. The rest of the group have to guess what it is. Alternatively, one student thinks of the food and other students ask yes/no questions to find out what it is, for example, *Is it spicy? Do you boil it?* Students could have a maximum of ten questions to find out what the food is. If they succeed, they get a point. If not, the person who chose the food gets the point.

2 Pairwork. Students look at the map and the names of the unusual foods eaten around the world. They discuss the food items and decide what they think they would taste like. Get feedback and see if anyone has actually eaten any of the items discussed.

3 📼 **44 SB p 156**

Students listen to an interview with someone who has eaten many strange things. They note down the words used to describe each thing. Check answers with the class.

fried grasshoppers and locusts in Thailand: crisp, tasty

crickets in North America: tasty, just the same as fried grasshoppers

roasted cockroaches in Indonesia: more chewy than crisp on the outside; sweet, fruity, rich liquid inside

roasted ants in Colombia: sweet and crisp, delicious

barbecued lizard in South America: bland, not particularly tasty

iguana eggs in South America: tasty, a bit salty, very good

fried grubs in Australia: a bit chewy, crunchy on the outside but chewy inside

shark fin soup in China: delicious, quite spicy, not particularly fishy

deep-fried Mars Bars in Scotland: greasy, horribly sweet, disgusting

📼 **44**

(I = Interviewer; M = Michael)

I: *Michael, you've had the opportunity to taste some of the more unusual dishes from around the world. Can you tell us something about them, and in particular, what they taste like?*

M: *Yes, well, I've just come back from Thailand and in the winter, sackloads of grasshoppers and locusts are brought into Bangkok from the countryside because the Thais love them. They make a really crisp and tasty snack. In fact, fried grasshoppers are tasty to most people, provided they don't know what they're eating. They eat crickets in parts of North America, and they taste just the same.*

I: *Hmm. I'm not sure I'd like to eat insects.*

M: *Well, you'd better not go to Indonesia then. Last time I was there, I had a feast of insects. The main course was roasted cockroaches.*

I: *Oh dear. What did that taste like?*

M: *They're rather more chewy than crisp on the outside and then there's a rich liquid on the inside which tastes quite sweet and fruity.*

I: *What other insects have you eaten?*

M: *Well, did you know that in Colombia, cinemas serve roasted ants instead of popcorn?*

I: *Really? What are they like?*

M: *Sweet and crisp ... delicious actually. I also ate barbecued lizard in South America, but that was a bit disappointing. It was a bit bland ... not particularly tasty. On the other hand, iguana eggs made a much more interesting dish. After ten minutes boiling in very salty water, they made a very tasty evening snack. A bit too salty for my taste, but very good.*

I: *I've heard that they eat grubs in Australia. I can't believe that. Is it true?*

M: *Yes. I've never eaten them raw, but I have eaten them fried. They're OK ... a bit chewy ... crunchy on the outside but chewy on the inside.*

I: *I'm sorry, I don't even want to think about it. Can we change the subject. How about shark fin soup? Have you ever tried that?*

M: *Only once, in China. It's very expensive and takes ages to prepare. But it's delicious. The taste depends on how the chef prepares it, but when I ate it, it was quite spicy and not particularly fishy. Anyway, what about you? Have you ever eaten anything strange?*

I: *Well, I'm not as adventurous as you, and I've never been out of Europe, but probably the strangest, and I must say the most revolting thing I've ever eaten was in Scotland recently.*

M: *Oh, you mean haggis?*

I: *No, no. Haggis is delicious. No, it was deep-fried Mars Bar.*

M: *What? You mean, like fish and chips ... Mars Bar and chips?*

I: *That's right. Greasy and horribly sweet. Disgusting!*

M: *Oh.*

4 Groupwork. Students discuss whether they would consider eating any of the dishes mentioned. They could number them with 1 being the dish they would most consider eating and 9 the dish they would least consider eating.

Whole class. Encourage students to tell the rest of the class the most unusual things they have ever eaten. When each student has described something, get the others to say whether or not they have eaten it or would eat it.

Bedtime (p 106) (Workbook p 62)

Groupwork. Students look at the picture and discuss it. They then have three minutes to write down all the words and expressions they associate with sleep. They compare and discuss their lists with other groups, explaining their words and expressions if necessary. Alternatively, each student writes down one word connected with sleep on a piece of paper and then passes the paper to their left. Students then write another 'sleep' word on the paper before passing it on again. Students cannot write a word already on the paper. This continues until there are, say, ten words on each paper. Papers are then compared and a class list written up on the board.

1 Pairwork. Students work individually to answer the questionnaire. They then compare their answers with a partner.

2 Students read the survey report and find expressions to match the figures in the list. Go through the instructions with the class first to encourage students to scan the text for the information needed to answer the question rather than read the text carefully. Check answers with the class.

> a) few   b) one in three   c) a large number
> d) over half   e) most   f) nearly half

3 Students match the figures to the facts in the report. This will involve a more careful reading of the text. Check answers with the class.

> Few – the number of people who understand the important role sleep plays in normal daily brain functions
>
> One in three – the number of people who admit they don't get enough sleep
>
> A large number – people who say that they need to be mentally alert in their work
>
> Over half – the number of people who sleep less than seven hours a night during the week
>
> Most – the number of people who sleep more than seven hours a night at the weekend, and the number of people who think the brain is resting or recuperating during sleep
>
> Nearly half – the number of people who believe that the brain rests when the body sleeps

Report writing (p 107)

1 Pairwork. Students write five questions about sleep habits. Go round offering help and encouragement where necessary.

2 Pairwork. Students ask the rest of the class their questions and note down their answers. If space permits, this can be done as a mingling activity with students moving around the classroom. Otherwise, divide the class into groups to ask and answer the questions.

3 Pairwork. Students write sentences reporting their results. Encourage them to use the Language toolbox for ideas and to use expressions they have just learnt, for example, *one in four, a large number of, less than half,* etc.

Test

> Scoring: one point per correct answer unless otherwise indicated.
>
> **1** (½ point each)
> meat: veal bacon turkey
> vegetables: pepper onion aubergine
> fish: trout salmon cod
> fruit: fig melon raspberry
>
> **2** 1 crunchy
>   2 bland
>   3 chewy
>   4 greasy
>   5 spicy
>   6 bitter
>
> **3** 1 reservation 2 house 3 everything 4 bill
>
> **4** 1 yawning 2 early bird 3 night owl
>   4 nap 5 insomnia 6 snores
>
> **5** (1–18 = ½ point each)
>   1 B   2 U   3 C   4 U   5 C   6 B   7 B
>   8 B   9 C   10 C 11 U 12 U 13 U 14 C
>   15 U   16 U 17 U 18 U
>   19 a few
>   20 a few
>   21 a little
>   22 a few
>   23 many
>   24 much
>   25 much
>   26 many
>   27 much

12 Basics *Test*

Name: _____   **Total:** _____ /40

---

1 Vocabulary – food *6 points*

Put the words in the box under the correct headings.

> pepper veal trout fig salmon bacon
> onion melon cod turkey aubergine raspberry

Meat   Vegetables   Fish   Fruit

2 Vocabulary – adjectives *6 points*

Here are some mixed-up words used to describe the taste or texture of food. What are they? The first letter is given.

1   ncyruhc   c _____

2   abldn   b _____

3   cehyw   c _____

4   sragey   g _____

5   sycip   s _____

6   rbtite   b _____

3 In a restaurant *4 points*

Here are four things you may hear or say in a restaurant. Add the missing word.

1   Do you have a r_____?

2   A bottle of h_____ red, please.

3   Is e_____ OK?

4   Can we have the b_____ , please?

4 Vocabulary – sleep *6 points*

Complete the missing words.

1   I'm exhausted – I can't stop y _ _ _ ing.

2   She's always up at the crack of dawn – she's a real
    e _ _ _ y b _ _ _.

3   He's certainly a n _ _ _ t o _ _. He's never in bed before one or two in the morning.

4   I usually have a n _ _ most afternoons.

5   Have you ever suffered from in _ _ m _ _ a?

6   He sn _ r _ _ all the time. I should get some earplugs!

5 Countable and uncountable nouns *18 points*

Are the following nouns countable (C), uncountable (U) or both (B), depending on the usage?

1	time _____	10	chair _____
2	money _____	11	sleep _____
3	dollar _____	12	news _____
4	rain _____	13	hunger _____
5	person _____	14	dream _____
6	glass _____	15	weather _____
7	beer _____	16	homework _____
8	lamb _____	17	knowledge _____
9	idea _____	18	food _____

Complete the sentences with *a few* or *a little*.

19   There were only _____ people at the party.

20   I've only got _____ dollars left.

21   I've got _____ money left.

22   Would you like _____ more potatoes?

Complete the following sentences with *many* or *much*.

23   I haven't got _____ CDs.

24   Did you have _____ homework last night?

25   I've drunk too _____ coffee today.

26   They didn't have _____ ideas.

27   How _____ was the ticket?

Communication Overview

The topics in this unit are telephoning, and men and women. The main grammatical focus is on real conditionals: first and zero conditionals, mixed conditionals and conditional imperatives.

Students practise taking down phone numbers, fax numbers, e-mail and website addresses. They go on to note down answering machine messages. They then listen to telephone conversations and study telephone language.

Students take part in a discussion of stereotypes of men and women. They do a survey questionnaire on how men and women really think and discuss the results. Finally they write their own questionnaire and report their findings.

Section	Aims	What the students are doing
Introduction page 108	*Listening skills*: note-taking	Listening and noting down phone numbers, fax numbers, and e-mail and website addresses. Practising saying these numbers and addresses.
After the beep pages 108–109	*Listening skills*: predicting; note-taking	Making predictions from a photo about the main character in a recording. Making notes from answering machine messages.
	Lexis: telephone language	Reviewing telephone language by choosing appropriate words and phrases to complete telephone messages.
	Listening skills: listening for detail	Listening to two telephone conversations to check comprehension. Practising telephone conversations. Listening to a further conversation to check comprehension.
Close up pages 110–111	*Grammar*: real conditionals	Identifying and practising real conditionals.
Stereotypes pages 112–113	*Reading skills*: scanning	Categorising statements that men and women say.
	Lexis: make & do	Reviewing collocations of *make* and *do*.
	Conversation skills: fluency work	Discussing male and female stereotypes. Talking about how women's lives have changed within three generations.
What do men & women really think? pages 114–115	*Reading skills*: for gist	Completing a questionnaire based on what men and women really think and guessing the answers for a partner.
	Writing skills: asking for information; summarising findings and paragraphing	Writing a multiple choice survey questionnaire, conducting the survey, collating the results and writing a report on the findings.

1 ☰ **45 SB p 157**

Before you play the recording, establish that students will be listening for the Internet website addresses and telephone numbers of various organisations. Go through the list of organisations with the class and elicit or explain what they are. (*BBC* = British Broadcasting Corporation, a British radio and television broadcasting company; *CNN* = an American news broadcasting company; *MTV* = a television company specialising in music; *Reuters Sport* = the sports section of the Reuters news agency; *Yahoo Travel* = the travel section of an Internet 'search engine'; *BTA* = British Tourist Authority; *Heathrow* = one of London's main airports). Ask students to say what kind of information they would expect to find on each website.

Students listen to the recording and complete the addresses. Check answers with the class and ask selected students to read out the addresses and numbers in turn. Check pronunciation and get the class to repeat them.

Pairwork. Students practise saying the complete addresses and numbers as fast as they can.

a) www.bbc.co.uk

b) www.cnn.com

c) 44 20 7557 1180

d) www.mtv.com

e) www.sportsweb.com

f) www.yahoo.com/recreation/travel

g) www.visitbritain.com

h) 020 8759 4321

☰ **45**

Welcome to the 'Inside Out' helpline for students of English. Here are some useful numbers and addresses for your information.

For news and current events, the BBC website is a good starting point at www.bbc.co.uk. An alternative is CNN at www.cnn.com.

To listen to BBC World Service radio you can find out about schedules and local frequencies by dialling 44 for the UK, then 20 7557 1180.

You can get the latest news and reviews on the music scene at www.mtv.com. Or if it's sports results you want then the Reuters site at www.sportsweb ... all one word ... .com will keep you right up to date.

For travel information try one of the major search engines like Yahoo at www.yahoo ... that's all one word ... Y A H double O ... .com/recreation/travel.

The British Tourist Authority has lots of information. You'll find them at www.visitbritain ... all one word ... .com. If you are already in the UK, the telephone number for flight enquiries to and from Heathrow is 020 ... if you are outside London ... 8759 4321.

2 Give students time to decide how many numbers or addresses they know. You could get students to say how many they think they can remember and then challenge those giving the highest numbers to say them to the class.

Pairwork. Students take turns dictating their numbers and addresses. Elicit a few of the questions they can ask about them using the expressions in the box, for example, *Whose address is this? How often do you e-mail this person? When did you last call them?*

After the beep ... (p 108)

1 Whole class. Students look at the photo and speculate about Richard by answering the questions. Encourage them to be imaginative and to give as much detail as possible.

2 ☰ **46 SB p 157 (Workbook p 66)**

Students listen to six messages on Richard's answering machine. They make notes of any clues they hear about his work, friends and lifestyle.

Pairwork. Students compare their notes and discuss their opinions about Richard. Check answers with the class. Have their ideas about Richard changed after listening to the messages?

Richard has a friend called Jeff and a girlfriend called Maggie, but she is unhappy with him because he spends more time with his computer than he does with her.

Richard and Maggie are planning to take an expensive holiday – ten days' scuba-diving in Egypt.

Richard spends a lot of time playing computer games. He works for a computer company, but possibly works from home.

Richard spends more money than he earns and has an overdraft at the bank.

📼 46

1

Hi, Rich. It's Jeff, six thirty Wednesday night. I'm in Bristol for a few days. Give me a call if you're around. 723688. Speak to you soon.

2

Hi there! This is Simon from Tim's Travel Company. We've finally got your tickets for ten days' scuba-diving in Egypt. Call by and pick them up any time. We're open from nine to five every day. Bye.

3

Richard ... it's Andrew. I've just had a call from Ian Watson at Smiths Insurance. They've got a problem with the programme we installed on their computer network last week, so I've told him I'll get somebody out there as soon as possible to sort it out. Could you phone him first thing tomorrow morning and arrange to go out there and see what you can do? The ... the number is 01225 302602. Give me a call at the office to let me know what you've arranged. Thanks.

4

Er, this is Alex at Virgin Megastore. The new computer game you ordered has come in. Please call by and pick it up. Thank you.

5

Hello, it's me ... Maggie. You may remember me. I'm supposed to be your girlfriend, although you wouldn't think so. Get off your computer for five minutes and give me a ring. By the way, have you heard anything about the tickets for Egypt?

6

Hello. This is Alison Moore from the South-Western Bank. Can you ring me to discuss your overdraft. 0117 515633 extension 300. Thank you.

Telephone language (p 109)

(Workbook p 64, p 67, p 68)

1 Encourage students to read through both conversations first, ignoring the gaps. This will give them a general idea of the content and degree of formality of each conversation. Once they have done this, making the right choices will be easier. Elicit that the first conversation is to Richard's girlfriend Maggie and the second to the bank. The first conversation is informal and the second formal. Establish that students should choose the correct alternatives from the choices. One choice is incorrect. The other two are grammatically correct but differ in degree of formality.

Pairwork. Students discuss the conversations and make choices for the gaps.

Phone conversation 1

a) Hello.

b) Is Maggie there?

c) Is that Richard?

d) Hang on, I'll go and get her.

e) It's me.

f) What are you up to later?

g) See you tomorrow.

Phone conversation 2

a) Good morning

b) I'd like to speak to Alison Moore, please.

c) Who's calling, please?

d) Hold on, please, I'll try to put you through.

e) This is Richard Swainston here.

f) Are you available later on today?

g) I'll look forward to seeing you tomorrow.

2 📼 **47 SB p 157**

Students listen to the recording and check their answers.

Groupwork. Students practise the conversations in threes, taking the roles of Richard, Jane, Maggie, the receptionist and Alison Moore.

📼 47

1

(J = Jane; R = Richard; M = Maggie)

J: *Hello.*

R: *Oh, hi. Is Maggie there?*

J: *Is that Richard?*

R: *Yes, hello, Jane. How are you?*

J: *Fine, thanks. Hang on, I'll go and get her.*

    ...

M: *Hello.*

R: *Hi! It's me.*

M: *You got my message then. I thought you'd forgotten about me.*

R: *Don't be silly. Of course I haven't forgotten you. I've just been busy, that's all.*

M: *Busy playing computer games, I suppose.*

R: *No, not all the time. Anyway, how are you?*

M: *Um, not too bad. Bit tired. Too much work as usual. Which reminds me, have you heard anything from the travel agent's?*

R: *Oh, yes. They've got the tickets.*

M: *Great! Oh, I really need this holiday.*

R: *Listen, I can't chat now, but what are you up to later?*

M: *I've got to work this evening, but I thought we could go to the cinema tomorrow.*

R: *OK, I'll come round at about seven.*

M: *See you tomorrow.*

R: *Bye.*

2

(Re = Receptionist; R = Richard; A = Alison)

Re: *Good morning. South-Western Bank. Can I help you?*

R: *Yes, I'd like to speak to Alison Moore, please.*

Re: *Who's calling, please?*

R: *My name's Richard Swainston.*

Re: *OK, hold on, please. I'll try to put you through ... Oh, Mr Swainston, I'm afraid she's on the other line. Would you like to hold?*

R: *Yes, thank you. ...*

...

A: *Alison Moore.*

R: *Oh, hello. This is Richard Swainston here.*

A: *Oh, yes. Mr Swainston. Thank you for getting back to me so promptly. There seems to be a problem with your account.*

R: *Oh, dear. What sort of problem?*

A: *Well, you're over your overdraft limit by more than £200. You really need to come to the bank to discuss it. Are you available later on today?*

R: *I'm afraid I'm rather tied up today. Er, would tomorrow be convenient for you?*

A: *Um, yes, that's fine. Ten thirty?*

R: *Yes, ten thirty's fine for me.*

A: *Well, thank you for ringing. I'll look forward to seeing you tomorrow.*

R: *Goodbye.*

3 Pairwork. Students look at the tapescript of Richard's messages on his answering machine on page 157 and write two telephone conversations. Before they start, elicit that the conversation with Andrew will be informal and the one with Smiths Insurance will be formal. Check that students are clear what the content of each will be. Go round offering help and encouragement where necessary. Get several pairs to perform their conversations for the class.

4 48 SB p 157

Whole class. Read the instructions and ask students whether they would phone their mothers if they were in Richard's shoes. Read through the sentences and encourage students to speculate on whether or not they are true before they listen to the recording. Students then listen and mark the sentences true or false.

a) False (Her husband is playing golf, but she's enjoying the peace and quiet.)

b) True (His mother says 'Have you got yourself into debt again?')

c) False (His mother thinks he spends it going out every night and buying expensive computers.)

d) True (Richard says his parents spent a fortune on her wedding.)

e) False (Richard tells his mother he isn't going to get married.)

f) True (She says he really must learn to budget and this is the last time she will help him out.)

g) False (She agrees to lend him the money, but only if he never says again that he isn't going to get married.)

h) False (Richard phones his mother when he wants something. She wishes he would phone just for a chat.)

 48

(MS = Mrs Swainston; R = Richard)

MS: *Hello?*

R: *Mum, it's Richard.*

MS: *Oh, is everything all right?*

R: *Yes, yes, fine. How are you?*

MS: *Oh, not too bad. Your father's playing golf so I'm enjoying the peace and quiet. How's Maggie?*

R: *She's OK. Working hard. Mum, I was wondering ... do you think you could lend me some money till the end of the month?*

MS: *Oh, Richard, have you got yourself into debt again? Because if you have ...*

R: *No, no. It's just a bit of an overdraft.*

MS: *Where does all your money go, Richard? I mean, you've got a good job ...*

R: *But Mum, it's expensive living in Bristol.*

MS: *Well, of course it is. What do you expect if you go out every night and buy expensive computers.*

R: *I haven't got a computer. It's a playstation.*

MS: *Oh, well, whatever. I mean, your sister never phones up asking for money.*

R: *But you spent a fortune on her wedding.*

MS: *Yes, and when you get married, we'll do the same for you.*

R: *Well, I'm not going to get married, so you might as well give me the money now!*

MS: *Richard! What would Maggie say! Now come on, this is silly. How much do you need?*

R: *£300.*

MS: *Oh, honestly, Richard, you really must learn to budget.*

R: *Look, Mum, if you can just help me out this time, I promise I'll try to be more careful in future.*

MS: *Well, we'll see about that. Listen, I ... I'll do it this time, but this really is the last time. If you get yourself into trouble again, you'll just have to sort it out yourself.*

R: *Oh thanks, Mum.*

MS: *But I'm doing this on one condition ...*

R: *Yes?*

MS: *You never say you're not going to get married again.*

R: *OK, I promise. Thanks, Mum. Bye.*

MS: *Bye ... and next time, you could phone up just for a chat!*

5 Pairwork. Students discuss what the conversation shows about the relationship between Richard and his mother. They then discuss their own relationships with their mothers. Encourage them to say whether they would ask their mothers for money in Richard's situation and how their mothers would react.

> *Possible answers*
>
> Richard's mother loves him and helps him out when he is in trouble but she wishes he was more responsible with money. She likes his girlfriend, Maggie, and hopes that they will get married. She is disappointed that her son only calls her when he wants something and she wishes he would call for a chat sometimes.
>
> Richard depends on his mother when he is in trouble. She has helped him before. He knows how to persuade her to help him again. He has quite a good relationship with his mother, but is inclined to take her for granted and take advantage of her.

Close up (p 110) (Workbook p 64, p 65)

Real conditionals

1 Play the recording again. Students look at the tapescript on page 157 and complete the sentences. Check answers with the class. There is information about forming real conditionals in the Language reference section on page 111.

> a) you go out every night and buy expensive computers.
>
> b) I promise I'll try to be more careful in future.
>
> c) you'll just have to sort it out yourself.

2 Pairwork. Students think of as many ways as possible of completing the sentence.

> *Possible answers*
>
> Because if you have ...
>
> don't expect me to help you.
>
> don't tell your father.
>
> don't ask me for money.
>
> don't expect sympathy from me.
>
> I'm not going to give/lend you any money.

> I'm not going to help you.
>
> you can sort it out yourself.
>
> you can ask your father to help.
>
> I won't help you.
>
> I won't give/lend you any money.

3 Students match clauses from A with clauses from B and write sentences using *if*. Check answers with the class. Remind students that the *if* clause can be at the beginning or at the end of the sentence.

Groupwork. Students discuss the sentences and decide what age the child would be for each of them. You could also ask them to say in what circumstances each sentence might be said. Check answers with the class.

> a) Take a front door key if you're going to stay out late.
>
> b) If you're going to listen to that awful music, shut your bedroom door.
>
> c) If you don't put your toys away, I'll give them all away.
>
> d) If you hurt yourself, don't come crying to me.
>
> e) You'll be late for school if you don't hurry up.
>
> f) If you've finished your dinner, you can leave the table.
>
> g) If you haven't finished your homework, you can't play computer games.
>
> h) If you're going to be silly, I'm not playing.
>
> i) I might buy you an ice-cream if you're good.
>
> j) If you're going to phone a friend, keep it short.

4 Students choose five sentences and rewrite them using *unless* instead of *if*. Do the first sentence as an example and to demonstrate the other changes that have to be made:

Take a front door key unless you're going to come home early.

Note: there may be several possible answers for each one and sentences d) and j) cannot be transformed using *unless*.

> b) Unless you're going to listen to some nice music, shut your bedroom door.
>
> c) Unless you put your toys away, I'll give them all away.
>
> d) Not possible
>
> e) You'll be late for school unless you hurry up.
>
> f) You can't leave the table unless you've finished your dinner.
>
> g) You can't play computer games unless you have finished your homework.
>
> h) I'm not playing unless you stop being silly.
>
> i) I won't buy you an ice-cream unless you're good.
>
> j) Not possible

5 Students look at the illustration down the side of the page. Ask if students think any of these things are lucky or unlucky. Elicit that being *superstitious* means believing that certain things bring good or bad luck. Find out if the students know what any of the things in the picture mean in Britain. (Some people believe it is lucky if a black cat crosses your path, if you blow out all the candles on your birthday cake with one breath, if you have a spider on your clothes, if you find a four-leaved clover. Breaking a mirror is supposed to bring bad luck, and it is said that the woman who catches a bride's bouquet will be the next one to get married.)

Pairwork. Students discuss some of the superstitions of their own country or countries.

6 Groupwork. Students read the sayings and try to decide what they mean. They write sentences to explain them using *if*. Give students one or two examples. Refer students to the Language reference section on this page if they are unsure about forming real conditional sentences. They then discuss if they have equivalent proverbs in their language(s).

> *Possible answers*
>
> a) If you get something without much effort, you aren't too upset if you lose it.
>
> b) If you don't concentrate, you won't succeed.
>
> c) If you don't make an effort, you won't succeed.
>
> d) If something bad has happened, it's no use wasting time worrying about it.
>
> e) If someone in authority is absent, everyone will relax and stop work.
>
> f) If lots of people help with a job, it is quickly and easily finished.
>
> g) If you eat an apple every day, you will stay healthy.
>
> h) If you act quickly, you are more likely to succeed.
>
> i) If too many people try to do something, the result is not good.
>
> j) If you haven't seen someone for some time, you will think about them more kindly.

Stereotypes (p 112)

1 Whole class. Read the definition of *stereotype* with the class and ask students for some examples. If they are slow in thinking of ideas, start them off with a few of your own, for example, *women aren't interested in football, men can't cook, blondes are not as intelligent as people with dark hair.* Read the instructions with the class. Elicit that the *Daily Mail* is a British tabloid newspaper.

Groupwork. Students discuss the stereotypes and say whether they agree with them or not.

2 Make it clear that students are to decide under which heading the *Daily Mail* put the statements, not which heading they personally would put them under. Providing they have understood the statements in 1, this should not be too difficult as stereotypes are by definition predictable and the *Daily Mail* is not famous for fresh ideas. The answers are opposite. Ask students if they agree with them. You could suggest that neither men nor women would say d) (because men rarely do the ironing and men rarely thank women for doing housework) or h) (because neither a man nor a woman is likely to admit that their partner is a better driver).

3 Students complete the statements. Emphasise here that the point is to make stereotypical statements based on the *Daily Mail* article, rather than statements the students themselves believe in. Women complete the sentences in A and men those in B.

Pairwork. Pairs should preferably consist of one woman and one man. Students compare their sentences and discuss them.

4 Pairwork. Students decide which two verbs can be used to complete the expressions in the two lists. They then discuss which member of their family they would associate with each expression.

> List A: do
>
> List B: make

5 Whole class. Students look at the cartoon. Ask them what they can see in it and if they think this is typical of male/female roles in their own society. Do they think this is typical of an older generation and have things changed? What happens in their own families?

6 Groupwork. Students discuss the questions. Go round offering help with vocabulary.

What do men & women really think? (p 114)

1 Pairwork. Establish who will partner whom, if possible having mixed sex pairs. Students work individually at first and answer the questionnaire for themselves. They then guess their partner's answers. Students compare their guesses about their partner with their real answers and see how accurate they were.

2 Whole class. Read the summary of the survey results and encourage students to decide as a class whether to put 'men' or 'women' in each gap. If there is disagreement, allow a few minutes for class discussion before moving on to the next gap. Students note down the class decision in each case.

Students can check the answers on page 141.

1	women
2	men
3	men
4	women
5	women
6	men
7	Women
8	men
9	women
10	men
11	men
12	women
13	men
14	women
15	men
16	women
17	men
18	men
19	women
20	men
21	women
22	women
23	men

3 Students discuss whether the results would have been different in their country or countries. If your students come from different countries, you could put them in country groups to discuss this. They can then report to the class on the situation in their country.

Report writing (p 115)

1 Groupwork. Students work together to devise a questionnaire on attitudes towards the items in the list. Go through the possible lines of enquiry with the class and elicit suggestions for suitable questions for the questionnaire about one or two of them.

2 Each group uses its questionnaire to do a survey with the rest of the class. They should divide the work so that each student interviews at least one other member of the class. They return to their groups and collate their results.

3 Students write reports summarising their findings, using the survey highlights text on page 115 as a model.

Test

Scoring: one point per correct answer unless otherwise indicated.

1   1 speak 2 calling/speaking 3 Hold 4 put
       5 through 6 there 7 'll 8 get/find

2   (½ point each)
       1 c 2 g 3 d 4 a 5 f 6 b 7 h 8 e

3   One point for identification and one point for correction.
       1 ✓
       2 ✓
       3 ✗ If you do that again, he will be annoyed.
       4 ✓
       5 ✓
       6 ✓
       7 ✗ When you arrive we will already have left.
       8 ✓

       9 don't get/haven't got
       10 start
       11 don't leave
       12 'll miss
       13 arrive
       14 wait
       15 are
       16 have already finished
       17 are going/went
       18 meet
       19 Unless she goes, I'm not going.
       20 If you don't start now, you might not get it finished in time.
       21 Unless you work harder, you won't pass your exams.
       22 You can go unless you haven't finished.

4   (½ point each)
       1 do the shopping
       2 do the driving
       3 make the bed
       4 do the cleaning
       5 make an effort
       6 make up your mind
       7 make a decision
       8 make a noise

13 Communication Test

Name: _____   **Total:** _____ /40

---

1 Vocabulary – on the phone *8 points*

Put an appropriate word in each space.

Receptionist: JKL Computers.

Nicola: Hi, I'd like to (1) _____ to Jonathan Wood please.

Receptionist: Who's (2) _____ please?

Nicola: My name's Nicola Moore.

Receptionist: OK. (3) _____ on please, I'll (4) _____ you (5) _____ .

Jonathan: Hello. Jonathan Wood speaking.

Dai: Hello.

Carla: Hi. Is Ngyen (6) _____ ?

Dai: Yes, he is. I (7) _____ go and (8) _____ him for you.

Ngyen: Hello. Ngyen here.

2 Proverbs *4 points*

Join the two halves to make some well-known proverbs.

1	Too many cooks	a	the iron is hot.
2	Easy come,	b	crying over spilt milk.
3	When the cat's away,	c	spoil the broth.
4	Strike while	d	the mice will play.
5	Absence makes	e	make light work.
6	It's no use	f	the heart grow fonder.
7	No pain,	g	easy go.
8	Many hands	h	no gain.

1 _____   2 _____   3 _____   4 _____
5 _____   6 _____   7 _____   8 _____

3 Real conditionals *24 points*

Only six of these sentences are correct. Mark them ✓ or ✗. Correct the two which are wrong.

1 If you've finished, will you let me know? _____

2 If he's still there, I'll ask him to phone you. _____

3 If you do that again, he is annoyed. _____

4 If we were just a minute late for class, the teacher got really angry. _____

5 Tell me if you can't do it. _____

6 If you're feeling tired, you should go to bed. _____

7 When you arrive, we have already left. _____

8 If it gets too hot, it stops working. _____

Put the verbs into an appropriate form.

If I (9) _____ (not/get) there by six, (10) _____ (start) without me.

If we (11) _____ (not/leave) now, we (12) _____ (miss) the train.

If you (13) _____ (arrive) early, (14) _____ (wait) for me in the bar next door.

You (15) _____ (be) free to leave if you (16) _____ (already/finish).

If you (17) _____ (go) on the trip to London, (18) _____ (meet) me in the students' room at 1.30.

Rewrite the following sentences beginning with the word given, so the meaning is unchanged.

19 If she doesn't go, I'm not going.

Unless _____

20 Unless you start it now, you might not get it finished in time.

If _____

21 If you don't work harder, you won't pass your exams

Unless _____

22 If you've finished, you can go.

You can go unless _____

4 Vocabulary – make and do *4 points*

Which verb, *make* or *do*, collocates with each of the following?

1	_____ the shopping	5	_____ an effort
2	_____ the driving	6	_____ up your mind
3	_____ the bed	7	_____ a decision
4	_____ the cleaning	8	_____ a noise

14 *Style* Overview

The topics in this unit are fashion, clothes and appearance. The main grammatical focus is on *I wish* and unreal conditionals: second conditionals. Students also look at adjective order.

The unit begins with students describing morning routines and how they get ready for particular events. They go on to describe favourite styles of clothes and then listen to people talking about their favourite clothes. Students then talk about a favourite item of clothes or accessory they have bought, and study idioms related to clothes.

Students read an extract, describing a girl, from the book *Come Together* and then use it as a model to write descriptions of people from an illustration.

Finally students listen to the song *Ugly* by Jon Bon Jovi and then read an interview with him.

Section	Aims	What the students are doing
Introduction page 116	*Lexis*: verb phrases	Forming verb phrases to describe morning routines.
	Reading skills: for detail	Choosing the correct verbs and verb phrases within two texts.
	Conversation skills: fluency work	Talking about getting ready in the morning and for a special event.
Suits you page 117	*Listening skills*: checking comprehension	Generating interest in a recording by talking about favourite styles of clothes. Checking listening comprehension by putting illustrations of clothes in the order they are mentioned in the recording. Discussing which item of clothing is the ugliest.
Close up pages 118–119	*Grammar*: adjective order	Reviewing, categorising and practising the order of adjectives to do with clothes.
	Conversation skills: fluency work	Anecdote: talking about a favourite item of clothing or accessory.
	Lexis: idioms	Categorising words to do with clothes. Reviewing idioms to do with clothes.
First impressions pages 120–121	*Pronunciation*: vowel sounds	Identifying pure vowel sounds and diphthongs.
	Lexis: adjectives	Reviewing adjectives to do with physical appearance.
	Reading skills: for detail	Checking comprehension by matching a description of a girl from an extract in the book *Come Together* with the correct person from an illustration.
	Writing skills: describing people	Completing a similar description for one of the other people in the illustration. Writing a description of a person.
Ugly page 122	*Listening skills*: listening for detail	Listening to the song *Ugly* to identify the mood of the song and for information. Checking comprehension of the song by matching the lines of the lyrics.
Close up page 122	*Grammar: I wish*	Identifying wishes from the lyrics and practising *I wish* sentences within different situations.
Interview with Jon Bon Jovi page 123	*Reading skills*: for detail	Checking comprehension by matching questions to their answers in an interview.
	Conversation skills: fluency work	Interviewing each other using the questions in the Jon Bon Jovi interview.
Close up page 124	*Grammar*: unreal conditionals	Identifying unreal conditionals from the Jon Bon Jovi interview, and from four dialogues. Distinguishing between real and unreal conditionals and *I wish* sentences.

1 Students look at the two illustrations on the left of the page and say what the person has done between the first picture and the second (had a shower, got dressed, had breakfast, etc). Students match the verbs with the words in the box to make expressions to describe what people do in the morning. Check answers with the class.

> have a shower, have coffee, have breakfast, have a cup of tea
>
> get the mail, get dressed, get breakfast, get the children ready, get the paper, get a cup of tea
>
> make coffee, make breakfast, make the bed, make a cup of tea
>
> do my homework, do the washing-up
>
> read the mail, read the paper
>
> put the radio on, put my make-up on, put the TV on

2 Pairwork. Students read the three points and make notes about their morning routines. They then compare and discuss their routines with a partner.

3 Students go through the two texts crossing out the unsuitable verbs. Do one or two with the class as an example. Check answers with the class.

> Person 1: 1 get dressed 2 wear 3 put on
> 4 fit 5 take them off 6 goes with
> 7 try on 8 looks 9 feels 10 match
> Person 2: 1 put on 2 had on 3 goes with
> 4 match 5 suit 6 look like

Pairwork. Students decide if the texts are written by men or women and discuss whether they fit anyone they know.

4 Students work individually to write accounts of their morning routines on pieces of paper. Make sure they don't write their names on their papers. Collect the accounts in, shuffle them and give them out. Students guess who wrote the account they have received.

5 Pairwork. Students choose two or three of the situations and discuss how they would get ready for them. Go round offering encouragement and help with vocabulary.

Suits you (p 117) (Workbook p 71, p 72)

Groupwork. Students discuss the kind of clothes they like. Encourage them to talk about styles, colours and individual items.

1 Whole class. Read the sentences to the class. Check that students understand the meaning of *smart* and *casual* by

eliciting examples of clothing for each category. Explain, or get the students to explain, any difficult vocabulary (*baggy* = very loose, *scruffy* = untidy). Students decide which of the sentences describe their style best.

2 ▭▭ **49 SB p 158**

Pairwork. Students look at the pictures and discuss the clothes shown in them. Encourage them to describe the clothes to each other as preparation for the listening. They could also discuss which of the clothes they like or dislike and which they would wear. Students listen to the recording and number the clothes in the order they are mentioned.

> A 1 D 2 O 3 L 4 N 5 Q 6 K 7 H 8
> E 9 M 10 G 11

▭▭ **49**

1
I think my favourite thing at the moment is my white polo-neck sweater. It goes with everything and it's really easy to wear.

2
I love my flowery silk waistcoat. I only wear it on very special occasions and I usually wear it with a suit. It cheers me up.

3
My favourite thing is my black leather jacket which I bought in America and is really old. It gets better as it gets older.

4
My baseball hat is my favourite thing. I've got very short hair and I feel really cold without it. The colours are great, bright orange and pink.

5
I spend quite a lot of money on clothes, but my favourite things aren't usually the most expensive. For example, I love my old short-sleeved T-shirt with a big banana on the front. I got that from the market for less than £5.

6
My favourite thing is definitely my leopard-print fake fur coat. I got it from a second-hand shop and it looks fabulous with my high-heeled boots.

7
I tend to like comfortable clothes best ... my favourite outfit is my baggy trousers and check shirt.

8
My gran sent me a beautiful tartan cashmere scarf for Christmas and I love it.

3 Pairwork. Students decide which clothes they like and which they find the ugliest.

Close up (p 118) (Workbook p 70)

Adjective order

1 Pairwork. Students put the clothes descriptions in the right order. Do the first one with the class as an example. If possible, get students to do the exercise without consulting the Language reference section on page 119. The order of adjectives is governed by rules, but is one of those things that native speakers decide by what 'sounds right'. Try to build up in your students a sense of what sounds right rather than sending them straight to the rules. Check answers with the class.

> a) an old, short-sleeved T-shirt
> b) a plain, green cardigan
> c) a beautiful, cashmere scarf
> d) a striped, v-neck sweater
> e) a flowery, silk waistcoat

Pairwork. Students use the words from 1 to create new combinations of adjectives and nouns. Check answers with the class.

> *Possible answers*
> an old, silk scarf
> a beautiful, cashmere sweater
> a plain, polo-neck sweater
> a black, v-neck T-shirt
> a beautiful, striped cardigan
> an old, green T-shirt
> a beautiful, flowery T-shirt

2 Whole class. Read the instructions. Students look at the adjectives and decide what categories they can put the adjectives in. They then look back at their answers to 1 and 2 and decide what order to put the categories in.

Age	Material	Pattern/colour
old	wool	stripy
second-hand	leather	check
new	silk	plain
Opinion	Style	
beautiful	short-sleeved	
horrible	full-length	
fabulous	Armani	

3 Read the two headings and the examples with the class. Explain that *I wouldn't be seen dead in this* is a colloquial way of saying that you dislike something. Students write combinations of adjectives and clothing nouns under the two headings.

Pairwork. Students take turns reading out items to their partner. The partner has to guess which heading the item belongs to.

Anecdote

See Introduction, page 4, for more ideas on how to set up, monitor and repeat 'anecdotes'.

4 Students prepare to tell a partner about a favourite item of clothing or accessory, using the list of questions. Go round and help with any language if necessary.

5 Pairwork. Students describe their item of clothing or accessory to a partner. The listening partner can ask questions to find out more information.

Idioms (p 119)

1 Whole class. Students look at the photo and identify the items shown (buttons, zips, buckles). They then look at the list of items and write down examples of items of clothing that have these features. You could set a time limit and see who can produce the longest list. This could also be done with pairs or groups competing to produce the longest lists.

> *Possible answers*
> a) coat, jacket, trousers, jeans, shorts, dress, skirt, boots, sweater
> b) dress, coat, jacket, trousers, jeans, shorts, skirt, shirt, T-shirt, blouse, sweater
> c) coat, jacket, trousers, dress, skirt, shorts, jeans, shirt, blouse, T-shirt
> d) trousers, jeans, shorts
> e) belt, shoes, boots, sandals
> f) shirt, T-shirt, sweater, blouse, dress, coat, jacket, anorak
> g) shoes, boots, sandals

2 Pairwork. Students read the sentences, choose the correct word to complete each idiom and discuss what the idioms might mean. Check answers to the first part with the class, but don't confirm their guesses about the meanings of the idioms at this stage.

> a) with   b) off   c) down   d) on   e) tighten
> f) given   g) collared   h) up

3 Students match the definitions with the expressions in 2. Check answers with the class.

> 1–d   wear one's heart on one's sleeve
> 2–e   tighten one's belt
> 3–g   collar someone
> 4–h   have something up one's sleeve

5–b   make an off the cuff remark

6–f   give someone the boot

7–c   buckle down to

8–a   get shirty with someone

4 Pairwork. Students take turns using one of the expressions in the previous exercise to tell their partner about an incident in which the idiom is appropriate.

First impressions (p 120) (Workbook p 72, p 73)

1 Pairwork. Students match words from column A with those in column B which have a similar underlined sound. Encourage students to read the words aloud to each other in order to decide what the sounds are. Check answers with the class.

/eɪ/ – a) 8   /ɔː/ – b) 6   /ɪə/ – c) 1   /ʌ/ – d) 7
/ɑː/ – e) 2   /æ/ – f) 5   /ɪ/ – g) 3   /uː/ – h) 9
/aʊ/ – i) 4

2 Students decide which of the adjectives can be used with hair, eyes or skin. Allow stud"ents to compare their ideas in pairs before checking answers with the class.

Answers in brackets are possible, but unusual

hair: brown, fair, dark

eyes: blue, deep-set, brown, (clear), dark, (pale)

skin: brown, clear, fair, pale, dark, tanned

3 Pairwork. Students use the words in the previous exercise to describe the people in the illustration.

4 Pairwork. Students look at the illustration again and discuss what the first thing they noticed about each person was.

5 Pairwork. Establish that a 'first impression' is the opinion you form the first time you see someone or something. Students discuss whether they can really tell anything about someone from a first impression and whether their first impressions are usually correct or not.

6 Students look at the pictures and say what they can see in them. They then read the text and decide which picture in 3 it matches.

The description is of the man in the middle.

7 Students choose one of the other people in the picture and complete the description with suitable words.

8 Pairwork. Students take turns to read their descriptions to their partner. The partner tries to guess which person is being described.

9 Students write descriptions of themselves or a classmate. They could use the frame in 7 or use their own ideas.

Ugly (p 122)

Closed books. Whole class. Write the saying *Beauty is in the eye of the beholder* on the board and see if anyone can tell you what it means (different people have different ideas about what beauty is). Students discuss whether or not they think this is true.

1   **50 SB p 158**

Open books. Whole class. Read the information about Jon Bon Jovi and the four questions. Students listen to the song and try to find answers to the questions. Check answers with the class.

Optional activity

Ask students if they are familiar with Jon Bon Jovi's music and whether they like it. See if they can name some other hits and if they can say what the lyrics are about.

a) The song is romantic, though it may not appear so at first.

b) The singer is talking to his girlfriend.

c) He thinks she is beautiful.

d) She thinks she is ugly.

50

Ugly by Jon Bon Jovi

If you're ugly, I'm ugly too!

In your eyes the sky's a different blue

If you could see yourself like others do

You'd wish you were as beautiful as you

And I wish I was a camera sometimes

So I could take your picture with my mind

Put it in a frame for you to see

How beautiful you really are to me

Ugly, ugly,

All of us just feel like that some day

Ain't no rainbow in the sky

When you feel U.G.L.Y.

And that's ugly

Yeah yeah yeah

Yeah yeah yeah

Ugly, ugly,

All of us just feel like that some day

Ain't no rainbow in the sky

When you feel U.G.L.Y.

And that's ugly, ugly

All of us just feel like that some day

Ain't no cure that you can buy

> *When you feel U.G.L.Y.*
> *And that's ugly*
>
> *So, if you're ugly, I'm ugly too*
> *If you're a nut, then I must be a screw*
> *If you could see yourself the way I do*
> *You'd wish you were as beautiful as you*
> *I wish I was as beautiful as you*

2   50 SB 158

Play the song again. Students listen and match the two halves of the lines. You might like to point out that the lines in the first column are in the correct order and that the rhyme scheme should give them some clues as to which lines go where. Check answers with the class.

> If you're ugly, I'm ugly too!
> In your eyes the sky's a different blue
> If you could see yourself like others do
> You'd wish you were as beautiful as you
> And I wish I was a camera sometimes
> So I could take your picture with my mind
> Put it in a frame for you to see
> How beautiful you really are to me

Close up (p 122)

I wish

1 Students look back at the Bon Jovi song and find the tense that is used after *I wish*. Check answers with the class. Note: *I wish I were* is more formal than *I wish I was*. It is the subjunctive form which is little used in speech.

> The past simple

2 Students look at the miserable-looking man in the illustration and make *I wish* sentences for him using the prompts. Check answers with the class.

> *Possible answers*
> a) I wish I lived in a big house in the country.
> b) I wish I had an exciting job.
> c) I wish I had a new car.
> d) I wish my wife understood me.
> e) I wish my children listened to me.
> f) I wish I had time to do the things I like.
> g) I wish I saw my friends more often.

3 Pairwork. Students write some wishes about their own lives. Encourage them to use the prompts so that they produce a variety of sentences, not just *I wish I was*. They then discuss their wishes with a partner.

Interview with Jon Bon Jovi (p 123)

1 Whole class. Students say what they know about Jon Bon Jovi.

2 Read the questions with the class and ask them to speculate on what they think Jon Bon Jovi's answers would be. Discourage them from finding the answers in the text. Students then match the questions with the answers. Give them a few minutes to do this, then check answers with the class.

> **1** c   **2** j   **3** d   **4** i   **5** g   **6** e

3 Groupwork. Students discuss their own answers to the interview questions.

Close up (p 124) (Workbook p 69, p 70)

Unreal conditionals

1 Students look at the Bon Jovi interview again and identify the tense used after *if*. Elicit why this tense is used.

> The past simple
> The sentences are in the conditional, used to talk about unreal situations. See the Language reference section on page 125 for the formation of these conditionals and more examples.

2   51

Students listen to the recording and read the sentences. They decide what the relationship between the people is in each conversation. Pause briefly after each conversation for students to note down their ideas.

> A) two friends
> B) child and parent
> C) two friends
> D) two sisters or two flatmates

> 51
> **A**
> Anna: *If you're looking for a new skirt, there's a sale on at DKNY.*
> Dan: *Is there? Well, come on. If we don't leave now, the shops'll be closed when we get there.*
> **B**
> Mark: *If I pass the exam, can I have a new pair of Doc Martens? And a CD? And …*
> Laura: *If you spent less time thinking about clothes and music and more time on your schoolwork, I'd be a lot happier.*
> **C**
> Paul: *This is really nice. If I had the money, I'd always wear Hugo Boss suits.*

Chris: *If you like it, why don't you buy it? You look great in it.*

D

Mel: *Right. Who's been wearing my Calvin Klein jacket?*

Julia: *Well, don't look at me.*

Mel: *Well, if it wasn't you, who was it?*

Julia: *Well, I don't know. Anyway what do you expect if you leave your things all over the house?*

Mel: *That's neither here nor there. If you're going to borrow things, you should ask. Look at this stain.*

3 Students read the conversations again and underline the conditional sentences. Check answers with the class.

a) If you're looking for a new skirt, there's a sale on at DKNY.

If we don't leave now, the shops'll be closed when we get there.

b) If I pass the exam, can I have ...

If you spent less time ... , I'd be a lot happier.

c) If I had the money, I'd always wear ...

If you like it, why don't you buy it?

Well, if it wasn't you, who was it?

d) Anyway, what do you expect if you leave your things ...

If you're going to borrow things, you should ask.

4 Pairwork. Students discuss the questions. Check answers with the class and refer students to the Language reference section for help and more examples.

a) two

b) some are real and some unreal:

If you're looking for a new skirt, there's a sale on at DKNY. (Real)

If we don't leave now, the shops'll be closed when we get there. (Real)

If I pass the exam, can I have ... (Real)

← If you spent less time ... , I'd be a lot happier. (Unreal)

← If I had the money, I'd always wear ... (Unreal)

If you like it, why don't you buy it? (Real)

Well, if it wasn't you, who was it? (Real)

Anyway, what do you expect if you leave ... (Real)

If you're going to borrow things, you should ask. (Real)

c) The verb backshifts, for example, present simple becomes past simple.

d) The past simple is also used after *I wish*. The things wished for are also unreal.

e) We use *would* in the main clause.

5 Students write sentences about themselves using the prompts. Go round offering help and encouragement where necessary. Check answers with the class.

Pairwork. Students talk about their sentences with a partner.

Test

Scoring; one point per correct answer unless indicated.

1 1 a beautiful, full-length, white dress

2 disgusting, black and white, leopard-skin trousers

3 a brand new, red, Italian sports car

4 It's a horrible, old-fashioned, tartan sofa.

5 He's wearing a second-hand, flowery, hippy shirt.

6 These twenty-year-old, faded, denim jeans are my favourites!

2 1 get 2 try 3 match 4 goes 5 put 6 fit
7 getting 8 suits

9 tight-fitting 10 casual 11 informal
12 neat and tidy 13 old-fashioned
14 long-sleeved

15 sleeve 16 belt 17 sleeve 18 boot

3 (½ point each)
1 /ɔ:/ – bald/broad
2 /aʊ/ – mouth/eyebrow
3 /eɪ/ – shave/weight
4 /a:/ – smart/scar
5 /ɪə/ – pierce/beard
6 /ʌ/ – scruffy/stubble
7 /u:/ – tooth/suit
8 /æ/ – baggy/hat

4 1 wasn't raining
2 was
3 won
4 wasn't
5 were
6 could

Possible answers

7 I wasn't a teacher.

8 didn't feel ill/felt better/wasn't feeling ill.

9 I liked my job/I had a new job.

10 I could afford it/I had more money, I would go. on holiday.

11 the sun was shining/the sun shone more.

12 I had some friends.

14 *Style* Test

Total: _____ /40

1 Adjective order *6 points*

Put the adjectives in brackets into an appropriate place in the sentence.

1   She was wearing a beautiful, white dress. (full-length)

2   He's just bought some disgusting, leopard-skin trousers. (black and white)

3   She's just got a red, Italian sports car. (brand new)

Reorder the sentences.

4   It's a tartan, horrible, old-fashioned sofa.

5   He's wearing a second-hand, hippy, flowery shirt.

6   These denim, faded, twenty-year-old jeans are my favourites!

2 Vocabulary – clothes *18 points*

Add the missing verbs in an appropriate form.

1   You'd better _____ dressed – the taxi will be here in a few minutes.

2   Excuse me. Can I _____ these jeans on? Sure, the changing rooms are over there.

3   I've got about a dozen socks here, but none of them _____ .

4   Do you think this tie _____ with the shirt?

5   In the morning, I usually _____ on the first pair of trousers I see.

6   I've put on a lot of weight since I last wore these jeans. I hope they still _____ me.

7   I generally start _____ ready at least an hour before I go out.

8   You should buy it – it really _____ you.

Match each word with one from the box with the opposite meaning.

9   baggy

10 smart

11 formal

12 scruffy

13 up-to-date

14 short-sleeved

old-fashioned   long-sleeved   casual
neat and tidy   informal   tight-fitting

Choose the correct words to complete the idioms.

15 He always wears his heart on his **collar/sleeve/tie**.

16 We're saving up for a new car so we've got to tighten our **belt/button/zip** for a while.

17 She's always got lots of ideas – I'm sure she'll have something up her **hat/trouser leg/sleeve**.

18 Marina and Pedro have split up. She gave him the **glove/boot/belt** last week.

3 Pronunciation *4 points*

Match a word in box A with a word with the same sound in box B:

A
bald   mouth   shave   smart   pierce   scruffy
tooth   baggy

B
scar   hat   weight   broad   suit   beard
eyebrow   stubble

4 Unreality – *wish* and *if* *12 points*

Put the verbs into an appropriate form.

1   I wish it _____ (not/rain). It want to go for a walk.

2   I wish it _____ (be) the weekend!

3   If I _____ (win) the lottery, I could leave this job!

4   She wishes she _____ (not/be) so tall.

5   If I _____ (be) you, I wouldn't do that!

6   I wish I _____ (can) see my parents more often.

Karl doesn't like his life and what is happening. Write his wishes.

7   I'm a teacher. I wish _____

8   I'm feeling ill. I wish _____

9   I don't like my job. I wish _____

10 I want to go on holiday, but I can't afford it. If _____

11 The sun never shines. I wish _____

12 I haven't got any friends. I wish _____

15 Age Overview

The topics of this unit cover regrets; age and dilemmas. The main grammatical focus is on *I wish* & *If only* + past perfect; unreal conditional, third conditionals and mixed conditionals and indirect questions.

Students read the poem *Age* from the Harley Davidson advertisement in which an elderly man looks back over his life. They go on to talk about age limits for different activities and life events. They then read an article about a woman who lies to her boyfriend about her age, and regrets doing so.

Students are given the opportunity to practise using conditionals in the game *Unreal! The Conditional Game*.

Students read five short stories describing different dilemmas and listen to the recording to find out what the people did. They then discuss whether they think these people did the right thing.

Finally students talk about the best age to be and listen to four people discussing the same topic.

Section	Aims	What the students are doing
Introduction pages 126–127	*Reading skills*: predicting; for detail	Making predictions from a photo about a man in the poem, *If*, taken from a Harley Davidson advertisement. Comparing descriptions with the description of the man in the poem.
Close up pages 127–128	*Grammar*: *I wish* & *If only*	Practising making wishes by using the 2nd conditional and *I wish* + past perfect. Analysing *I wish* and *If only* structures to describe past regrets. Practising *I wish* and *If only* structures by commenting on illustrations and situations.
Act your age pages 129–130	*Reading skills*: scanning; summarising; predicting	Generating interest in a text by talking about age limits. Scanning an article for specific information and summarising the text by putting sentences in the correct order. Listening to a conversation to check predictions.
Close up page 130	*Grammar*: unreal conditionals	Analysing unreal conditional sentences and practising writing unreal conditionals from prompts.
Unreal! The Conditional Game page 131	*Grammar*: unreal conditionals	Playing a game: *Unreal! The Conditional Game*, to practise unreal conditionals.
What would you have done? page 132	*Reading skills*: for gist; predicting	Reading for gist. Discussing the dilemmas in four texts and how to solve them. Listening to compare solutions.
Sweet sixteen page 133	*Conversation skills*: fluency work	Talking about the best age to be.
	Listening skills: note-taking; listening for detail	Listening to an interview with four people discussing the best age to be and taking notes from their answers. Checking comprehension by matching the person interviewed to the questions they were asked. Distinguishing between direct and indirect questions.
	Functions: delicate questions	Practising indirect questions.

15 Age *Teacher's notes*

1 Groupwork. Students look at the photograph of the man in the advertisement. Discourage them from reading the text at this stage. They work together to decide on an identity for the man, using the questions for guidance. Encourage them to use their imaginations and invent as many details as possible. Students then compare their ideas with other groups.

2 Groupwork. Students read the text of the advertisement. Some of the difficult vocabulary is glossed. They decide if the words fit the character they have invented and answer the question. Tell students that 'less beans' is ungrammatical but is used in the actual advert ('fewer beans' is correct). Tell students that 'prophylactically' is very rarely used.

> He feels he has led a rather sensible and safe life. He wishes he had had more fun and taken more chances.

3 Whole class. Establish that the advertisement is for Harley Davidson motorbikes. Ask students why the company chose this poem and whether they think it is an effective advertisement. Ask them to describe the sort of person the advertisement is aimed at.

Note: most advertising is based upon presenting the public with an image of a lifestyle that they would like to have and suggesting that purchase of a certain product will produce that lifestyle.

> *Possible answers*
>
> The lifestyle that the writer of the poem wishes he had had is one that will appeal to many people. The company are suggesting that to achieve this lifestyle you should buy a Harley Davidson motorbike and it is probably a very effective advertisement.
>
> It is aimed at middle-aged people who have achieved some success in life in terms of money (Harley Davidsons are not cheap!), but who perhaps are looking back at their lives with some regrets about not having had enough fun. Some middle-aged people have a sense of time running out and they want to relive their youth by doing more fun activities and worrying less about being safe and secure.

Wishes (p 127) (Workbook p 77)

1 Students think about their own lives and make lists of five things they would like to do in the future and the reasons why they can't do them now. Read the examples with the class and elicit a couple more examples before students start work.

2 Students rewrite their lists using conditional sentences. Read the examples with the class and remind them of the structure of unreal conditionals: *if* + past tense + *would*.

3 Pairwork. Students compare and discuss their sentences.

4 Give students a few minutes to complete the sentences for the man in the advertisement. They should only use each word in the box once. Check answers with the class. Don't comment on the various ways of expressing wishes and regrets at this stage.

> a) I wish I'd been more adventurous.
> b) I wish I'd been less anxious/sensible.
> c) I wish I'd taken more risks.
> d) If only I'd had more fun.
> e) I wish I hadn't been so sensible/anxious.
> f) I wish I hadn't taken life so seriously.
> g) If only I'd done more of the things I enjoy.

Close up (p 127) (Workbook p 74)

I wish & if only

1 Pairwork. Students look back at the sentences in the last exercise and discuss questions a)–c). They then read the sentences in d) and answer the question. Check answers with the class or refer students to the Language reference section on page 128.

> a) the past perfect tense
> b) the past
> c) no
> d) The verbs change from the past simple to the past perfect when you change from a fact to a wish.

2 Pairwork. Students look at the pictures and decide what the people might regret. They then write a sentence with *I wish* or *If only* for each picture. Allow pairs to compare their sentences before checking answers with the class.

Possible answers

A   I wish I hadn't got involved in a fight.

B   If only I hadn't had children.

C   I wish I hadn't had my hair cut so short.

D   If only I hadn't stolen that car.

E   I wish the horse I bet on had won.

F   If only I hadn't got that tattoo.

G   I wish I hadn't got dressed up.

H   If only I hadn't become a teacher.

3   Pairwork. Students read the situations and write wishes for the people. Do the first one with the class as an example and elicit as many wishes as possible. Students should write at least two for each one, but you might want to have a competition to see which pair can think up the most wishes for each situation. Check answers with the class.

Possible answers

a)   I wish I hadn't agreed to play with Jack. I wish I could play with Nico. I wish Jack hadn't asked me to play. I wish Jack was a better tennis player and a nicer person.

b)   I wish we hadn't gone to see it. I wish we had gone to see a nicer film. I wish we had gone to see *Bambi*. I wish she hadn't told her mother it was my idea to go.

c)   If only I had gone to university. If only I hadn't listened to my dad's advice. If only the business hadn't gone bankrupt. If only I had got a different job.

d)   If only I could stop smoking. If only I had never started smoking. If only someone could invent a harmless cigarette.

e)   I wish I hadn't got married so young. I wish I had married someone else. I wish we got on better. I wish we didn't fight so much.

4   Pairwork. Students talk to their partners about any bad decisions they have made which they regret. Go round offering help with vocabulary where necessary. Encourage them to give as much detail as possible and to use the *I wish* and *If only* structures as much as possible.

Act your age (p 129)

Whole class. Students look at the two photographs and say how old they think the two people are. Elicit whether they think beauty pageants are acceptable for young children (if not, at what age do they become acceptable?) and whether they think ageing rock stars are fine or whether they are embarrassing and should be made to retire (if so, at what age?).

1   Whole class. Read the list of activities and elicit whether students think there should be an upper or lower age limit for each of them. If they think there should be, try to get a consensus on what the limits should be. Write them on the board next to the name of each activity.

Pairwork. Students discuss the activities, saying whether they agree that they should have limits and whether they agree with the limits set by the class.

2   Whole class. Read the definition of 'ageism' in the margin and ask students for their comments. Do they know anyone who has experienced ageism? Do they think it is ever right to discriminate against older people? Read the statements and make sure everyone understands them. Students then read the article and mark the statements which are true for the writer. Check answers with the class.

Statements b, c and e are true for the writer.

3   Students read the sentences and number them in the correct order to summarise the article. Check answers with the class.

1   She has always had friends

2   of all ages. In fact, one of the most attractive

3   men she knows is in his mid fifties. Her fortieth birthday was a deeply

4   traumatic event. But she got

5   over the shock and tried

6   to convince herself that life begins

7   at forty. She met him playing badminton but didn't come

8   clean about her age. Silence has made the problem

9   much greater and now she thinks that the longer she remains silent

10   the more likely he is to find out. She thinks it's unfair that society judges older

11   women so harshly. But she knows that she has no one to blame

12   but herself for the situation she's in.

4   Groupwork. Students discuss how they would feel and what they would do if they were the writer. Encourage them to predict what the outcome would be of the various suggestions they make.

5   Pairwork. Students decide how the man will react when the woman tells him the truth and they write the conversation using the beginning given. Go round giving help and encouragement where necessary. Students practise the conversation in their pairs. Encourage some pairs to perform their conversations to the class. Try to choose some pairs who portrayed a positive reaction and some a negative reaction to the news.

6 📼 **52 SB p 158**

Students listen to the conversation and see how it compares to the ones they wrote. Ask them which they prefer.

> 📼 **52**
>
> (M = Man; W = Woman)
>
> M: *You look worried. What's on your mind?*
>
> W: *Actually, there is something I've been meaning to tell you ...*
>
> M: *Look, if it's about last night, it really doesn't matter. I shouldn't have said anything.*
>
> W: *No, no, it's nothing to do with that. Or rather I suppose it is, in a way.*
>
> M: *I knew it. If only I'd kept my mouth shut.*
>
> W: *Look, I agree with you. The Rolling Stones are old-fashioned and I wish I'd never put that record on.*
>
> M: *It's not a bad record. It's my fault. I shouldn't have called them boring old dinosaurs.*
>
> W: *No, it's my fault. I shouldn't have reacted like I did. It's just that that record brings back special memories for me.*
>
> M: *Look, I understand. My parents used to play The Rolling Stones too.*
>
> W: *No, you don't understand. I was in my teens when that record first came out.*
>
> M: *Ah, right. I see what you mean. Well, you look very good for your age.*
>
> W: *Oh, shut up.*
>
> M: *No, no, no. What I mean is that I don't care how old you are ... and anyway, I've got something to tell you. I'm not 31, I'm 26.*
>
> W: *What!*

7 Groupwork. Students discuss the questions. Encourage them to give as much detail as possible about any situations they are familiar with or experiences they have had.

Close up (p 130) (Workbook p 75)

Unreal conditionals

1 Students read the woman's comments and match them to the time sequences. Check answers with the class.

> a) past situation ➡ past result
>
> b) past situation ➡ present result
>
> c) present situation ➡ past result

2 Students use the prompts to write conditional sentences. Do one or two with the class before allowing them to work individually on their sentences. Check answers with the class.

> *Possible answers*
>
> a) If I hadn't eaten so much last night, I wouldn't feel ill/be feeling ill.
>
> b) If he hadn't gone to university, he wouldn't have got such a good job.
>
> c) If she hadn't got such a fast car, she wouldn't have got here in under two hours.
>
> d) If you had had more to eat at lunch time, you wouldn't be hungry now.
>
> e) If I had seen you, I would have said 'hello'.
>
> f) If there hadn't been a power cut, I wouldn't have lost two vital computer documents.
>
> g) If you had asked someone for directions, we wouldn't be lost.
>
> h) If he didn't love her so much, he wouldn't have forgiven her.

Unreal! The Conditional Game (p 131)

Whole class. Go through the rules of the game with the class and answer any questions. Make sure you have enough dice and counters for the number of groups who will play.

Groupwork. Students play the game in small groups. Go round monitoring and helping where necessary. The winner in each group is the student who reaches the *Finish* square first. As the number of sentences that can be made with the cues is infinite, this game can be played more than once by the same class. You can use it whenever students need reminding of the structure of conditionals.

What would you have done? (p 132)

1 Groupwork. Students read the letters and discuss what they would have done in each situation. Go round offering help and encouragement. Allow time for a spokesperson from each group to present the group's findings to the class.

2 📼 **53 SB p 158**

Students listen to the writers of the stories saying what they did. Then in the same groups they decide if they think it was the right thing or not.

> 📼 **53**
>
> **a**
>
> *Of course I didn't say anything ... I mean, the cashier should have asked to look in her bag, shouldn't she? If it had been a small shop, I probably would have said something, but a big supermarket like that can afford it.*

b

Well, I picked it up, brushed the cat hairs off and served it. Well, what you don't see you don't worry about, do you?

c

So I said, 'It looks lovely' and then spent the rest of the day wishing I'd told her the truth.

d

I was so shocked. It took me a few days to decide what to do, but once I'd made up my mind, I was sure it was the right thing. I cashed the cheque and went straight to the travel agent's where I bought tickets to Egypt for myself and a couple of friends. At least they love me as I am. The divorce will be through next month.

e

I don't know if he saw me, but I didn't want to embarrass him so I just carried on walking. I often think about him and wonder how he ended up on the streets.

Sweet sixteen (p 133) (Workbook p 76)

1 Groupwork. Students discuss the three questions.

2 ▭ **54 SB p 158**

Students look at the photos. Ask them to predict how they think the people in the photos would answer the questions in 1. Students listen to the recording and make notes on the answers the people give.

> Freddie ...
> thinks 12 is a good age to be.
> wishes he was older so he didn't have to tidy his room.
>
> Jem ...
> would prefer to be 18.
> thinks the best age is when you're really young.
> wishes he was older so he could go to bars and clubs and vote.
>
> Yvette ...
> thinks being 21 means you have to be responsible.
> thinks the best age is 5.
> wished she was older when she was 15 so she could go out.
>
> Carmel ...
> thinks being in her mid thirties is good but she only feels 25.
> thinks the best age is between 25 and 30.
> wouldn't want to be older or younger.

▭ **54**

Freddie

(I = Interviewer; F = Freddie)

I: *How old are you now, Freddie?*

F: *Twelve.*

I: *Is that a good age to be?*

F: *Yeah ... you're grown up enough to be semi-independent but still young. At school I've just gone from being one of the oldest in my old school to being one of the youngest in secondary school.*

I: *Oh, and which do you prefer?*

F: *Well, it was good being the oldest because I could boss people around but it's quite good being the youngest too because we're let out early for lunch and we get to go home at two o'clock on Wednesday afternoons. Also having an older brother in the same school helps.*

I: *What are the advantages of being 12?*

F: *You're not a teenager yet so you're not annoyed and uptight about everything.*

I: *How old's your brother?*

F: *Sixteen.*

I: *What differences are there between being 12 and being 16?*

F: *He smells and I don't. Hah. Also, he's got exams and I haven't.*

I: *Have you ever wished you were older or younger than you are?*

F: *Yeah ... I'd like to be old enough not to tidy my room.*

I: *Hah. But you have to tidy your room whatever age you are.*

F: *Yeah, but if I was old enough to leave home and have my own place, I wouldn't have to tidy my room.*

Jem

(I = Interviewer; J = Jem)

I: *How old are you, Jem?*

J: *Sixteen.*

I: *What's it like being 16? Is that a good age to be?*

J: *Er, well, I'd prefer to be 18.*

I: *Why?*

J: *Because of the things I could do legally, like go to bars and clubs ... oh yeah, and vote.*

I: *Are you looking forward to voting?*

J: *Yeah.*

I: *Do you mind if I ask you who you might vote for?*

J: *Well, I don't really know. Um, it might all have changed in two years.*

I: *What do you think is the best age to be?*

J: Er, probably when you're really young, before you go to school. You don't have a care in the world.

I: You've got a brother who's 12, haven't you?

J: Yes, unfortunately.

I: Hah. In what way are your lives different?

J: I've got a lot more responsibilities. I've got a part-time job at the weekend and I've got more of a workload from school. But I've also got a lot more freedom. He's not allowed out after six o'clock.

I: Ah. Do you mind if I ask you whether you've got a girlfriend?

J: Er, not really.

Yvette

(I = Interviewer; Y = Yvette)

I: You've just had an important birthday, haven't you?

Y: Oh, well, not really. These days 18 is the important one.

I: So, how does it feel to be 21?

Y: Oh, exactly the same as 20.

I: Is there anything you can do now that you couldn't do before you were 21?

Y: Um, no, not really. But I suppose when you're 21, you have more responsibilities. You're supposed to be more independent and er, you can't depend on your parents so much. Er, like I have to pay for my holidays myself now, so these are the disadvantages. And er, people expect grown-up behaviour from you.

I: Ah. What do you reckon is the best age to be?

Y: Um, maybe five years old. You go to play school and you play all day. Everybody spoils you and life is just fun.

I: Have you ever wished you were older or younger?

Y: Oh, yes. When I was about 15, my brother was allowed out and I wasn't. He's three years older than me and I wanted to be the same age as him.

Carmel

(I = Interviewer; C = Carmel)

I: Do you mind if I ask you how old you are?

C: Actually, I'd rather not say. But put it this way, I'm the wrong side of 30.

I: Is that a good age to be?

C: Um yes, pretty good. But it's a lot older than 25, which is how old I feel.

I: What's life like when you're in your thirties?

C: Well, not very different from my twenties except that I'm seriously thinking of buying more expensive face creams, and wondering if they really work.

I: What do you think is the best age to be?

C: I think between 25 and 30 is a good age, because you've kind of sorted out what you want and you know how to get it and you've got some experience of trying to get it. At that age you don't think about the consequences of what you do whereas when you're a bit older you do tend to worry about the consequences.

I: So do you wish you were still 25?

C: No, I'm happy at the age I am now. I mean, I had a good time in my twenties, but I wouldn't necessarily want to relive them.

I: Hah.

3 Students put the name of the person next to the question they were asked.

Check answers with the class. Then elicit which question uses the most polite form. You might like to point out that this question is asked to the oldest person. We tend to use polite forms more often to adults than to children.

Carmel:	Do you mind if I ask you how old you are?
Freddie:	How old are you now?
Yvette:	You've just had an important birthday, haven't you?
Jem:	How old are you?

The most polite question is 'Do you mind if I ask you how old you are?'

Delicate questions (p 133) (Workbook p 75)

Read the introduction and the examples with the class. Something 'delicate' is something the other person might be embarrassed about or might not want to talk about.

1 Students complete the polite questions using the prompts. Check answers with the class.

Pairwork. Students ask and answer their questions with a partner.

Possible answers

a) Do you mind if I ask you where you bought your shirt?

b) Do you mind if I ask you why you are studying English?/why you studied English?

c) Do you mind if I ask you why you didn't get here on time?

d) Do you mind if I ask you where you are going after the lesson?/where you went after the lesson?

e) Do you mind if I ask you if you are enjoying this lesson?/have you enjoyed this lesson?

f) Do you mind if I ask you what you are doing this evening?/going to do this evening?

2 Read the definition of *taboo* in the margin. Elicit a couple of examples of taboo subjects in the students' culture.

Groupwork. Students read the questions and discuss which ones they think are taboo with someone you don't know well. You could also ask them to discuss if there are any which they would never ask anyone, no matter how well they knew them.

3 Groupwork. Students add more taboo questions to the list.

4 Pairwork. Students transform the list of questions in 2 and any others they have added into indirect questions, using *Do you mind if I ask you ...?* Check answers with the class.

a) Do you mind if I ask you what perfume you are wearing?

b) Do you mind if I ask you how much you earn?

c) Do you mind if I ask you where you bought your shoes?

d) Do you mind if I ask you how much you weigh?

e) Do you mind if I ask you who you voted for in the last elections?

f) Do you mind if I ask you if you are married?

g) Do you mind if I ask you if that is your natural hair colour?

h) Do you mind if I ask you how much your house cost?

5 Students look at the Language toolbox to find ways of responding to an indirect questions, either agreeing to answer or politely refusing to answer.

Pairwork. Students then take turns asking and answering the indirect questions they formed in 4, using these expressions.

Test

Scoring; one point per correct answer unless indicated.

1 1 Do you mind if I ask you how old you are?

2 Do you mind if I ask you what you are doing here?

3 Do you mind if I ask you if you have got a girlfriend?

4 Do you mind if I ask you what you were just reading?

5 Do you mind if I ask you where you got those shoes?

6 Do you mind if I ask you how much you earn?

7 Do you mind if I ask you how you know her?

8 Do you mind if I ask you when you gave it to them?

2 One point for identification and one point for correction.

1 ✗ I wouldn't be feeling so terrible if I had gone to bed earlier last night.

2 ✓

3 ✓

4 ✓

5 ✗ If she had seen you ...

6 ✗ If I'd got some ...

7 ✓

8 ✓

9 ✓

10 had earnt

11 'd go

12 hadn't gone

13 didn't have

14 wouldn't be feeling

15 wouldn't have bought

3 (1–4 ½ point each)
1 b
2 d
3 a
4 c

4 (5–10 2 points each)
5 I hadn't come
6 she didn't live/wasn't living/liked living
7 I was sitting in a bar watching
8 I could speak
9 there was some wine
10 I had been listening

15 *Age* Test

Name: **Total:** _____ /40

1 Indirect questions *8 points*

Rewrite the questions using *Do you mind if I ask you... ?*

1   How old are you?

_____

2   What are you doing here?

_____

3   Have you got a girlfriend?

_____

4   What were you just reading?

_____

5   Where did you get those shoes?

_____

6   How much do you earn?

_____

7   How do you know her?

_____

8   When did you give it to them?

_____

2 Unreal conditionals *18 points*

Three of these sentences are incorrect. Mark them ✓or ✗.
Correct the three which are wrong.

1   I wouldn't be feeling so terrible if I went to bed earlier last night. _____

2   If I didn't earn so much, I would seriously consider leaving this job. _____

3   I wouldn't have fallen over if I'd been looking where I was going. _____

4   He wouldn't be in this mess now if only he'd listened to Federica. _____

5   If she saw you, she'd have told you yesterday.

_____

6   If I've got some, I'd give you some. _____

7   If it wasn't so late, I'd have gone with them. _____

8   If he didn't have such good friends, he would've got into a real mess. _____

9   If I didn't like it, I wouldn't have bought it. _____

Put the verbs into an appropriate form and use any modal verbs necessary.

10 If I _____ (earn) more in my last job, I probably wouldn't have left.

11 If I were you, I _____ (go) with them. You'll love it!

12 I wouldn't have met her if I _____ (not/go) to the party.

13 If I _____ (not/have) a family and a mortgage, I'd go travelling around the world.

14 If he hadn't drunk so much last night, he _____ (not/feel) so terrible now.

15 If she hadn't needed it, she _____ (not/buy) it.

3 Wishes *14 points*

Match the situations on the left with the wishes.

1   The barbecue last week was ruined.   a)   I wish it didn't rain so much.

2   I want to go for a walk.   b)   I wish it hadn't rained.

3   It always rains here!   c)   I wish it hadn't been raining.

4   It was raining so we couldn't go out.   d)   I wish it wasn't raining.

Complete the wishes.

5   I regret coming to the UK.

If only _____ to the UK.

6   She doesn't like living in London.

She wishes _____ in London.

7   I'm not sitting in a bar watching the football.

I wish _____ football.

8   I can't speak German.

I wish _____ German.

9   There isn't any wine left.

I wish _____ left.

10 I wasn't listening to him.

I wish _____ to him.

16 Review 2 Teacher's notes

Who said what? (p 134)

1 You may need to explain to students who the famous people are/were:

Walt Disney – American producer of cartoon films. Born 1901, died 1966

Salvador Dalí – Catalan surrealist painter and eccentric. Born 1904, died 1989

Groucho Marx – One of four brothers who made comedy films in the 1930s. Born 1895, died 1977

Pablo Picasso – Spanish painter, perhaps the greatest artist of the 20th century. Born 1881, died 1973

Oscar Wilde – Irish writer. Born 1854, died 1900

Zsa Zsa Gabor – Film actress, famous for marrying many times

Albert Einstein – German born phycisist and Nobel prize winner. Born 1879, died 1955

Rudyard Kipling – English writer born 1865, died 1936

Napoleon Bonaparte – French Emperor and military leader in the 18th and 19th centuries, born 1769, died 1821

Andy Warhol – American painter of the 1960s and 1970s, leader of the pop art movement, born 1928, died 1987

Frank Sinatra – American popular singer, died May 1998

John Lennon – member of the Beatles, married to Yoko Ono, shot dead in 1980

> a) John Lennon   b) Andy Warhol
> c) Frank Sinatra   d) Salvador Dalí
> e) Napoleon Bonaparte   f) Rudyard Kipling
> g) Walt Disney   h) Zsa Zsa Gabor
> i) Pablo Picasso   j) Groucho Marx
> k) Albert Einstein   l) Oscar Wilde

2

a) John Lennon once said that the Beatles were more popular than Jesus Christ.

b) Andy Warhol once said that in the future everyone would be famous for fifteen minutes.

c) Frank Sinatra once said that rock 'n' roll had no future.

d) Salvador Dalí once said that painting a picture was either easy or impossible.

e) Napoleon Bonaparte once said that England was a nation of shopkeepers.

f) Rudyard Kipling once said that words were the most powerful drug used by mankind.

g) Walt Disney once said that he loved Mickey Mouse more than any woman he had ever known.

h) Zsa Zsa Gabor once said that she had never hated a man enough to give diamonds back.

i) Pablo Picasso once said that there was no such thing as a bad Picasso.

j) Groucho Marx once said that he didn't want to belong to any club that would accept him as a member.

k) Albert Einstein once said that he never thought about the future.

l) Oscar Wilde once said that there was no sin except stupidity.

I predict ... (p 136)

will

1

2 I will have got married by the time I'm thirty.

3 In five years, I will be speaking English every day.

4 By this time next week, I will have probably fallen in love yet again!

5 I won't have forgotten how to speak English twenty years from now.

6 By the end of the year I will have travelled to a new country.

7 I will be a millionaire in ten years' time.

8 Before I die, I will have visited the moon!

The world of languages (p 136)

Questions

2

a) 3500 BC

b) 3,500 years ago.

c) around 4,000

d) Mandarin Chinese, English, Hindi, Spanish, Russian

e) at least a million

f) *the, be* and *thing*

g) ketchup: Malay, shampoo: Hindi

h) India

(I = interviewer; KT = Kim Thomas)

I: ... so, if we could turn to the origin of language? Um, do we know when, where and how language originated?

KT: Ah, that's a difficult question to answer, or rather the answer is no one really knows. What we do know, is when language was first written down.

I: Ah hah, and that was ...

KT: That was about five and a half thousand years ago, in about 3500 BC. The Sumerians, who lived in Mesopotamia, were the first people to write down their language. They used symbols called pictographs to represent everyday objects – a bit like Egyptian hieroglyphics – and the first actual alphabet was developed around 3,500 years ago by the Phoenicians, who lived on the eastern coast of what is now Syria. Today there are around 65 alphabets in the world. Interestingly, the shortest of them, the one used in the Solomon Islands, has only 11 letters.

I: Hah, hah. And the longest?

KT: Er, the Cambodian, I think. I believe it's got 74 letters.

I: So, how many languages are there in the world today?

KT: Somewhere in the region of 4,000. I don't think we'll ever find out the exact figure.

I: Um, and which of these are the most spoken?

KT: Well, Mandarin Chinese has about a billion speakers. English is next with about half a billion speakers and Hindi, Spanish and Russian are not too far behind. These five languages account for half of all the conversations in the world!

I: Hah, hah, hah. And is it true that Mandarin is the biggest language? I mean the one with the most number of words?

KT: Again, it's difficult to say, but the latest thinking is that English is actually the biggest, largely due to the number of technical and scientific words it contains. There are at least a million words in English. Most native speakers only use about 10,000 words, that's one per cent of them.

I: Hah. Only 10,000?

KT: Yeah, and can you guess which are the most common of these? The most used words in English.

I: Huh. Let me think. Um, maybe 'be'?

KT: Well, according to recent research, where tens of thousands of hours of conversation have been fed into computers and analysed, the most common word is 'the'.

I: Oh, and 'be'?

KT: Well, 'be', we think, is the most used verb in English. But of course there are different forms of these verbs. Er, what do you think the most common noun in spoken English is?

I: Mm. The most common noun? Erm, maybe something like ... er, oh, I've no idea. You're going to have to tell us.

KT: Hah, hah, hah. Well, you just said it, actually. Apparently, it's 'thing'.

I: Mm. Hah ... OK. ... hah. What about the origins of words? Where does English come from?

KT: Well, modern English, which is about 500 years old, is a mixture of mainly Romance and Germanic languages. Greek and Arabic have also provided English with many words. Er, did you know 'sugar' comes from Arabic? And, surprisingly, so does 'alcohol'. In fact many, many words have been 'borrowed' from other languages. For example, did you know that 'coffee' comes from Turkish and that 'chess', the game, is a Persian word?

I: Oh, no.

KT: Where do you think 'ketchup', as in tomato ketchup, comes from?

I: Er, I've never really thought about it. I've no idea. Hah, hah, hah. America?

KT: Hah, hah, hah. It's from the Malay language. A traditional Malaysian sauce, I believe.

I: Ah.

KT: How about 'shampoo'?

I: Mmm, it sounds a bit oriental to me. Maybe Japanese?

KT: It's actually a Hindi word, from India. The list is endless.

I: Er, you mentioned India just then. Isn't that a country with hundreds of languages?

KT: Well, I don't know about hundreds. I think Papua New Guinea has got the most with over eight hundred and fifty separate languages, but India has got dozens of languages. The bank notes there have got thirteen languages written on them. I suppose they're the main languages. Um, most people there speak at least two or three languages.

I: Um, talking of which ... and one final question. To speak two languages fluently is difficult enough, but have you any idea what the highest number of languages spoken by one person is?

KT: There is, or was, a Frenchman, I, er, can't remember his name, but he spoke 31 different languages. All of them fluently!

I: Oh. On that note, Professor Thomas, we'll say thank you very much and, er, au revoir, auf Wiedersehen, arrivaderci, sayonara, adios ...

Doing the right thing (p 137)

Modals

1
1. false, it's often essential to get things done.
2. true
3. false, it's three times.
4. true, it symbolises death.
5. false, it's 20.
6. true   7 true
8. false, but you can with animals.
9. false   10 false   11 true
12. false, except on someone's 20th birthday, when you give them 20.
13. true, but you don't have to vote.
14. false, in most states it is 16.
15. false, you should never do this.
16. false, as in most countries, there's no age restriction.
17. false, but you must never deface a picture of the Queen.
18. false   19 false
20. true, for a prayer.

Greetings from Vietnam (p 138)

General revision

1 're having 2 wonderful   3 beautiful, small
4 amazing   5 said   6 were   7 had   8 many
9 've been   10 'd   11 arrived   12 've been
13 exhausted   14 absolutely   15 who   16 which
17 likes   18 can't   19 stay   20 few   21 have left
22 be lying   23 doing   24 a few   25 were
26 were   27 'd   28 hadn't broken   29 might
30 is getting   31 you are   32 them   33 lots of
34 get   35 'll finish   36 Tell   37 to her

End of Course Test

Scoring: one point per correct answer unless otherwise indicated.

1
1 see   2 've finished   3 Would he go   4 'll help
5 phone   6 isn't raining   7 'd tell
8 hadn't rained   9 hadn't missed   10 are
11 didn't like   12 arrives   13 's won   14 're not
15 had got up   16 wants   17 had   18 sees
19 wasn't feeling/hadn't been feeling   20 didn't
mean   21 ✓   22 ✗ I'd go   23 ✗ We would have
finished   24 ✓   25 ✓   26 ✗ I'd seen

2
1 shone   2 hadn't gone   3 wasn't   4 could
5 was lying   6 didn't live
7 hadn't bought   8 had talked   9 were/was
10 played

3 (1/2 point each)
1 at   2 at   3 on   4 in   5 at   6 in   7 in
8 on   9 in   10 in

4
1 She said she was Spanish.
2 He told me she played the guitar in a band.
3 He says he's almost finished.
4 He asked me if I had ever been to Argentina.
5 She told us she would be in New York tomorrow/the next day.

5
1 be lying   2 be packing   3 have finished
4 show   5 ring   6 be flying   7 have left
8 be having   9 be swimming   10 be

6
1 ✗ much money   2 ✗ many children   3 ✓   4 ✓
5 ✗ a few   6 ✓   7 ✓   8 ✗ much food
9 much/a little   10 a little   11 much   12 a little
13 a few   14 much   15 many   16 a few

7
1 Can you go …
2 I must go …
3 would you do …
4 don't have to do it …
5 I had to go …
6 mustn't do …
7 I couldn't leave …
8 Will you be …
9 wouldn't do that …
10 It might be him …

8
1 might   2 can't   3 had to   4 mustn't
5 must   6 could   7 has to   8 can
9 don't have to   10 should

11 Can   12 can't/must/have got to
13 have to/must   14 can't   15 don't have to
16 must/might/could   17 must   18 have to
19 can   20 can't   21 might not   22 must

9
1 is Sarah doing   2 think   3 is writing   4 Have
you ever been   5 went   6 Does anyone know
7 was   8 was talking   9 Were you still living
10 got   11 were   12 had been
13 have you worked/have you been working
14 came   15 Are you doing   16 'm meeting
17 Do you want   18 've spilt   19 Do you need
20 'll get

10
1 breathtaking   2 try   3 make   4 after
5 business   6 thoughts   7 right   8 idea
9 talk   10 sleeve   11 put   12 calling   13 in
14 mid   15 early   16 broke   17 faithfully
18 up   19 on   20 do   21 second   22 bland
23 to sleep   24 bird   25 up   26 made

16 *End Of Course Test*

Name: **Total:** _____ /150

1 Conditionals *26 points*

Choose the correct alternative.

1   If I **see/will see** them, I'll tell them.

2   When you've **finished/'d finished**, you are free to leave.

3   **Would he go/Will he go** if he had enough time?

4   If you wait a few minutes, I'**d/'ll** help.

5   If you **phone/would phone** me later, I'll be able to tell you.

6   If it **isn't/wasn't raining**, we can go for a walk.

7   I'**d/'ll** tell you if I knew.

8   If it **didn't rain/hadn't rained** this morning, we'd have played golf.

9   They would be there by now if they **didn't miss/hadn't missed** the bus.

10 If you **will be/are** late once more, you are in serious trouble!

11 If she **doesn't like/didn't like** it, she wouldn't have bought it.

12 When he **arrives/will arrive**, let me know.

13 If she wins this point, she **won/'s won** the match.

14 If they **won't be/'re not** here, they're too late.

Put the verbs into an appropriate form.

15 If we _____ (get up) in time, we wouldn't have been late.

16 If he _____ (want) it, he'll ask for it.

17 I'd love to learn another language if I _____ (have) more time.

18 Don't worry! She'll give him the message if she _____ (see) him.

19 If she _____ (not/feel) so ill, we could have gone out tonight.

20 Why did you say it if you _____ (not/mean) it?

Three of the following sentences are wrong. Mark them ✓ or ✗. Correct the sentences which are wrong.

21 If you don't like it, don't eat it. _____

22 If I were you, I'll go with them. _____

23 We'd finished already if we started on time. _____

24 If you don't agree with the arrangements, can you tell me please? _____

25 If we didn't do our homework, the teacher got very angry. _____

26 I'd have told him if I saw him. _____

2 *wish* *10 points*

In each sentence the verb is in the wrong form. Put the verbs into the correct form.

1   I wish the sun *shines* a bit more in this country.

2   I imagine he wishes he *didn't go* to that party last night.

3   I bet she wishes she *isn't* here right now!

4   I wish I *can* give up smoking.

5   I wish I *am lying* on a beach at the moment.

6   I wish I *hadn't lived* here any more.

Complete the wishes by putting the verbs into the correct form.

7   She hates the dress. She wishes she _____ (not/buy) it.

8   We didn't say much. I wish I _____ (talk) to them more.

9   I'm too old to take up skiing. I wish I _____ (be) younger.

10 I've had enough of the guitar. I wish I _____ (play) the drums instead.

3 Prepositions of time *5 points*

Complete the following sentences by adding appropriate prepositions.

1   I saw her _____ the weekend.

2   Do you ever work _____ night?

3   The party is _____ the 24th.

4   I hope the ambulance gets here _____ time.

5   I'll be arriving _____ around six thirty.

6   He was born _____ 1987.

7   I think her birthday's _____ March.

8   I'm seeing them a week _____ Friday.

9   I'll be with you _____ ten minutes.

10   They arrived yesterday, _____ the afternoon.

4 Reporting *5 points*

Report the following, beginning with the words given.

1   'I'm Spanish.' She said _____

2   'She plays the guitar in a band.' He told me _____

3   'I've almost finished.' He says _____

4   'Have you ever been to Argentina?' He asked me _____

5   'I'll be in New York tomorrow.' She told us _____

5 *will* *10 points*

Choose the correct form.

1   Just think. This time tomorrow I'll **lie/be lying** on a beach in Greece.

2   Don't come at six – I'll **be packing/pack** my suitcases then, but ...

3   ... hopefully, I'll **be finishing/have finished** it by seven thirty.

4   I'll **show/be showing** you my new dress when you get here.

5   I think I'll **be ringing/ring** for a taxi in a minute.

6   At ten thirty, we'll **fly/be flying** over the English Channel and ...

7   ... we will **have left/leave** rainy old England behind us.

8   While you are still asleep, I'll **have had/be having** breakfast on the beach ...

9   ... and as you are on your way to work. I'll **swim/be swimming** in the clear blue sea!

10   And then I'll **be/have been** back here before you know it!

6 Countable and uncountable nouns; *some, a lot of, much, many, a few* and *a little* *16 points*

Four of the following sentences are wrong. Mark the sentences ✓ or ✗. Correct the sentences which are wrong.

1   I haven't got many money. _____

2   How much children have they got? _____

3   Can I have some more wine please? _____

4   He had a few good ideas. _____

5   There were a little people at the party. _____

6   I saw a couple of people I knew. _____

7   There was a lot of rain last week. _____

8   There wasn't many food at the party. _____

Complete the following by adding *much, many, a few* or *a little*.

9   Is there _____ bread left?

10   Can I have _____ more milk in my coffee?

11   How _____ does it cost?

12   I've only got _____ money left, I'm afraid.

13   It'll only take _____ minutes.

14   How _____ sleep did you get?

15   How _____ times have you seen it?

16   He's only been there _____ times I think.

7 Modal verbs – general *10 points*

Correct the grammar mistakes in the following sentences.

1   Do you can go to the party?

2   I'm afraid I must to go now.

3   What would do you if you were me?

4   You haven't to do it if you don't want to.

5   Sorry I wasn't here yesterday, but I must go to Paris.

6   You don't must do that again!

7   I didn't can leave until I had finished.

8   Will be you there at six thirty?

9   I wouldn't to do that if I were you.

10   It might him be, but I'm not sure.

8 Modal verbs – obligation, prohibition, permission, deduction *22 points*

Choose the correct modal verb.

1   He **can/might** be from Spain – I heard him speaking Spanish.

2   It **can't/mustn't** be her. She wasn't here at the time.

3   Sorry I'm late. I **had to/must** stop at the shops on the way here.

4   You **mustn't/don't have to** arrive any later than 4 o'clock or you won't be allowed in.

5   You haven't eaten since breakfast – you **must/have to** be really hungry.

6   Well, I suppose it **can/could** be him, but I'm not sure.

7   It **can/has to** be them who did it – who else can it be?

8   You **can/could** leave if you've finished your work.

9   You **mustn't/don't have to** get there early, but it's a good idea to do so.

10 You **should/have to** go to bed if you're tired.

Add an appropriate verb. Choose from *must (not), have (got) to, don't have to, might (not), may (not), can, can't* or *could*. In some cases there is more than one possibility.

11 _____ I leave now, please?

12 I _____ go now, I'm afraid.

13 I _____ take some clients out to lunch.

14 She _____ be Australian – she doesn't speak a word of English.

15 You _____ go to the meeting, but it would be useful if you did.

16 He _____ be French – he certainly speaks it well.

17 They _____ be out – I've rung them three times and there's still no answer.

18 In most schools you _____ wear a uniform …

19 … but in some you _____ wear whatever you like.

20 This _____ be their house. They said it had a blue door and this one's red.

21 I'm afraid I _____ get there in time. If so, start without me.

22 You _____ be crazy to try that!

9 General tenses and verb forms *20 points*

Put the verbs into an appropriate tense/form.

Tom: What (1) _____ Sarah _____ (do) at the moment?

Boris: She's in her room. I (2) _____ (think) she (3) _____ (write) a letter.

Akiko: (4) _____ you ever _____ (be) to Greece?

Maya: Yes, a couple of years ago. I (5) _____ (go) there on a school holiday.

Gerta: (6) _____ anyone _____ (know) where Andrés is?

Petra: He (7) _____ (be) in the students' room a few minutes ago. He (8) _____ (talk) to Olaf.

Sanjay: (9) _____ you still _____ (live) in Brighton when you (10) _____ (get) married?

Maya: No, we (11) _____ (be) in London. We (12) _____ (be) there for about a year actually.

Joelle: How long (13) _____ you _____ (work) here?

Mario: Too long! I (14) _____ (come) here in 1997.

Walter: (15) _____ you _____ (do) anything this evening?

Gordon: Yes, I (16) _____ (meet) Harry for a few drinks. (17) _____ you _____ (want) to join us?

Francis: Aaaargh! I (18) _____ (spill) coffee all over my desk.

Pitma: (19) _____ you _____ (need) a hand? I (20) _____ (get) a cloth.

10 General vocabulary *26 points*

Choose the correct alternative.

1   The views were absolutely **breathtaking/breathstopping**.

2   Can I **test/try** these jeans on, please?

3   We need a decision fast. Come on, **make/do** your mind up.

4   I'm seeing him the day **after/following** tomorrow.

5   I'm not telling you – it's none of your **affair/business**.

6   Hang on! On second **thoughts/thinking**, let's meet at seven thirty.

7   It serves you **just/right**!

8   I've no **clue/idea** where she lives.

9   Let's **talk/speak** this over before it's too late.

10 We'll be OK. He's always got something up his **trouser leg/sleeve**.

11 Annick: Could you **give/put** me through to Sergio Hernandez please?

12 Gregor: Certainly. Who's **ringing/calling**, please?

13 She's my sister-**in/at**-law.

14 He's in his **middle/mid** twenties.

15 She's in her **low/early** thirties.

16 She **broke/stole** his heart when she ran off with his best friend.

17 Dear Sir, ... Yours **faithfully/sincerely** ....

18 He has recently split **apart/up** with his girlfriend.

19 Hang **on/off** a minute, I'll see if she's there.

20 I'll be with you in an hour or so, I've just got a few odd jobs to **make/do** first.

21 New? No, it's **second/twice**-hand. Do you like it?

22 This soup tastes a bit **blank/bland** actually.

23 When did you finally get **asleep/to sleep** last night?

24 He's always up before seven – he's a real early **bird/worm**.

25 I don't mind where we go – it's **up/out** to you.

26 I hope I haven't **done/made** any mistakes.